Differentiated Instruction

*Content Area Applications and
Other Considerations for Teaching in
Grades 5-12 in the Twenty-First Century*

Edited by Ervin F. Sparapani

University Press of America,® Inc.
Lanham • Boulder • New York • Toronto • Plymouth, UK

Copyright © 2013 by University Press of America,® Inc.
4501 Forbes Boulevard, Suite 200, Lanham, Maryland 20706
UPA Aquisitions Department (301) 459-3366

10 Thornbury Road, Plymouth PL6 7PP, United Kingdom

British Library Cataloguing in Publication Information Available

Library of Congress Control Number: 2012956198
ISBN: 978-0-7618-6084-6 (cloth : alk. paper)—ISBN: 978-0-7618-6085-3 (electronic)
ISBN: 978-0-7618-6554-4 (pbk : alk. paper)

This book is dedicated to my wife, Carol, my brother, Jim,
and to Todd and Richelle, my children,
for their constant support and interest in anything I've ever tried to do.

Contents

List of Figures

List of Tables

Foreword

Pamela L. Ross McClain

The Five Senses of Learning

I hear my teacher teaching
Knowledge enters in my ears
My nose knows there is a chance for learning
I smell the words I hear
My hands touch understanding
I feel stronger the more I know
My eyes see a bright future
Where my appetite continues to grow
My tongue tastes the flavor of learning
A variety of morsels so sweet
Hear, Smell, Touch, See, and Taste Learning
Where all fives senses meet

My nine-year-old son came home from school with a look of elation on his face. He announced proudly when I asked why he was so happy, "I love the smell of learning!" When I inquired further, he described an engaging class activity on fractions that his teacher had taught using a surprise pizza party as the backdrop for her lesson. My son is in the midst of a pre-adolescent growing spurt and is enthralled by most anything that involves eating. When I witnessed how excited he was to explain his mastery of fractions, I thought, "This is what learning should sound, smell, taste, look, and feel like every day." Clearly his teacher understood that she needed to differentiate her instructional approach for teaching fractions so all of her students had an opportunity to master her learning objectives. The poem, *The Five Senses of Learning*, printed above was inspired by my son and written to capture the spirit and promise of differentiated instruction.

Teaching involves multiple interactive exchanges across diverse cultural, linguistic, and socio-economic terrains. The idea that all youth can learn is a healthy belief for educators; however, the notion that all children can learn in the same way and at the same time is quite another matter. Unfortunately, there is often a tendency to resist customizing teaching strategies and learning indicators in favor of standardizing the educational process. In other words, it is easier to approach education from the posture of "one-size-fits-all" than it is to make differentiated instruction the norm. Differentiation poses a challenge to the status quo approach of "one-size-fits-all" curriculum development and delivery. It attacks the paradigm of "business as usual" that looms in schools in spite of mounting educational research on best practices to promote student learning. In order for differentiated instruction to fully take root in any school culture, it will take more than the work of individual teachers. Differentiated instruction properly adopted and implemented will touch all aspects of schooling including: curriculum development, delivery of the curriculum, student-teacher interaction, student assessment, job-embedded professional learning for educators, and community partnerships with schools.

Curriculum development that utilizes differentiated instruction calls for advanced subject matter knowledge. Ironically, the more you learn about any subject, the more you become aware of what you do not know about the subject; therein lies an educational paradox. The master educator does not aspire to simply be an expert on the content area(s) taught. To do so would yield intellectual inertia and the subsequent stagnation of students. Ideally, teachers who differentiate instruction are also willing to expand their content area knowledge to teach in ways that are interdisciplinary. Master educators adept at differentiating constantly strive to raise the bar higher, to unearth another layer, to reach the next level. For them, there is always something new to be discovered, uncovered, or undiscovered.

Differentiated instruction expands the delivery of instruction beyond typical teacher-centered approaches that provide many teachers with a false sense of security because they can manage a controlled learning environment. Many teachers may fear that differentiating instruction poses management issues when students are afforded shared decision-making authority. On the contrary, when students have multiple ways to represent their understanding of content, they are less apt to become behavior problems because they are likely to feel like a valuable contributor in the learning community. In the differentiated instruction classroom, students are not viewed as passive receptacles that teacher's fill up with cultural capital by a process of osmosis that allows knowledge to be diffused based on the students' capacity to absorb knowledge. The presumption that students are empty vessels waiting to be filled with information is replaced with the perception that students are full vessels waiting to assimilate new information into their existing schemata. Students are viewed as complex beings that are capable of co-creating knowledge while learning, if teachers are willing to serve as the catalyst for the synergism innate to the learning process.

Few people would disagree with the adage that "You can't teach what you don't know." The argument could also be made that "You can't teach 'who' you don't know." Differentiated instruction cannot exist without building authentic relationships with students. Fundamentally, effective teachers must understand the value of developing meaningful relationships with learners to encourage students to take advantage of the full benefit of instruction. Although schools cannot totally insulate students from all variables that might adversely impact their classroom performance, they can foster an environment that is more conducive to learning. When teachers fully embrace differentiated instruction, they are capable of restructuring and re-culturing their individual classroom community by creating a diverse and dynamic learning climate.

If we expand the belief that all students "can learn" to include the fundamental premise that all students are inescapably and perpetually in a learning mode, we are forced to rethink the purpose and utility of student assessment. Traditionally, assessments have been used to distinguish what knowledge students have or have not mastered as measured by a very restricted body of information. Likewise, the manner in which students have been allowed to convey their understanding has been limited. Differentiated instruction cannot flourish without a differentiated assessment process that includes multiple assessment strategies that yield a constant flow of information regarding student learning and teacher effectiveness. Differentiated assessment is more than a means to ultimately evaluate student learning, it is also an essential variable in determining teacher efficacy. Effective teacher leaders are wise to spend more attention and resources on refining the quality of differentiated assessments to avoid having to devote an inordinate amount of time to remediation.

Schools provide the social setting/learning context that can either advance or restrict efforts to differentiate instruction. In spite of the autonomy that compartmentalized classrooms provide, master teachers do not operate within a vacuum. The master educator, in any and all subjects, exhibits content mastery infused with pedagogical creativity. They are more cognizant that there is always more on the horizon to discover. To approach being an educator in any other way would mean having missed the point of being a lifelong learner alongside one's students. It is with a sense of awe and innovation that master teachers are capable of embracing the challenge of differentiation, knowing that they are capable of adapting instruction to accommodate the ever-changing learning needs of diverse students. The viability of a professional learning community is promising when educators hold the relevant content knowledge, a diverse pedagogical skill set, a culturally responsive disposition, as well as the commitment to continually invest in their professional learning over the entire span of their career as an educator. Educators that do not embrace differentiated instructional practices are ultimately creating unproductive learning environments for students with atypical learning styles who routinely experience school as if they are square pegs being shoved into round holes.

Educators have a professional obligation to be adaptive and responsive to the varied needs of students as products of their varied cultural contexts. In order to educate every child holistically, we must also educate the whole community. The general public counts on schools to act in the best interests of all youth by helping students and families make informed decisions regarding the educational experiences and training needed in an ever-evolving technological workforce and service sector. Educators should be comfortable learning from cultural informants who can enlighten and enhance their professional practices and success with students. Schools must commit to supporting teachers as they differentiate teaching and assessment strategies to meet the varied needs of their diverse students and communal stakeholders.

I often hear educators state with conviction that schools will be transformed when teachers want the same school experience for every child as they would want for their own child. I generally cringe in silence at the forwarding of this line of thinking because I believe that schools will be reformed when teachers create a different school experience for every child. By differentiating instruction and assessments, teachers empower youth by providing an educational experience based on their individual learner profile. My two sons are a daily reminder of how learners differ, even when they reside in the same household. My oldest son enjoys the "smell of learning" while my youngest son has a kinesthetic learning style, and responds to instruction that involves touching, feeling, and movement. As an educator, I never presume that what works best for my sons works best for every child. Instead, I strive to build relationships with my students that allow me to learn from them so that I can help them learn from me.

Differentiated instruction does not mean doing something different for the sake of being different. It does not mean "out with the old and in with the new." It is more than multiple ways to deliver and explore subject matter. It means diversifying the pedagogical repertoire to utilize a variety of teaching methods and assessments that appeal to multiple learning modalities and thereby enrich the learning community for all participants. At the heart of differentiated instruction, there is the belief that every learner is distinct and entitled to an education that honors their uniqueness and is responsive to their individual developmental learning curve.

Acknowledgments

It is surprising how the process of completing a book, from start to finish, always involves a large number of people. This book, especially, has involved a great number of people. I want to thank all the writers who contributed chapters. There are nineteen of you. Thank you for your willingness to share your expertise, your diligence in completing the chapters, and, in particular, your patience with me.

Thanks, too, to all the people who supported me and helped me stay focused. These people often asked, "How's the book coming along?" So, thank you to Mark and Connie Oswald, Warren Martin, Max Foster, Ron Schmidt, Dale Myers, Gregg Rollwagen, and Dennis Hoppe.

A very huge thank you goes to Dennis Strobel. Without his technical assistance, it's unsure how long it would have taken to complete the book. Thank you, Dennis.

Introduction

Ervin F. Sparapani

No man is an island entire of itself. Each is a piece of the continent, a part of the main
—(John Donne, 1624).

Teachers of the twenty-first century, and the students they teach, live in a common-core-curriculum world laced with assessment and accountability. The philosophy of this "common core" curriculum, with its "one-size-fits-all" mentality, seems to be that somehow the United States' educational system will magically transform itself into the leading educational system in the world, which it probably already is. It appears that, lost in this common core/assessment mentality, is the uniqueness of people, especially students. This uniqueness is captured excellently by the exclamation of Ross Mcclain's son (in the Foreword), "I love the smell of learning!"

The United States of the twenty-first century is a society of diversity, probably the most diverse society in the history of the world, which naturally leads to high diversity within schools. This diversity is not only racial and ethnic diversity, but also intellectual diversity. With the U.S. striving to rise above other countries and be "the best," change needs to occur in schools and classrooms. Unfortunately, even though the U.S. is one of the most culturally diverse countries, what happens in schools and classrooms is not very diverse, and typically does not address the unique capabilities of the diversity of students.

The diversity in society places special demands on the educational system in all states. This diversity emphasizes the need to provide twenty-first century learners with the knowledge and skills that will allow them to live and act as global citizens, citizens of an increasingly dependent world (Garii, 2002).

It is up to teachers to see that all students are provided an adequate education in order for them to become global citizens.

The twenty-first century teacher is confronted with a level of complexity, uncertainty, and diversity that requires a clear direction in schools (Martin, 2010). This is one explanation for the strong belief in a common core curriculum, a curriculum that provide the necessary twenty-first century knowledge and skills. With up-to-the-minute media sources (such as the internet), classroom teachers are no longer the main providers of information, but remain important factors in how this information is processed by students.

A main issue with middle schools and high schools in the U.S., though, is that they are not designed for diversity, or the uniqueness of students, but for conformity to a common standard. The desire to mass-produce proficient students has resulted in an assembly-line mentality in schools that aims to use a standardized process to develop students that are all proficient within an approved framework.

This "economics-of scale" mentality is not without logic; it provides opportunities for all students to be raised to the same standard and ensure an equal opportunity for them. As suggested above, however, each student is unique, racially, culturally, and intellectually. Decisions made to standardize education are made with a "color-blind" mentality, which runs counter to the uniqueness of the individuals who inhabit schools.

Middle school and high school teachers need to have the freedom to decide when to use a standardized approach in their classrooms, and when to use a personalized approach. Wolk (2010) argues that the standardization found in most classrooms is one reason for the failure of many schools to be successful, as determined by high-stakes assessments. Wolk argues that personalizing the curriculum allows the learning process to be more relevant to the student, and can allow for individual differences in intelligence, learning styles, cultural identities, and personal interests. With such a focus, middle school and high school classrooms may be less "standardized" and seem somewhat chaotic, but such a focus may seem more valid to the students who are experiencing their learning in that classroom.

The focus of this textbook is not to speak against the common core curriculum, or assessment. Indeed, in many instances the common core curriculum and the legislatively-mandated assessments have improved the quality of learning in many middle schools and high schools. Rather, the intent of this book is to provide teachers in middle schools and high schools with a basic understanding of the purpose for the common core standards, and provide suggestions for how teachers can design lessons (differentiate instruction) so that the uniqueness of learners is addressed, while still teaching the standards so that students can be successful, not only on the high-stakes assessments, but also in a twenty-first century society that is interconnected and global.

With that the book is divided into three sections, i.e., parts. Part I provides an overview of instruction (Chapter 1), reviews the essentials of differentiated instruction (Chapter 2), compares standards and benchmarks with differentiating instruction (Chapter 3), and shows how a variety of assessments can assist teachers with differentiation (Chapter 4).

Part II, which is the main focus of the text, explains how instruction can be differentiated in the content area disciplines. Chapter 5 discusses differentiating instruction in the English language arts. Chapter 6 discusses differentiating instruction in mathematics. Chapter 7 discusses differentiating instruction in science. Chapter 8 discusses differentiating instruction in social studies. Chapter 9 (the last chapter in Part 2) discusses differentiating instruction in the arts. Each of the chapters discusses the influence of the common core standards and provides examples of lessons (or vignettes of lessons) that differentiate instruction, but still target the essential knowledge expectations of the standards of the discipline.

The third section of the book (Part III) examines how to differentiate for "other" classroom considerations. Chapter 10 discusses teaching for higher-level thinking and presents an instructional system (the Thinking/Learning System) that can help teachers design lessons that differentiate instruction while expecting students to use higher-level thinking skills. Chapter 11 discusses technology and presents ideas for differentiating instruction by using technology in the classroom. Chapter 12 discusses response to intervention (RTI) and how that can be used to differentiate instruction. Chapter 13 discusses how differentiating instruction can be used with "at-risk" learners and (perhaps) affect the drop-out rate. Chapter 14 (the last chapter in Part III and the last chapter in the book), discusses students with cognitive impairments and how differentiating instruction can have a positive effect on the learning experiences of these students.

The twenty-first century world is one of change and diversity. Schools must adapt so that students are prepared for that change and diversity. To do this, schools must change the way they view how instruction is delivered, while maintaining high expectations for students. This book can assist schools in doing that. This book provides a strong foundation in common core standards, assessment, and, especially, differentiating instruction. It can be a valuable instructional resource for middle school and high school teachers and principals, for district-level curriculum designers, and also for teacher educators.

REFERENCES

Garii, B. (2002). Growing good citizens with a world-centered curriculum. *Educational Leadership, 60* (2), 10-13.

Martin, C. (2010). Going global: Adaptive education for local and global citizenship. *Independent School, 70* (1), 68-74.

Wolk, R. (2010). Education: The case for making it personal. *Educational Leadership, 67* (7), 16-21.

I

About Differentiated Instruction

Chapter One

The Nature of Instruction

Ervin F. Sparapani

INTRODUCTION

Instruction, in some form, exists in every facet of life. This chapter on instruction examines what instruction is, how instruction can be delivered, instruction and assessment, and the relationship between the purpose for instruction and differentiated instruction as a concept for thinking about instruction. Instruction is at the core of what teachers do. It goes without saying that effective instruction results in something being taught and something being learned. In education, this generally means delivery of the curriculum in a manner that engages most of the students in a classroom in the learning process. Engaging students in learning can best be done by differentiating the processes of instruction.

Delivery of the curriculum is best understood in the context of a discipline. A teacher teaches the content of a curriculum; students learn the content, and are assessed on what they know about that content. Delivery of the curriculum, though, needs to be understood as including more than content. Differentiated instruction, as delivery of the curriculum, must embrace a person's entire being, mind, body, and spirit. In order to effectively differentiate instruction, teachers need to see students as individuals and build a sense of community in the classroom.

DEFINITION OF INSTRUCTION

Instruction is a fascinating word, which is used in many ways, and can be seen in many forms, from "stand up" teaching, to modeling, to demonstrating, to discussing. In educational settings "stand up" teaching is the most common form of instruction. Outside of an educational setting though (e.g., in the animal kingdom, in families, on the job), modeling, demonstrating, and discussing are more common. Whatever the setting, instruction can be defined as giving information in such a way that another being not only can learn the information, but understands what they are expected to do in a given situation.

As one expects, there are varieties of instruction. Instruction can be directive or explanatory. Instruction can be demonstrating or modeling. Instruction can be discussion. Instruction can be role modeling or mentoring.

In a narrow sense, instruction is directive. Directive instruction is generally very specific, and more like an order, with the person giving the "directive" expecting that the "order" be followed quite specifically. For example, such directive instruction happens when commands are given, as when someone in the military receives a "command" from their superior, or when a person working with a computer gives a "command" to the computer.

Another type of directive instruction is explanatory. Explanatory instruction happens when guidelines or procedures are given. A judge in a courtroom, for example, provides such explanations to a jury when they are ready to begin deliberations on a case. Similarly, a teacher in a classroom uses explanatory instruction to provide guidance for completing an assignment or clarification of information.

Demonstrating and modeling types of instruction occur when an individual (or group of individuals) display for others (those who are watching and learning) how something can be accomplished. Demonstrating and modeling occur "on the job" or in a laboratory when one person is showing others (demonstrating and modeling) how something is to be done. Demonstrating and modeling is also seen when parents or older siblings demonstrate or model acceptable (or unacceptable) behavior. Demonstrating and modeling is also seen in the animal kingdom when an animal mother demonstrates or models hunting, gathering, and safety behaviors for her young.

Discussing as instruction occurs when two or more people have a conversation in order to understand a task. Demonstrating and modeling also involve conversation. Unlike demonstrating and modeling, in which there is someone considered the "leader," in discussion all individuals involved participate as equals. In formal discussion, there is a designated leader. The responsibility of the discussion leader, though, is not to provide answers, but to keep the discussion focused and moving, and, most importantly, to make sure that all voices are heard in the conversation.

Another type of instruction is role modeling or mentoring. In this type of instruction, a person considered to have experience and knowledge with something (an expert) provides another person with advice and counsel when learning or completing a task. Expert role modeling and mentoring are particularly important in circumstances in which a person is new at something and inexperienced, in other words, a novice.

PROVIDING INFORMATION

As noted above, in an educational setting, the actual purpose for instruction is providing information through the delivery of the prescribed curriculum. Typically, in an educational setting, all the aspects of instruction mentioned can be observed at one time or another.

The most appropriate way to deliver the curriculum, or to "differentiate" instruction, is always open for debate. What may work as "best" practice for one teacher is not "best" practice for another. Most teachers agree, however, that the "best" way to deliver the curriculum is by making it meaningful and relevant to the learner. Indeed, the main precept of differentiating instruction is meeting the needs of the learners so that the curriculum is meaningful and relevant.

Instruction Is Communication

Instruction is a communicative process. Communication implies interaction. To have communication there must be a communicator and a recipient of the information being communicated. There are three important features to communication. One, the communicator must communicate in a manner that is understandable to the recipient; two, the communication must be meaningful and relevant to the recipient; and three, if not meaningful and/or relevant, the recipient eventually "tunes out" the communication. In an educational setting, the best way to make learning meaningful and relevant to a recipient (the student) is to select an instructional process that is interactive, engaging, and student centered, i.e., instruction that is differentiated.

Interactive Instruction

Instruction that is interactive allows for constant and open communication between the teacher and the learner. Instruction that is centered on discussion, using questioning strategies, is where the teacher uses pause/wait time appropriately and students are given time to discuss issues with guidance and focus from the teacher, and limited interruption leads toward active communication between teacher and recipient. Grouping strategies that are open-ended, but task-oriented, also tend toward active communication. Such instruction (using questioning strategies or grouping strategies) actively engages the students (is differentiated) and can lead to meaningful, relevant learning.

Engaging instruction divides the time available for instruction into fifteen- to twenty-minute time segments, which means that every fifteen to twenty minutes the students are involved in a different activity focused on the information and the objective(s) for the lesson. Changing activities in this manner keeps the students alert and involved, and keeps their interests elevated, which is especially helpful in middle schools and high schools.

Engaging the Passion of the Learner

Instruction that is differentiated captures the interests and passions of the learner. To engage the passion of the learner, the teacher must be passionate. It is difficult for students to be interested in or be excited about a subject if the teacher does not seem interested or excited. Often teachers are expected to teach material that is not particularly engaging or exciting. The material is in fact, boring, for the teacher to teach and the students to learn. No matter, the teacher still must show passion for teaching and joy in learning. If the teacher shows passion and excitement even for the most tedious material, students will follow the teacher's lead and show excitement about learning, even though not especially interested.

Student-Centered Instruction

Student-centered instruction is differentiated and focused at the ability levels of the learners. Student-centered instruction attempts to nurture the whole child, mind, body, and spirit. Even in activity type classes, instruction concentrates on the mind, which is learning a body of knowledge. Focusing on the mind is appropriate in any educational setting, but for information to be meaningful and relevant (i.e., differentiated) the instruction needs to address the learners' physical and spiritual needs as well. Students, especially in middle level schools, need movement time. Students also need spiritual time, during which they have opportunities as people to explore the mysteries of learning.

VICARIOUS AND EXPERIENTIAL LEARNING

Exploring the mysteries of learning can be either vicarious or experiential. Vicarious learning happens a lot in the classroom. The teacher expects the students to take the knowledge being presented and somehow see it "living" in the real world. Except for a very few learners, that transition is difficult to accomplish. At these times, students often ask, "Why do we need to know this?" or "What is this good for?" Here is where a teacher's passion for the topic is important, and the art of teaching needs to be at its highest.

Taking vicarious learning and making it experiential requires a great deal of creativity. It is easy for learning to be vicarious. Often that is exactly what learning is. For the teacher to take learning and make it come alive in the classroom, though, takes time and energy. Preparing instruction that lives (is interactive, engaging, and student-centered) does not just happen. It is not impossible to do, but it takes planning, usually a great deal of planning. It is easier for the teacher to just leave the learning at the vicarious level, and let the learners figure out how to connect the learning to the real world, than it is to plan experiential lessons where the learners get an opportunity to live the learning. The latter is probably much more beneficial for the learner than the former, but, unfortunately, vicarious learning is simpler to plan and easier on both student and teacher; some form of vicarious instruction is typically what is found in most middle level schools and high schools.

DIDACTIC INSTRUCTION

Instruction can be either didactic (traditional) or flexible. Didactic instruction is where the teacher is the "sage on the stage" imparting their knowledge and wisdom to a group of usually passive students. Flexible instruction is differentiated and considers the diverse needs of the students based on the material to be presented.

Didactic/Traditional Instruction

Didactic/Traditional instruction is stand-up lecture/discussion, with the teacher talking most of the time and the students passively listening (Smerdon, Burkham, & Lee, 1999). Although it does not necessarily have to be, typically didactic/traditional instruction is quite formal and structured. The lecture/discussion (didactic/traditional) method of instruction is the most common pedagogical practice in the world, particularly at the secondary level.

Central to didactic/traditional instruction is lecture with the focus on a textbook, completing worksheet type assignments, with an objective-type test (multiple choice, true/false, fill in the blanks, matching, short-answer) to measure performance at the end of learning. Students are expected to take notes as a way of keeping a record of their learning, which, again, is passive. Students identified as "at-risk" prefer traditional instruction because it is passive. Few expectations are placed on them other than to sit and quietly pretend they are paying attention.

With today's focus on standards and accountability and "getting through the curriculum," traditional instruction comprises the vicarious learning that is typical in secondary schools. A point that must be made, though, is that there is nothing inherently wrong with vicarious learning or traditional instruction. There are times when traditional instruction is necessary. When traditional instruction is the only instruction, then there is a problem.

Explicit Instruction

Another form of didactic/traditional instruction is explicit instruction. Explicit instruction has been around since at least the 1960's. Unlike lecture, which can tend to wander and lack focus, explicit instruction is very systematic and structured, textbook/worksheet oriented, and teacher-centered. Additionally, the explicit instruction process leans toward differentiating instruction by incorporating several of the types of instruction mentioned at the beginning of the chapter, i.e., directing, demonstrating, modeling, discussing. Explicit instruction, though, is still very teacher-centered, in that the teacher is "in charge."

With today's push toward literacy in reading and mathematics, explicit instruction is commonly used in the teaching of basic reading and mathematics skills. Because of the perceived need for structure in presentation of information to students with limited skills in reading and mathematics, teachers who work with students identified as learning disabled, "at risk" learners, or second language learners are especially encouraged to use the explicit instruction format (Hudson, Miller, & Butler, 2006; McCleery & Tindal, 1999; Schmidt, 1993). Also, administrators who want classrooms that are quiet and orderly and seemingly focused at the curriculum, support the use of explicit instruction.

Hudson, et al. (2006) explain the four phases of explicit instruction. Depending on the complexity of the new information, the four phases are intended to last one to two class periods.

Phase one of the explicit instruction process is an advance organizer (this can be a graphic organizer), which presents information that gives the students a foundation for learning the new material to be presented in the lesson. The purpose of the advance organizer is to help students "bridge the gap" from previously learned information to the new information to be learned.

Phase two of the explicit instruction process is demonstration. During this phase the teacher models in an overt manner what the students are expected to learn, as well as the metacognitive and cognitive skills necessary to work appropriately with the new material. Specific to the modeling process, the teacher asks questions and engages students in discussion. The discussion not only keeps students attentive, but helps the teacher monitor student understanding.

The third phase is guided practice. This phase gives an opportunity for students to practice the new learning with the teacher as the guide. The teacher helps students work with the information that has been modeled. At the beginning of this phase the teacher provides a high level of support, with the support decreasing as students become more and more adept at understanding and working with the new information.

Phase four, the final phase of the explicit instruction process, is independent practice. This phase uses a variety of formats, including worksheets, peer tutoring, computer software programs, cooperative learning, and self-correcting material.

Although very systematic and structured, explicit instruction is a practical instructional system. It gives teachers an organized lesson format to design and implement lessons that moves through the curriculum in an orderly fashion, and tends to keep students focused and on task.

FLEXIBLE INSTRUCTION

Flexible instruction is just that—"flexible." Flexible instruction does not function under the didactic/traditional "one-size-fits-all" umbrella, but considers the most appropriate way to deliver information. Flexible instruction differentiates the delivery of the curriculum by attempting to meet the needs of all learners. Flexible instruction can include didactic/traditional means of instruction, but does not begin from the didactic/traditional premise. Rather, flexible instruction considers first the specific needs of the learners, second the information to be learned is considered, and, third, instructional practices are selected that best meet the needs of the learners and the material to be learned. It can be argued that didactic instruction starts from the same premise, but that is inaccurate. Didactic instruction begins with the needs of the teacher and the curriculum. The needs of the learners are secondary.

Two flexible instruction practices are brain-based instruction and constructivist instruction. Slavkin (2003) writes, "The nature of cognition, the functioning of the human brain, and the construction of knowledge are tied to one another" (p. 20).

Brain-Based Instruction

The brain is the center for learning. Everyone knows that. The brain is also very social. It wants to (typically) interact with other brains. It is important, therefore, that teachers understand the way the brain functions as a brain and the manner in which the brain accesses and uses the diverse bits and pieces of information that it encounters.

Given (2002) explains that the brain accesses and works with information through the brain's natural learning systems. According to Given, these learning systems are (1) the emotional learning system, (2) the social learning system, (3) the cognitive learning system, (4) the physical learning system, and (5) the reflective learning system.

Caine and Caine (1994, pp. 88-95) suggest twelve principles essential to brain-based instruction. These are (1) the brain is a parallel processor; (2) when the brain learns a person's entire physiology is engaged; (3) the brain wants to learn; the search for meaning is innate; (4) the search for meaning occurs through patterning; the brain attempts to discern and understand patterns and gives expression to creative patterns of its own; the brain resists the imposition of meaningless patterns; (5) what we learn is influenced and organized by emotions; (6) the brain processes parts and wholes simultaneously; in healthy people, both hemispheres of the brain are interactive and both reduce information into parts and perceive and work with information as a whole; (7) learning involves both focused attention and peripheral perception; (8) learning always involves conscious and unconscious processes; (9) we have at least two different types of memory, a spatial memory system and a set of systems for rote learning; we have a natural, spatial memory system that does not need rehearsal for "instant" memory of experiences, such as what we had for dinner last night; we also have a set of systems specifically designed for storing relatively unrelated bits of information; (10) we understand and remember best when facts and skills are embedded in natural, spatial memory; (11) learning is enhanced by challenge and inhibited by threat; (12) each brain is unique.

Sylwester (2007), when discussing the adolescent brain (indeed any brain), says that the brain is always active and engaged. The brain is constantly accessing information and interpreting its environment. Price (2005) says that the brain is continuously interacting with its surroundings to "learn" how to function appropriately in the environment in which it finds itself. The brain takes in information through the senses (sight, smell, touch, taste, sound) and translates that information into a response. Sometimes the response is appropriate; sometimes the response is inappropriate.

Each brain constructs information that it takes in from its environment in a way athat makes sense to that brain only. The curriculum of a "brain-based" classroom, then, should be thematic and integrated, with a great deal of interaction with others.

The concept of brain-based learning and brain-based instruction in education has been around for quite some time (at least since the early seventies); the idea has not, however, become part of the day-to-day practice of most teachers. There are several reasons for this. First, it is difficult to explain what brain-based instruction is in terms of how it is different from what teachers "normally" do, in that everything a teacher does in the classroom in some way involves the brain and therefore can be categorized as "brain-based." Second, if the brain and the concept of brain-based learning is discussed with those who do research about the brain, it is quickly understood that, even though more is learned everyday about how the brain functions, what is known about the brain is actually limited, particularly when it comes to how a brain learns.

There is, however, a great deal of information known about the brain that is useful knowledge for teachers and how teachers need to think about instructional practice. One such piece of information is that each brain is unique (Caine & Caine, 1994; Hart, 2002). This in itself is probably not new information. How a teacher understands the uniqueness of the brain in classroom practice, though, is important.

For example, a high school teacher designs a lesson, and delivers the lesson in a manner that makes sense to that teacher's brain, and for the brain of that teacher, it very probably is an excellent lesson. The problem comes in the communication of knowledge from the teacher's brain to the learner's brain. As the teacher teaches the lesson, all learners hear and experience the same information; however, the teacher has to remember that each brain is unique, and each learner's brain understands the information in a manner different from how the teacher understands the same information. When a learner does not seem to understand what the teacher is trying to communicate, both the teacher and the learner become frustrated. The problem comes in re-teaching. The teacher uses the same instructional procedures, which both the teacher and learner already know has not worked, but is used anyway.

A teacher must always remember that each brain receives, understands, and processes information in a manner that makes sense to that brain only. It becomes the responsibility of the teacher to have enough variety in the lesson so that during instruction each "brain" has sufficient opportunity to learn the material being presented.

Another piece of information that is helpful for teachers in classrooms has to do with allowing for refreshments or physical movement. Providing time during instruction for a drink of water or some other refreshment (Jenkins, 1995) revitalizes the brain, and, as a result, keeps the learners alert and focused on learning. Physical movement (Given, 2002) is also revitalizing. Intentionally giving time (three to five minutes) during instruction for focused physical movement (through conversation or actually moving) awakens the brain and, again, helps learners stay focused.

It is also well known that learning is affected by emotions (Marzano, 2007; Goleman, 2006; Given, 2002; Hart, 2002, Caine & Caine, 1994). Instruction that resonates with learners in a positive manner awakens their emotions, and will more than likely be learned and remembered. Learners whose emotions are engaged in a positive manner are generally enthusiastic, highly motivated, and interested in learning the information. This does not mean that a teacher must be an entertainer, in the sense of "entertaining the troops." What it does mean is that in some way, through instruction, the teacher's passion for the subject must come through. Learners need to recognize that the teacher has a strong emotional attachment to the topic, so that regardless the information presented (e.g., basic grammar or math skills are not particularly exciting or fascinating topics for the teacher or the learner), the learner may also become emotional (passionate) about the topic, and motivated to learn.

Emotions can also have a negative influence on learning. In a classroom where other learners (or even the teacher), humiliate, degrade, or show disrespect to an individual, that person may not perform well. The learner may become aggressive, or, since they will probably not be able to leave the situation, may shut out all outside activity and find their "safe place" in seclusion. In fact, the only thing the learner may learn is that they need to try to avoid that situation by not showing up for class or being absent from school.

Brain-based instruction goes against the traditional roles of teacher as the information giver and the student being the information receiver. When brain-based instruction is followed the teacher is still the provider of information and the student is still the recipient of the information, but first and foremost in the instruction is the awareness and recognition of the uniqueness of the brain. Brain-based instruction understands that the brain is flexible in its approach to learning and often uses illogical reasoning to be successful in daily experiences. Brain-based instruction knows that learning is not a result of logical and sequential experiences (Hart, 2002). Teachers who consider brain-based instruction as the core of their teaching understand that learning is not immediate. Learning happens after numerous, random experiences.

When instruction is brain-based, learning is facilitated from a variety of trial and error approaches. Through these trial and error activities, students determine what skills are necessary for success. Generally, the more instructional approaches used (i.e., the more differentiated the instruction), the more learning that takes place. The freedom to learn through discovery and practice fits with the natural ways of the brain; the traditional ways of the classroom do not.

Constructivist Instruction

A second flexible approach to instruction is constructivist. Constructivism emphasizes the personal environment of the learner and, based on their environmental backgrounds, how knowledge is constructed by the learner.

Constructivist learning theory applied to education comes from the writings of Jerome Bruner (1973, 1966, 1960) and Lev Vygotsky's socio-cultural theory (Schunk, 2004). Bruner claims that learning is an active process in which learners construct new ideas or concepts based on their current as well as past knowledge. To Vygotsky, learning happens as a person interacts with the environment and others in that environment.

For Vygotsky, two concepts are fundamental, the zone of proximal development (ZPD) and scaffolding. The zone of proximal development is the area between what a learner knows and what the teacher wants the learner to know. Scaffolding occurs within the ZPD as the teacher scaffolds (builds on) experiences so the learner gains the necessary knowledge.

Marlowe and Page (2005, pp. 7-9) explain that constructivism is "about constructing knowledge, not receiving it…; it's about thinking and analyzing, not accumulating and memorizing…; it's about understanding and applying, not repeating back; it's about being active, not passive."

Constructivism, then, can be defined as "a philosophy of learning founded on the premise that, by reflecting on our experiences, we construct our own understanding of the world we live in. Each of us generates our own 'rules' and 'mental models,' which we use to make sense of our experiences. Learning, therefore, is simply the process of adjusting our mental models to accommodate new experiences" (Funderstanding, 2003, p. 1).

Constructivist instruction is a flexible practice that begins with the understanding that all learners live in the world and construct their understanding of the world in a way that makes sense to that learner (Brooks & Brooks, 1999a). Constructivist instruction is not linear. In constructivist practice, information is presented as concepts to be learned in a holistic (Gestalt) manner rather than specific information to be learned in a systematic manner.

Patterns of instruction following constructivist practice (problem-based and authentic learning) have been quite popular. Within constructivism, however, there is much controversy and debate surrounding constructivist practice and its applicability to learning in schools (Phillips, 2000). Central to that debate is the belief that learners, whether or not authentic/problem-based learning is used, will not be exposed to the essential information and fundamental principles of a discipline.

As with brain-based instruction, constructivist instruction is hard to understand, and difficult for teachers to visualize as a viable instructional model. In today's world of standards and curriculum alignment to standards, the expectation is that teachers make sure what students learn is directly connected to state tests used to determine "adequate yearly progress." Teachers cannot see how they can get through the assigned curriculum by using a practice that seems to lack a definite goal or purpose (Brooks & Brooks, 1999b).

Teachers find constructivist instruction problematic because it allows the learner to lead the teacher, and, as such, the learning can take a variety of directions. Teachers typically want to know where instruction is going to take them, and are uneasy when learners are leading the way. Constructivism, though, gives the learner the opportunity to take responsibility and direct their learning, which is what teachers want. In essence, when a teacher implements constructivist instructional practices, the teacher becomes the "guide on the side" rather than the "sage on the stage" (Smerdon et al., 1999).

Taking on the role of "guide on the side" does not mean that in constructivist instructional practice, the teacher stands by and watches while the students "do" something. That is not it at all. Implementing constructivist instruction means that the teacher has to be just as actively involved as the learners. The teacher's role is still guiding and directing, encouraging the learners to an understanding of the information being presented. The guiding and directing happen differently. When using constructivism, the teacher "constructs" and learns along with the students. For many teachers, constructivist instruction is freeing because it gives them the feeling of "teacher" consistent with the way they imagined teaching to be.

Perkins (1999) recognizes three distinct roles of the learner in constructivism. He identifies these roles as the "active learner," the "social learner," and the "creative learner."

The "active learner" along with the teacher, is fully engaged in the learning process, and fully involved in gaining and understanding the information they are expected to learn. Rather than only reading, writing, listening, doing work sheet exercises, and the like, active learners "discuss, debate, hypothesize, and take viewpoints" (Perkins, 1999, p. 7).

The "social learner" is not an isolated learner. Constructivism understands that learning is a social process, and is constructed by interaction with other learners. In constructivist practice, learning is "co-constructed in dialogue with others" (Perkins, 1999, p. 7). Additionally, the teacher understands the social aspects of learning, and builds social learning opportunities into the instructional process.

The "creative learner" not only investigates knowledge, but sees (or discovers) other possibilities for using the knowledge. In constructivism, learners, with the help of the teacher, are more than active; as they engage in the learning, the learners create or "recreate" their own understandings of the principles being learned. By so doing they begin to take ownership of the knowledge.

"Under the theory of constructivism, teachers focus on making connections between facts and fostering new understanding in learners. Teachers shape their teaching strategies to learner responses and encourage learners to analyze, interpret, and predict information. Teachers also rely heavily on open-ended questions and promote extensive dialogue among students" (Funderstanding, 2003, p. 2).

The research literature (e.g., Howard, McGee, & Schwartz, 2000; Tucker & Batchelder, 2000; Cobb, 1999) has shown that learners can be quite successful in learning situations that follow a constructivist design model. The research points out, however, that in order to be successful, constructivist learning situations need knowledgeable subject matter experts as teachers, and learners who are motivated, independent, and self-directed.

Constructivist learning, constructivist thinking, constructivist instruction is based on people addressing a common problem (an issue of importance and relevance) and learning from each other, with input from an expert. When people discuss, they learn from each other. Each person has an insight that another may not have. Or, if two or three people have the same insight, one person sees the issue in a different way, or with more depth.

PERSPECTIVES ON INSTRUCTIONAL PRACTICE

Planning for Instruction

Appropriately planning for instruction, whether instruction is didactic or flexible, is always important. Probably the most important responsibility of a teacher is planning for instruction. Planning for instruction is a major part of what any teacher experiences in undergraduate or graduate teacher preparation programs.

When using didactic/traditional instruction, instruction does not need much planning. With didactic methods much of the planning is already accomplished, and the kind of planning a teacher learns in their teacher preparation program is not used to its fullest extent. With didactic methods, the teacher becomes a facilitator of canned information rather than using their knowledge and expertise to design their own classroom instruction.

Because of the order and structure it provides, the public, many school district administrators, and often teachers, seem to like didactic instruction. Didactic instruction has the school district providing a curriculum (which has been aligned with state standards) providing a textbook, and expecting teachers to "teach" the curriculum as identified by the textbook. A high-stakes test assesses whether teachers have "taught" the curriculum. Ultimately, responsibility for learning is placed with the teacher.

Unlike the didactic method, flexible instructional practices place more responsibility for planning with the teacher. A curriculum plan and a textbook are still provided by the school district. Also, the curriculum plan is aligned with state and/or national standards, and student learning is assessed by a high-stakes test that determines whether the teacher has "taught" the curriculum. There are two major differences between didactic instruction and flexible instruction.

One major difference between didactic and flexible instruction is that with flexible instruction a school district's curriculum plan serves as a guide for teachers rather than the rule that teachers need to follow. A flexible instruction model expects teachers to know, based on their teacher training and subject matter expertise, (1) how to plan, (2) what students should learn, and (3) the appropriate instructional strategies for helping students learn.

The second major difference between didactic and flexible instruction is that with flexible instruction students are more actively involved in determining what information they want to learn and how they want to learn that information. Flexible instruction takes on the character of differentiated instruction. As such, responsibility for learning is placed with the student and the teacher together as partners in the learning process.

Implementing Instruction

The manner by which instruction is implemented is as important as how instruction is planned. Doubtless it is apparent that flexible instructional practice is considered more appropriate than didactic instruction. One size, however, does not fit all. There are times when didactic instruction is appropriate and serves a purpose.

Didactic instruction, though, should not be the guiding pedagogical practice. The secondary teacher should always begin from the perspective of flexible instruction.

Flexible instruction, though, demands more of the teacher. Also, flexible instruction demands more of the learner. Further, flexible instruction may take more time to cover the curriculum, which can create problems for the teacher. Teachers, generally, want to be flexible, but they also are expected to "teach" the curriculum in a timely manner. To feel comfortable with what they are expected to do, teachers need a structure, or at least a guide. Understanding by design (Wiggins & McTighe, 1998) and habits of mind (Costa & Kallick, 2000a; 2000b) are curriculum design concepts that provide structure for teachers and the kind of instructional variety inherent to brain-based and constructivist practice. In addition, Barell (2007) and Crawford (2007) are valuable resources for helping secondary teachers design problem-based lessons and units.

Both "understanding by design" and the "habits of mind" provide coherence for the curriculum. Teachers who want more structure should look to understanding by design. Teachers who want more flexibility should look to the habits of mind.

ASSESSMENT AND INSTRUCTION

Instruction is not complete without assessment. Somehow the teachers and the students need to know that the information, which has been delivered, investigated, and experienced, has been "learned." Whenever learning is considered, assessment enters the picture. Assessment includes evaluation and measurement, and refers to the collection and analysis of information and the use of the information to make a decision of or on competent performance of the learner.

The "measurement" part of assessment is the data-gathering part; such data-gathering is usually accomplished by students taking tests, or completing worksheets, or performing a multiple of possible tasks. Data, then, are gathered through a variety of assigned tasks that show level of performance or change in behavior.

The "evaluation" part of assessment takes the measurement data and uses those data to place a value on performance. The typical designator of performance is either a grade level (e.g., an eighth-grade reading level) or a letter grade. The "value" placed on performance is then used by many (teachers, administrators, students, parents/guardians, the public) as a numerical quantity used for comparative purposes.

There are two main types of assessments, performance assessments and standardized assessments. Performance assessments can include constructed response items, essays, writing, oral discourse, exhibitions, experiments, and portfolios. Standardized tests are assessments based on some national norm (or standard) for a particular grade level, and used by school districts and states to show annual progress of students at each grade level. Scores from standardized tests are also used as one criterion for entry into a college/university or a vocational/technical school.

A huge issue among assessment people has to do with validity and reliability of measure. In order to provide an acceptable indicator of performance, assessments need to be appropriately valid and reliable. An appropriately valid and reliable instrument lends credibility to a learner's performance based on the score on that instrument.

Standardized instruments have established validity and reliability; however, items on standardized instruments are general across the nation rather than specific to the curriculum of a certain state, school district, or teacher. Also, standardized instruments are often in multiple- choice format, which, if one agrees with information on brain-based learning, does not work well for all learners. Consequently, for some learners, a score on a standardized test, even though the test itself has high validity and reliability, may not be a valid or reliable indicator of performance for that learner. For those who believe in explicit/traditional instruction, however, standardized assessments fit quite well.

Performance assessments, on the other hand, are more closely connected to the curriculum of a teacher or a school district. On the face of it, performance assessments are supposed to be connected to the specific objectives of a school district's or teacher's curriculum, but often the alignment between curriculum objectives, assessments, and what is actually taught by the teacher or experienced by the student is not very strong. As a result, even if rubrics are used to score a performance assessment, validity and reliability of performance assessments can be suspect.

School districts and the public want (and deserve) an annual accounting of student performance. They want to know that students are learning the curriculum the students are expected to learn. Any assessment plan should include a balance of performance assessments and standardized assessments. One type of assessment should not overshadow the other.

Performance assessments should be the most powerful indicators of performance. Due to the alignment issues mentioned above, as well as subjectivity in scoring, performance assessments are not always viewed as the best indicators. Additionally, it takes a great deal of resources on the part of states and school districts, and a great deal of time on the part of teachers, to develop quality performance assessments.

The publishers of standardized instruments have already invested the time and resources to develop a quality instrument. As a result, even though there are still high costs accrued by a school district, and even though standardized assessments may not be as closely aligned to the curriculum as performance assessments, standardized tests tend to be more efficient. Also, data from standardized tests are often viewed as more accurate measures of year-to-year performance. Additionally, a factor inherent to standardized assessments that is not a factor in performance assessments is that data from a standardized assessment can be compared across a school district, across a state, and across the nation.

INSTRUCTION AND DIFFERENTIATED INSTRUCTION

In education, instruction is what happens in a classroom on a daily basis as a teacher delivers the curriculum and students experience the curriculum. Differentiated instruction is not a specific instructional practice, but a concept that targets delivering the curriculum using a variety of approaches. Differentiated instruction works from the premise that there is no "one size fits all" curriculum and it is the responsibility of the teachers to understand the uniqueness of each individual student and provide opportunities in the classroom for all students to learn and be successful. Instruction is a given, whether the instruction is differentiated is another matter.

CONCLUDING THOUGHTS

Effective instruction in the secondary classroom of the twenty-first century, unlike the past, cannot be folded into a one-size-fits-all format. Society has changed. Cultures have changed. What is understood about how people learn has changed. It should be well known by now that there is not one best way to deliver the curriculum.

All teachers approach the classroom in a manner that fits their personality and what they believe is the best way to deliver the content of their curriculum. Some teachers believe in explicit instruction; others believe in flexible instruction. Whether instruction begins from an explicit perspective or a flexible perspective, the learners and the content to be learned need to be considered first. The "same-old/same-old" gets "old" in a hurry, for everyone.

Teachers want learners to be focused and engaged. To be an effective teacher in the twenty-first century, instruction for all learners needs to start with how instruction will be assessed and always be differentiated.

REFERENCES

Barell, J. (2007). *Problem-based learning: An inquiry approach.* Thousand CA: Corwin Press.

Brooks, J. G. & Brooks, M. G. (1999a). *The case for constructivist classrooms.* Alexandria, VA: Association for Supervision and Curriculum Development.

Brooks, M. G. & Brooks, J. G. (1999b). The courage to be constructivist. *Educational Leadership, 57* (3), 18-24.

Bruner, J. (1960). *The process of education.* Cambridge, MA: Harvard University Press.

Bruner, J. (1966). *Toward a theory of instruction.* Cambridge, MA: Harvard University Press.

Bruner, J. (1973). *Going beyond the information given.* New York, NY: Norton Publishers.

Caine, R. N. & Caine, G. (1994). *Making connections: Teaching and the human brain.* Menlo Park, CA: Addison-Wesley Publishing Company.

Cobb, T. (1999). Applying constructivism: A test for the learner-as scientist. *Educational Technology Research and Development, 47* (3), 15-31.

Costa, A. & Kallick, B. (Eds.). (2000a). *Activating & engaging habits of mind.* Alexandria, VA: Association for Supervision and Curriculum Development.

Costa, A. & Kallick, B. (Eds.). (2000b). *Discovering & exploring habits of mind.* Alexandria, VA: Association for Supervision and Curriculum Development.

Crawford, G. B. (2007). *Brain-based teaching with adolescent learning in mind* (2nd ed.). Thousand Oaks, CA: Corwin Press.

Funderstanding. (2003). *Constructivism.* Available at www.funderstanding.com/constructivism.cfm.

Given, B. K. (2002). *Teaching to the brain's natural learning systems.* Alexandria, VA: Association for Supervision and Curriculum Development.

Goleman, D. (2006). *Emotional intelligence.* New York, NY: Bantam Books.

Hart, L. A. (2002). *Human brain & human leaning* (3rd ed.). Covington, WA: Books for Educators.

Howard, B. C., McGee, S., & Schwartz, N. (2000). The experience of constructivism: Transforming teacher epistemology. *The Journal of Research on Computing in Education, 32* (4), 455-465.

Hudson, P., Miller, S. P., & Butler, F. (2006). Adapting and merging explicit instruction within reform-based mathematics classrooms. *American Secondary Education, 35* (1), 19-32.

Jenkins, E. (1995). *The learning brain.* Del Mar, CA: The Brain Store.

Marlowe, B. A. & Page, M. L. (2005). *Creating and sustaining the constructivist classroom* (2nd ed.). Thousand Oaks, CA: Corwin Press.

Marzano, R. J. (2007). *The art and science of teaching: A comprehensive framework for effective instruction.* Arlington, VA: Association for Supervision and Curriculum Development.

McCleery, J. A. & Tindal, G. A. (1999). Teaching the scientific method to at-risk students and students with learning disabilities through concept anchoring and explicit instruction. *Remedial and Special Education, 20* (1), 7-18.

Perkins, D. (1999). The many faces of constructivism. *Educational Leadership, 57* (3), 6-11.

Phillips, D. C. (Ed.). (2000). *Constructivism in education: Opinions and second opinions on controversial* issues. Chicago, IL: The University of Chicago Press.

Price, L. F. (2005). The biology of risk taking. *Educational Leadership, 62* (7), 22-26.

Schmidt, R. (1993). Awareness and second-language acquisition. *Annual Review of Applied Linguistics, 13* (1), 129-158.

Schunk, D. 2004). *Learning theories: An educational perspective* (4th ed.). Upper Saddle River, NJ: Pearson Education.

Slavkin, M. (2003). Engaging the heart, hand, brain. *Principal Leadership (Middle School Edition), 3* (9), 20-25.

Smerdon, B. A., Burkam, D. T., & Lee, V. E. (1999). Access to constructivist and didactic teaching: Who gets it? Where is it practiced? *Teachers College Record, 101* (5), 5-34.

Sylwester, R. (2007). *The adolescent brain*. Thousand Oaks, CA: Corwin Press.

Tucker, G. R. & Batchelder, A. (2000). *The integration of technology into a constructivist curriculum: Beyond PowerPoint*. Arlington, VA. (ERIC Document Reproduction Service No. ED 444 592).

Wiggins, G. & McTighe, J. (1998). *Understanding by design*. Alexandria, VA: Association for Supervision and Curriculum Development.

Chapter Two

About Differentiated Instruction

Ervin F. Sparapani, Ryan H. Walker, & Marie E. Van Tiflin

INTRODUCTION

The people of the United States live in a diverse society, and that diversity brings a variety of learners to the secondary classroom (VanSciver, 2005). The challenge to help all students succeed is present for secondary teachers every day in every classroom. Often secondary teachers have the belief that focusing on diversity and attempting to differentiate instruction to address that diversity brings chaos and instability to the classroom. Teachers want order and continuity, not complexity and uncertainty.

The field of education is constantly growing and changing. Society's expectations for the education of its youth have been increasing for decades (Kovalik & Olsen, 2002). Students are expected to exhibit independent critical thinking skills. The same students are also expected to function in group settings as positive, contributing members (Simpson, 2005; Tomlinson, 2006). Schools have been given the responsibility to teach young people the skills society deems necessary to function. Therefore, educators have sought new methods to increase the quality of student's educational experiences in relation to society's expectations. Although not a specific instructional method as such, an idea that can intentionally address classroom diversity is the concept of differentiated instruction.

Mastering the art of differentiating any curriculum according to the needs of any given set of students is the challenge that diversity can bring. It is our belief, and the premise of this book, that the most appropriate way to address the diverse composition of learners in the classroom is through differentiating instruction. Our understanding of differentiating instruction, and our way of defining differentiated instruction, is that it is a way to address (1) students' readiness needs, (2) students' interests, and (3) students' ways of learning. As Tomlinson (1999b) maintains, at its core, differentiated instruction is a means of addressing ways by which students vary as learners.

In order to begin any kind of differentiation, teachers first need to examine what they truly believe about the learner and what they can learn. Preconceived ideas about particular students or student groups must be addressed. A teacher needs to approach all students with an optimism that encourages them to learn.

If a teacher believes that students can learn, they will be more apt to arrange a positive environment for learning, and be more willing to be flexible in their delivery of material. Positive teachers see diversity as a challenge and opportunity instead of a problem. Positive teachers know that their students can succeed and take it upon themselves to make sure they do. Differentiating instruction can be a way to make this happen because essentially, as already has been stated, differentiated instruction is based on the premise that teachers should adapt instruction to each student's individual needs, abilities, and interests (Willis & Mann, 2000).

BACKGROUND

Since the dawn of formal education, educators have sought to implement teaching strategies that would both inspire and motivate their students to learn at the highest levels of their potential. New "best practices" are constantly being introduced, tested, critiqued, and discarded; each having failed to live up to the publicity and hype (Wolfe, 2001). As a result, teachers remain frustrated with a lack of student effort, stressed by the pressure to raise standardized test scores, and overwhelmed by the variety of abilities found in their classrooms (Jerald, 2006; VanSciver, 2005; Posner, 2004).

The appeal of differentiated instruction is that through this concept, teachers can use a variety of "best practices" to tailor instruction to meet the various strengths of each student in a diverse classroom (VanSciver, 2005; Strong, Thomas, Perini, & Silver, 2004). Differentiated instruction is not a ready-made kit that will revolutionize classroom activities and student performance (Pettig, 2000; Tomlinson, 1999a). Rather, differentiated instruction describes a wide variety of teaching strategies and practices that seek to recognize and celebrate individual student preferences and strengths.

While there are varieties of instructional practices that differentiate for instruction, they do share several characteristics in common (Tomlinson, 1999b). First, each variety of differentiated instruction begins by identifying students' strengths and weaknesses. Then, by addressing the tenets of differentiated instruction (see below), teachers develop lesson plans that accentuate students' strengths and downplay students' weaknesses. This ultimately creates an environment in which all students can experience academic success.

Central to differentiated instruction are three principles. These principles are that (1) students differ in their learning profiles, (2) classrooms in which students are active learners, decision makers, and problem solvers are more natural and effective than those in which students are served a "one-size-fits-all" curriculum and treated as passive recipients of information, and (3) making meaning out of important ideas is as important as "covering information" (Sparks-Langer, Starko, Pasch, Burke, Moody, & Gardner, 2004; Tomlinson, 1999b).

ESSENTIAL FACTORS TO CONSIDER WHEN DIFFERENTIATING INSTRUCTION

When planning to differentiate instruction, whether the planning involves a school-wide curriculum design or lesson plans designed by teachers, there are five essential factors that must be considered. These are:

- Key Questions/Important Skills/Learner Outcomes. The first essential factor is the key questions (what Wiggins & McTighe, 2005, refer to as essential questions) are fundamental to framing curriculum and lesson planning. The key questions are the major questions that learners need to understand about a discipline, and lead to the important skills and learner outcomes central to unit and lesson design.
- Assessment. The second essential factor is assessment. In the twenty-first century, assessment-based decision making drives curriculum planning. Assessment must include pre-assessment, formative assessment, and summative assessment.
- Standards and Benchmarks of the Discipline. The third factor essential to differentiating instruction is the standards and benchmarks of the discipline. It goes without saying that in all instruction, including differentiated instruction, the standards and benchmarks of the discipline must be addressed.
- Twenty-First Century Knowledge and Skills. The fourth essential factor is the twenty-first century knowledge and skills that learners must have in order to be successful in the twenty-first century world. The curriculum should address all the twenty-first century skills, but lesson planning should focus particularly on the skills of critical thinking, problem solving, creative thinking, and knowledge of technology and the ethical use of technology.
- The Uniqueness of the Learner. The fifth essential factor is the uniqueness of the learner. When differentiating instruction, the curriculum and the

lessons that deliver the curriculum must consider the learner first, and the contextual factors that affect learner success.

Society has changed, thus students have changed (Simpson, 2005). Education must follow this pattern and alter the traditional instruction path common to past students (Noble, 2004). Differentiated instruction is a concept that can increase student understanding and result in higher student achievement scores on standardized tests (Faulkner & Cook, 2006; Willis & Mann, 2000).

Students who truly understand concepts, ideas, and information will naturally perform higher on assessments of achievement. More importantly, students will experience academic success, which encourages them to continue to succeed academically (Tomlinson, 2006; Dreher, 1997). The point is that by using differentiated instruction all students can learn.

MEETING INDIVIDUAL STUDENT NEEDS

Doctors tailor each diagnosis to each patient's individual symptoms, mechanics work on automobiles based on targeted problems, and architects design buildings based on the customer's likes and/or dislikes (Keck & Kinney, 2005). Similarly, teachers should design curriculum and classroom methods that are intended to meet all students' educational demands (Tomlinson, 1998). The public, as legislated by state governments, expects that schools develop ways to ensure the academic success of all students (Faulkner & Cook, 2006).

It is certain that with such legislation, measured by student performance on high-stakes tests, many teachers are left scrambling to teach to the test because their job is at stake ("The intelligence," 2007; Higgins, Miller, & Wegman, 2006; Odland, 2006; Scott, 2005). Not only are teachers concerned about their jobs, they are finding that because of the high-stakes tests, they are not able to develop appropriate programs so that students can learn (Rothstein & Jacobsen, 2006).

Educators are also not allowed flexibility in the way that they teach, and students are being forced to squelch their creativity and miss out on exploring their own potential (Odland, 2006; Rothstein & Jacobsen, 2006; Brown, 2006). In a lecture situation where students are taking notes, it is probable that if students are not focused on the task at hand, none of the lecture is processed into the memory of the brain (Wolfe, 2001; Banikowski & Mehring, 1999). Teachers are conscious of the error in policy and are aware that preparing students for a test limits their abilities on their job and degrades their position (Lewis, 2006; Scott, 2005; Berliner, 2005; Wilson, Cordry, Notar, & Friery, 2004).

Jones (2005) proposes that endless hours spent memorizing specifics for a test does not assist memory, but hinders it by decreasing the ability to memorize extensive information. Jones also notes that a lot of time spent going over information does not necessarily mean that students will remember it unless there is an emotional event that is surrounding the information. The task at hand then is that teachers are to create a context-rich environment where students are able to remember specific details and imprint them into their brain's recollection (Wolfe, 2001; Banikowski & Mehring, 1999).

In fact, student's brains are looking to make a connection with the material that is being presented, and if they are not able to, the information is discarded. It is also known that the physiological basis for memory is connected with an experience that changes the way synaptic connections are made, thus creating a significant impact on the brain's memory. Therefore, a teacher's task is to create an environment where students can remember what they have learned.

Teachers have to differentiate instruction to provide interesting and new experiences for their students that engage them on an emotional level (Armstrong, 2009; Brier & Hall, 2007; Green, 1999; Banikowski & Mehring, 1999). When they are shown different ways to remember material and are presented with a variety of learning strategies, each student has the capacity to learn.

Teachers used to believe that all students learned the same material in the same manner (Dreher, 1997). Differentiated instruction has provided an avenue to connect the content of the curriculum to a student's strengths. Differentiated instruction has created a positive effect for students in all content areas (Bishop & Pflaum, 2005; Tomlinson, 1998).

INSTRUCTIONAL PRACTICES THAT DIFFERENTIATE INSTRUCTION

The key to a differentiated classroom is that all students are regularly offered choices and students are matched with tasks compatible with their individual learner profiles. Tomlinson (1999b) and Willis and Mann (2000) say that the curriculum in such a classroom should be differentiated in three areas, (1) content (The teacher provides multiple options to students for taking in information), (2) process (The teacher provides multiple options to students to make sense out of the ideas being presented), and (3) product. (The teacher provides multiple options to students for expressing what they know about what they have learned).

In this section of the chapter, three instructional practices (multiple intelligences, the 4MAT, and the Teaching/Learning System) are presented that can assist secondary teachers in differentiating instruction. Each practice provides a different way to differentiate. For more information about differentiated instruction practices, Tomlinson (1999b) gives a somewhat complete list. For examples of differentiated instruction related to specific content areas (the core curriculum and the arts) see chapters 5, 6, 7, 8, and 9.

Multiple Intelligences

The traditional view of how people display their intelligence is through language and mathematics. Gardner (1983), however, questions this tradition and suggests that there are multiple ways people show their intelligence. Gardner initially suggests seven intelligences (linguistic, logical-mathematical, spatial, musical, physical, intrapersonal, and interpersonal). He has since added an eighth intelligence (naturalist) and has implied the possibility of a ninth (existential).

Typically, as mentioned earlier, secondary teachers design instruction that focuses at the traditional view of intelligence (linguistic and logical-mathematical), and ignore the other six; however, a teacher who differentiates their instruction begins with the traditional lesson design (linguistic and/or logical mathematical) and adds two to three of the other intelligences.

A differentiated lesson design using the multiple intelligences would be framed around the linguistic or logical-mathematical intelligences. In addition, the lesson would include the spatial intelligence, either the musical, naturalist, or physical intelligences, and either the intra-personal or interpersonal intelligences.

Armstrong (2009) contains a wealth of information on the multiple intelligences. He is an excellent source of suggestions for designing multiple intelligence lessons that are differentiated.

The 4MAT System

The 4MAT system, designed by Bernice McCarthy (1990; 1980), is an excellent, practical tool for implementing differentiated instruction. The 4MAT system differentiates instruction by addressing McCarthy's four learning styles, i.e., imaginative, analytical, common sense, and dynamic. The 4MAT system is divided into four quadrants (corresponding with McCarthy's four learning styles), which become a cyclical, eight-step unit of instruction. Each quadrant has a minimum of two lessons.

In addition to considering the four learning styles, the 4MAT takes into consideration the right/left-mode functioning of the brain. As such, each of the quadrants includes at least one lesson that is designed in a manner that addresses left-brain functions and at least one lesson designed in a manner that addresses right-brain functions.

Units that follow the 4MAT system begin "on the street," move into "school," and end back "on the street." The first step in any 4MAT unit is to simulate a "real world" experience in the protected environment of the class-room. In this simulated environment, the students encounter the information to be learned in the unit in a manner that shows how the information exists in the world. The result is that all students have some prior "real-world" knowl-edge of the information before learning the information "in school." Once students experience the topic in a "real-world" manner, the topic is learned in the typical "school" manner.

After learning the subject matter "in school," students develop ownership of their learning by bringing it back "to the street;" in essence, the students take the information back "out to the world." This time, though, the experi-ence is not simulated. Students design and make a project that shows their understanding of the subject matter learned and bring it out "to the street."

The 4MAT System takes time to learn, but it is a fascinating way to design units and address learner diversity. More information about the 4MAT System and designing lessons based on the 4MAT System can be found at McCarthy's web site www.aboutlearning.com.

The Thinking/Learning (T/L) System

The Thinking/Learning (T/L) System is another quality approach to differen-tiate instruction. The T/L System, designed by Peter Edwards and Ervin F. Sparapani (see Sparapani, 2000; Edwards & Sparapani, 1996), differentiates instruction by designing lessons that address higher-level thinking. The T/L System differentiates instruction by combining specific levels of Bloom's taxonomy (knowledge, application, analysis, evaluation) with four higher-level thinking skills (information gathering, critical thinking, creative think-ing, decision making) and left-, right-, and whole-brain modes of brain func-tioning. Each T/L System lesson includes the four levels of Bloom's taxono-my, the four higher-level thinking skills, and the modes of brain functioning.

As with the 4MAT System, the T/L System takes time to learn, but it is an excellent way of addressing learner diversity and providing students with depth and breadth of knowledge. The T/L System is explained in more com-plete detail in chapter 10.

ASSESSMENT AND DIFFERENTIATED INSTRUCTION

For differentiated instruction to be effective, it is important that assessment is done appropriately and consistently. Assessments need to be timely so accu-rate feedback can be communicated to students to help them adjust their learning and for teachers to understand how information is being processed by their students (Wormeli, 2008). It is important that assessments always focus on the unit and/or lesson objectives. Whenever differentiated instruction is practiced, three methods of assessment are recommended, pre-assessment, formative assessment, and summative assessment. Each is discussed below. A thorough discussion of the relationship between assessment and differentiating instruction can be found in chapter 4.

Pre-Assessment

Pre-assessment is used at the beginning of each lesson or unit. Pre-assessments come in many forms. They can be pre-tests, in which the teacher administers a brief test (ten to fifteen items long) to determine prior knowledge of the topic. Another type of pre-assessment is teacher observation. When teachers use observation, the teacher gives the students a task to perform and observes how well the students do the task, which parts of the task the students seem to struggle with, and which parts of the task the students seem to understand. A third pre-assessment a teacher can use is by simply asking questions about the topic. A fourth type of pre-assessment is using checklists. When using checklists, the teacher gives the students a list of topics that might be included in a lesson/unit and asks the students to check off what they know and what they do not know.

Formative Assessment

Formative assessment is important in differentiated instruction because it provides feedback to both students and teacher about student learning. Formative assessment serves the purpose of tracking the progress of student learning, and checking where students are in their learning. Basically, formative assessment is used to provide an ongoing record of how well each student understands the material they are expected to learn.

Formative assessment can include peer evaluations, talk arounds, exit cards, portfolio checks, and journal entries. Obviously there are other types of formative assessments, but those listed have been selected because they provide a more holistic view of student learning, and include voices other than the teacher.

Peer evaluations begin with a specified set of criteria, based on a rubric. Each student submits their work according to the rubric criteria, and then student work is randomly assigned to peers for evaluation based on the rubric. After peers evaluate, it is recommended that the teacher re-evaluate each peer-evaluated rubric for accuracy and possible subjectivity.

A "talk around" begins with a specific set of questions that deal with specific lesson objectives. After pre-reading assigned information, or taking notes from teacher lecture, or after discussion of some topic, the teacher goes around the room, asking questions, and having students name or identify one aspect of the information the question addresses. A key to a successful "talk around" is that no questions are repeated.

Exit cards are used at the end of class to make sure students understand the key aspects of that day's information. Either 3 x 5 cards or post-it notes can be used. On the 3 x 5 cards or post-it notes, students are asked to write down the three main topics learned that day, plus a topic from the day's instruction about which they need more information or clarification, and then hand the cards in to the teacher at the end of class. The teacher reviews the exit cards and responds to questions or provides additional information the following day.

Portfolio checks include examples of work collected during a specific lesson that demonstrate student knowledge, application, and synthesis of the lesson. A rubric is used to assess competency.

Journal entries are similar to exit cards except that students write a paragraph or two about the key points learned in class that day. The teacher checks the journal entries for understanding and provides additional information as necessary.

Summative Assessment

Summative assessment is assessment that takes into consideration all a student has done to learn the material being taught. Whereas formative assessment provides feedback on a particular task, summative assessment takes into account performance on all tasks, and provides a comprehensive gauge for determining the totality of learning. Summative assessment is an indicator of cumulative performance over a period of time.

Summative assessments include, but are not limited to, unit tests, demonstrations, and performance tasks. Regarding summative assessment and differentiated instruction, it is important to keep in mind that one summative assessment, like just using a unit test, is not a good indicator of student learning. Differentiating instruction in a unit involves students in a variety of learning tasks. With that, it is important that at least two summative assessments are used. More than one summative assessment (e.g., a unit test and a demonstration assignment) provides a more accurate measure of student learning.

CONCLUDING THOUGHTS

Economic factors, social issues, technological advancements, and a myriad of other agents of change have drastically altered the face of education (Simpson, 2005). Changes in social, economic, and family issues are ensuring that students will come to institutions of education from a wide variety of backgrounds and with vastly different experiences (Armstrong, 2009; Simpson, 2005). Because of this, educational needs, skills, abilities, and interests for students today tend to be more complex than the needs of students in the past (Bishop & Flaum, 2005). Differentiated instruction not only takes this into consideration, it is the basis for its existence (Willis & Mann, 2000; Tomlinson, 1999b).

Differentiated instruction is an exciting concept, and can be a successful educational tool when administration, teachers, parents, and, ultimately, students work in harmony. Schools, from superintendents to principals to teachers to parents, need to work together and support each other. When all constituencies are coordinated in their efforts, differentiated instruction can have a tremendous influence on student interest in and attitude toward their learning. This can be accomplished by differentiating instruction in order to purposefully address the standards and benchmarks established for the content areas, as well as the other essential factors for differentiating instruction. Chapter 3 discusses standards and benchmarks and their relationship to differentiating instruction. Chapter 4 discusses assessment and its relationship to differentiated instruction. Additionally, chapters 5-9 discuss the key questions, standards and benchmarks, assessments, twenty-first century knowledge and skills, and the uniqueness of the learner as they relate to the specific content areas covered in each chapter.

REFERENCES

Armstrong, T. (2009). *Multiple intelligences in the classroom,* (3rd ed.). Alexandria, VA: Association for Supervision and Curriculum Development.

Banikowski, A. & Mehring, T. (1999). Strategies to enhance memory based on brain-research. *Focus on Exceptional Children, 32* (3), 16-36.

Berliner, D. (2005). The near impossibility of testing for teacher quality. *Journal of Teacher Education, 56,* 205-209.

Bishop, P. A. & Pflaum, S. W. (2005). Student perceptions of action, relevance, and pace. *Middle School Journal, 36* (4), 4-12.

Brier, G. & Hall, M. (2007). From frustrating forgetfulness to fabulous forethought. *The Science Teacher, 77* (1), 24-27.

Brown, D. (2006). It's curriculum, stupid: There's something wrong with it. *Phi Delta Kappan, 87,* 777-783.

Dreher, S. (1997). Learning styles: Implications for learning & teaching. *Rural Educator, 19* (2), 26-29.

Edwards, P. & Sparapani, E. F. (1996). The thinking/learning system: A teaching strategy for the management of diverse learning styles and abilities. *Educational Studies and Research, 14* (2), 2-12.

Faulkner, S. & Cook, C. (2006). Testing vs. teaching: The perceived impact of four assessment demands on middle grades instructional practices. *Research in Middle Level Education Online, 29,* (7). Available at www.nmsa.org/Publications/RMLEOnline/Articles.

Gardner, H. (1983). *Frames of mind: The theory of multiple intelligences.* New York, NY: BasicBooks, A division of HarperCollins Publishers.

Green, F. (1999). Brain and learning research: Implications for meeting the needs of diverse learners. *Education, 119,* 682-688.

Higgins, B., Miller, M., & Wegmann, S. (2006). Teaching to the test...not! Balancing best practice and testing requirements in writing: High-quality, evidence-based instruction need not be sacrificed in preparing students to succeed on standardized writing assessments. *The Reading Teacher, 60,* 310-320.

Jerald, C. D. (2006). *'Teach to the test'? Just say no.* Arlington, VA. (ERIC Document Reproduction Services No. ED 456 087).

Jones, W. (2005). Music, the brain, and education. *Montessori Life, 17* (3), 40-45.

Keck, S. & Kinney, S.C. (2005). Creating a differentiated classroom. *Learning & Leading with Technology, 33* (1), 12-15.

Kovalik, S. & Olsen, K. (2002). *Exceeding expectations: A user's guide to implementing brain research in the classroom* (2nd ed.). Covington, WA: Books for Educators, Inc.

Lewis, A. (2006), Clean up the test mess. (No Child Left Behind Act of 2001). *Phi Delta Kappan, 87,* 643-646.

McCarthy, B. (1990). Using the 4MAT system to bring learning styles to schools. *Educational Leadership, 48* (2), 31-37.

McCarthy, B. (1980). *The 4MAT system: Teaching to learning styles with right/left mode techniques.* Barrington, IL: EXCEL, Inc.

Noble, T. (2004). Integrating the revised Bloom's taxonomy with multiple intelligences: A planning tool for curriculum differentiation. *Teachers College Record, 106* (1), 193-211.

Odland, J. (2006). NCLB: Time to reevaluate its effectiveness. *Childhood Education, 83,* 98-100.

Pettig, K. L. (2000). On the road to differentiated practice. *Educational Leadership, 58* (1), 14-18.

Posner, D. (2004). What's wrong with teaching to the test? *Phi Delta Kappan, 85,* 749-751.

Rothstein, R. & Jacobsen, R. (2006). The goals of education: In the NCLB era, accountability has focused almost exclusively on basic academic skills. *Phi Delta Kappan, 88,* 264-270.

Scott, T. (2005).Consensus through accountability? The benefits and drawback of building community with accountability: Through interview's and class observations, the author of this article examines the building of community among teachers and students through high-stakes assessment. *Journal of Adolescent & Adult Literacy, 49* (1), 48-60.

Simpson, E. (2005). Evolution in the classroom: What teachers need to know about the video game generation. *Tech Trends: Linking Research & Practice to Improve Learning, 49* (5), 17-22.

Sparapani, E. F. (2000). The effect of teaching for higher-level thinking: An analysis of teacher reactions. *Education, 121* (1), 80-89.

Sparks-Langer, G. M., Starko, A. J., Pasch, M., Burke, W., Moody, C. D., & Gardner, T. G. (2004). *Teaching as decision- making* (2nd ed.). Upper Saddle River, NJ: Pearson Education.

Strong, R., Thomas, E., Perini, M., & Silver, H. (2004). Creating a differentiated mathematics classroom. *Educational Leadership, 61* (5), 73-78.

The intelligence we never measure. (2007). *Roeper Review, 29* (2), 83-85.

Tomlinson, C.A. (1998). For integration and differentiation choose concepts over topics. *Middle School Journal, 30* (2), 3-8.

Tomlinson, C. A. (1999a). Mapping a route toward differentiated instruction. *Educational Leadership, 57* (1), 12-16.

Tomlinson, C. A. (1999b). *The differentiated classroom: Responding to the needs of all learners.* Alexandria, VA: Association for Supervision and Curriculum Development.

Tomlinson, C. A. (2006). An alternative to ability grouping. *Principal Leadership,* (Middle School Edition), *6* (8), 31-32.

Vansciver, J. H. (2005). Motherhood, apple pie, and differentiated instruction. *Phi Delta Kappan, 86,* 534-535.

Wiggins, G. & McTighe, J. (2005). *Understanding by design* (expanded 2nd edition). Alexandria, VA: Association for Supervision and Curriculum Development.

Willis, S. & Mann, L. (2000). Differentiating instruction: Finding manageable ways to meet individual needs. In *Curriculum Update, Winter,* pp. 1-8. Alexandria, VA: Association for Supervision and Curriculum Development.

Wilson, J., Cordry, S., Notar, C., & Friery, K. (2004). Teacher truths: Speaking from the heart of educators. *College Student Journal, 38* (2), 163-170.

Wolfe, P. (2001) *Brain matters: Translating research into classroom practice*. Alexandria, VA: Association for Supervision and Curriculum Development.

Wormeli, R. (2008). Show what you know. *Principal Leadership, 9* (1), 48-52.

Chapter Three

Standards and Benchmarks and Differentiated Instruction

Integrating Approaches to Teaching and Learning

Nicole M. Rogers & Barbara Garii

INTRODUCTION

As discussed in the two previous chapters, differentiated instruction allows teachers and other educators to personalize and customize instruction to meet the individual needs of all students. Differentiated instruction acknowledges student variance and encourages teachers to respond to individual students' learning needs as a way to increase student achievement, performance, self-worth, and self-esteem (Cox, 2008; Hertberg-Davis, 2009; Protheroe, 2007). In this chapter, we will consider the role of standards and benchmarks as a tool to guide teachers as they consider how to differentiate their curricular planning. Student success is assessed and evaluated through a myriad of techniques that are integrated into daily lessons and long-term assessment strategies. Understanding how differentiated instruction supports student success in terms of reaching identified content and process standards that is accurately, reliably, and validly assessed allows teachers to make viable pedagogical decisions that support all students. The challenge that teachers face is how to ensure that they are meeting students' learning needs while simultaneously ensuring that students are learning the academic content in ways that can be measured by state-mandated assessment paradigms (Levy, 2008). Thus, in order to effectively understand how to integrate differentiated instruction into the classroom, teachers must also understand how to interpret standards and benchmarks across content areas.

DEFINING STANDARDS AND BENCHMARKS

Standards are clear and concise statements that describe what students should know and do at each grade level in each academic content area. They act as long-term goals that guide teachers' practices across the academic year. Standards help teachers articulate the specific content that students must know, the processes of teaching and learning that are to be accomplished, and the products that students will use to demonstrate that they have learned the content and skills they have been taught (Levy, 2008). Thus, standards are one of the tools we use to structure the curriculum we teach.

Recently, the term "benchmarks" has entered the educational lexicon. "Benchmarks," like standards, are another way to measure student progress and identify and integrate the most effective practices into teachers' repertoires (National Governors Association, the Council of Chief State School Officers, and Achieve, Inc., 2008). When a standard has been "benchmarked" we mean that this particular academic, process, or product goal has been deemed necessary for student success, such as the benchmarked standards articulated by the Common Core State Standards (Council of Chief State School Officers, and the National Governors Association Center for Best Practices, 2010a, 2010b).

Most states have identified standards or benchmarks that structure the curriculum at each grade level within every academic area. Student attainment of competence of these standards is assessed on a regular basis through state-supported standardized testing. These state-based standards are often based on benchmarks identified by national organizations, such as the National Council for the Teaching of English (NCTE), the National Council for the Teaching of Mathematics (NCTM), or the National Council for Social Studies (NCSS) (NCTE, 1998-2011; NCTM, 2011; NCSS, 2010). More recently, there has been a movement to identify a core of academic and process standards to guide educational practice nationwide (Council of Chief State School Officers, and the National Governors Association Center for Best Practices, 2010a, 2010b). Although there is still discussion about whether this is viable, useful, and necessary (Meier & Finn, 2009), as of July 2011, 44 states have adopted the Common Core Standards (Council of Chief State School Officers, and the National Governors Association Center for Best Practices, 2011).

Assuring That Differentiated Instruction Has Supported Student Success

Differentiated instruction focuses on the academic knowledge and process skills that students are expected to learn. When teachers differentiate how they support student learning, they are ensuring that all students have access to the content and skills that have been identified in the standards and that educational opportunities are equitable for all students. Thus, differentiated instruction suggests that teachers have identified and integrated into their practices a variety of tools, strategies, and methods that enable them to individualize the learning pathways for each student in the classroom (Levy, 2008).

In order to demonstrate student success, teachers must assess students (both informally and formally) on a regular basis in the classroom and use the assessment results to evaluate student progress and implement pedagogical supports to strengthen student performance in areas that are identified as challenging for the individual student. Additionally, students must demonstrate the knowledge and skills they have learned in the specific ways that are mandated by the state's assessment paradigms, regardless of their specific strengths or challenges. Thus, differentiated instruction in conjunction with the identified standards ensures that there is clear alignment between what students actually learn and the specific content, process, and product goals articulated in the standards.

Expanded Assessments

Differentiated instruction requires that teachers be more vigilant than ever about ensuring that all students have access to the curriculum. Thus, the frequency of assessment and evaluation of student success is increased in classrooms where differentiated instruction is incorporated (Protheroe, 2007). It is important to recognize here that differentiated instruction relies on increased utilization of constant, informal assessments, such as targeted observations, small group discussions, and pre-assessments of readiness and interest, that allow teachers to be aware of what students are learning, how they are learning, and what interventions may be most effective for specific students at any given time. The flexibility of differentiated instruction, in conjunction with on-going assessment of every student and a sharp eye on the goals, standards, and benchmarks, allows for student success to be consolidated across the whole classroom.

HISTORIC BASES FOR STANDARDS AND BENCHMARKS

Differentiating instruction to ensure that students meet academic standards is not new to educational practice. Teachers have been differentiating instruction since the one room school house. However, in the late twentieth century and early twenty-first century, the implementation of standards and benchmarks has been formalized thus creating a greater need to practice differentiation.

Standardizing Schools: Nineteenth Century

While formal education in the United States grew out of colonial school
initiatives, the standardization of schooling is a relatively recent phenomenon. Horace Mann, an attorney in the eighteen-thirties, and, notably, the first
Secretary of the Massachusetts Board of Education, identified the need to
restructure schooling to better serve communities, the nation, and the individual students. Mann traveled through Europe seeking a viable method to improve schooling and identified the Prussian class-grade, state-supported system as the model to adopt. Based on this model, Mann introduced the "common school" system in 1837 to create unity and standardization across curricular goals and educational expectations. Mann and his supporters believed
that common schooling was necessary to preserve republican institutions and
create a political community (Salomone & Minow, 2010). Two over-arching
principles guided this system. These over-arching principles were (1) non-
partisanship, which ensured that no single political party maintained educational oversight; and (2) non-sectarianism, which established Christian (specifically, Protestant) bible-based morality as an underlying educational vision while explicitly avoiding the influence of any specific Christian belief.
These guiding principles were meant to ensure that all students shared a
similar understanding of what it meant to be an American (Salomone &
Minow, 2010). It is Mann's Common School Movement that led to the more
profound standardization of curriculum and pedagogies of the early twentieth
century.

Twentieth Century Legislation to Support Non-Hegemonic Populations

By the early twentieth century, the United States understood itself to be a
Protestant nation; however, there was a steady growth in immigration (Mirel,
2002), and this growth brought a large number of non-Protestant students to
the schools. In the nineteenth century, the development of the common
schools was understood as a way to socialize students and help them understand what it meant to be an American. Similarly, as non-Protestant (and,
therefore, non-hegemonic) immigration increased, schools were seen as a
place to ensure that these new immigrants were, and their families had the
opportunity to become, "Americanized" (Mirel, 2002; Salomone & Minow,
2010). In the common schools of the early twentieth century, "Americanization" suggested that immigrants could hold onto their traditions and values as
they became one as a nation. Americanization in the common schools focused on English language courses, civics classes, Anglo-American literature
classes, and American history courses, as well as continued exposure to
Protestant values (Mirel, 2002).

As the century progressed, students from a wider variety of religious and cultural backgrounds continued to move into schools and classrooms. Many of these students experienced academic difficulties and performed poorly on IQ tests and other tests of aptitude and achievement, often due to their lack of academic English and/or unfamiliarity and/or discomfort with "typical" American culture, values, and expectations. These students were often deemed "slow" or "intellectually challenged" and segregated into separate classes. Similarly, American-born students with a variety of physical disabilities as well as those from non-hegemonic backgrounds (e.g., students of color, students of poverty) were also segregated from mainstream classrooms and placed into "special education" classes that often focused on vocational training rather than academic learning. Thus, public schools "tracked" students based on perceived differences and held these students accountable to different standards and expectations of achievement.

In 1965, however, the Elementary and Secondary Education Act (ESEA) was enacted by the federal government to provide equal educational opportunity for all students. Between 1965 and 2001, when the reauthorization of ESEA was enacted, there was growing recognition that the tests used to identify students with intellectual and/or learning disabilities included cultural biases. These biases were associated with an over-identification of students whose backgrounds were non-hegemonic who, therefore, were inappropriately placed in special education classes.

The reauthorization of ESEA in 2001 created substantial changes for special education students (Means, 2006). These changes, supported by federal law, took into consideration the needs of students with physical and/or mental impairments that required them to have special assistance through Title I funding to succeed in a general education classroom. Title I funding were federal funds which were provided to increase access to remedial instruction to meet educational needs of at-risk students (Salomone & Minow, 2010), allowing support services and mechanisms to enable special education students to successfully demonstrate their knowledge and abilities in state and district assessments. ESEA, through the Individuals with Disabilities Act (IDEA) (Thurlow, 2002) thereby supported and promoted equitable expectations for those students who had not been held to the same standards as students in the general education population. In summary, IDEA ensured a free appropriate public education (Maag & Katsiyannis, 1997), while also mandating that teachers and schools hold all students accountable to the same set of academic standards in every grade.

IDEA was reauthorized in 1997, becoming the first federal law of its kind requiring students with disabilities to receive testing accommodations, thereby allowing them access to the supports deemed necessary for them to sit for and do well on standardized tests. The types of accommodations were specified in students' individualized education programs (IEP) and included in general state and district-wide assessment programs (Kohl, McLaughlin, & Nagle, 2006). Today, IDEA has been revised, revamped, reauthorized, and renamed as "The Individuals with Disabilities Education Improvement Act" (IDEIA) of 2004. IDEIA aligns closely with "No Child Left Behind" (NCLB) (No Child Left Behind Act of 2001, 2001) in many ways, but most strongly in terms of creating access to the general education curriculum for students with disabilities. Thus, schools are held accountable for enabling and ensuring that all students are given appropriate education and educational supports that will enable them to demonstrate AYP, adequate yearly progress. Kohl, et al. (2006), however, report that states continually change how they define and implement their alternate assessments for students with the most severe cognitive disabilities.

Entering the New Millennium: Role of No Child Left Behind (NCLB)

In the late 20th century, international educational comparisons (e.g., TIMMS, PISA) suggested that U.S. students were no longer as "competitive" in the world marketplace. Additionally, analyses of U.S. student "success" indicated that the achievement gap was widening between white middle class students and African American students, Hispanic students, students living in poverty, and other students from non-hegemonic backgrounds (Holmes Group, 1995). NCLB responded to these, and similar, concerns by calling for an annual testing regimen between grades 3 and 8 to ensure that all students were making AYP based on academic standards identified by each state for each grade level.

Constitutional limits on federal power prevent the federal government and the Department of Education from mandating national testing protocols for students in public schools. Through NCLB, however, federal education dollars paid to each state is tied to each state's voluntary participation in assessment of student progress on an annual basis. Thus, each state identifies specific standards or benchmarks that students are expected to reach each year. While these standards are nominally based on recommendations promulgated by various professional organization (e.g., NCTE, 1998-2011; NCTM, 2011; NCSS, 2010), the assessments and evaluations used by each state are themselves not "standardized" across state lines so different states have different expectations and varying criteria for success at each grade level and across the academic lifespan. This ensures that these annual assessments are not federally regulated but still assess student progress on an annual basis, thereby enabling states to receive federal education monies.

As mentioned previously, a recent move to identify common and consistent standards in mathematics and English language arts has been endorsed (as of July 2011) by 44 states (Council of Chief State School Officers, and the National Governors Association Center for Best Practices, 2011). Implementation is still in progress, however, and it is not yet clear how the participating states will enact assessment and evaluation of the common core standards. Thus, there are questions about consistency of educational standards and benchmarks across state lines, although the intent of the common core movement is to ensure similar educational attainment throughout the United States.

STANDARDS AND BENCHMARKS IN CURRENT PRACTICE

Standards and Benchmarks guide teaching to ensure that all students in a given state (and, more recently, across the country (Council of Chief State School Officers, and the National Governors Association Center for Best Practices, 2011)), regardless of their economic class, are being prepared to meet similar academic objectives. However, the mandated identification of standards and associated benchmarks raises some concerns across the educational community.

Standards-Based Curriculum

To ensure all students are provided the same high-quality education, NCLB has encouraged state departments of education and individual school districts to reframe their curricula within a standards-based context in an effort to ensure that all students show proficiency in specific academic areas in each grade level (Bloomfield & Cooper, 2003; Hoover & Patton, 2004). Student progress is measured through the use of state-selected or state-developed tests that measure student performance against the state standards. Students are to be tested annually in reading and mathematics in grades 3 through 8 and at least once during the four years of high school (Harrison-Jones, 2007). State-developed standards in each content area articulate specific grade-level benchmarks, thereby identifying the specific skills and knowledge that students are expected to demonstrate in each academic discipline each year (Murnane, 2007; Salomone & Minow, 2010). All students, regardless of socioeconomic status, language ability, academic, social, and/or mental disability, or other differences, are, on an annual basis, held to the same standard and are required to illustrate grade-level learning growth. In other words, all students in every grade level are held to the same academic expectations (Hoover & Patton, 2004; Levy, 2008; Philips & Wong, 2010).

The federal government holds schools and educators responsible for students' progress through an annual high-stakes testing and reporting system to determine adequate yearly progress (AYP) to show that students have made sufficient growth over the course of each academic year (Arce, Luna, Borjian, & Conrad, 2005; Champagne, 2006; Liston, Whitcomb, & Borko,

2007). High-stakes tests measure individual academic mastery of state-developed standards (Jorgensen, 2002); students who do not "pass" are not promoted and/or are unable to graduate until they show mastery of the standards through the testing procedure, regardless of the students' classroom abilities.

Issues Associated with Standards and Benchmarks

Standards and benchmarks offer both teachers and students a clear path to academic success in this era of standardization. Evaluating students' ability to demonstrate mastery of specific benchmarks with both formative and summative performance measures allows teachers to identify students' strengths and challenges at precise points during the academic year. Thus, student growth can be charted and teachers' pedagogy can be targeted to specific needs in the classroom. A major challenge, however, is the overreliance of a single high-stakes assessment tool to monitor student academic growth.

In regard to the singularity of assessment measures, the specific aspect of NCLB that raises controversy is the reliance on standardized testing. Ultimately, for school and teacher assessment purposes, student success is measured solely on the basis of these standardized tests, which become the primary measure of student performance in terms of student achievement of the identified standards (Townsend, 2002).

In some cases, especially in schools in high poverty areas or in neighborhoods with large non-English speaking immigrant communities, much of the classroom pedagogy focuses on "teaching to the test" as an attempt to ensure that students will attain mastery of the mandated standards and benchmarks (Lombardi & Burke 1999). Creative pedagogies are often eschewed due to the fear that students will not recall the specific content that is assessed in the testing regimen. Anecdotally, this is described as 'only that which can be measured is deemed to be important' (Koppich, 2004). This, then, devalues the other equally important learning that occurs in classrooms and ignores the developmental differences that students bring to the educational process.

Role of Differentiated Instruction in Teaching to Standards and Benchmarks

All students, regardless of background, language proficiency, and/or readiness to learn, are held to the same standards in each grade level. Differentiated instruction offers many opportunities for a child to achieve classroom-based academic success by acting on what is fair, equitable, and appropriate for each student (Wormeli, 2006). In many classrooms, students of widely varied intellectual abilities, home cultures, and linguistic backgrounds are taught together (Hoffman, 2003), often in inclusive settings. In such settings, students with special needs are integrated into general education classes, thereby expanding the ability and capacity ranges in the classroom. Thus, differentiated instruction provides several learning options which take into consideration students' learning strengths while simultaneously creating scaffolding opportunities that allow students to organize the information being taught and make sense of the concepts and skills at hand. Specifically, Mastropieri, Scruggs, Norland, et al. (2006) define differentiated instruction as a way of teaching in which the teacher tries to address students' particular needs, interests, and preferred ways of learning through a variety of teaching approaches and strategies. In a classroom environment that stresses differentiated instruction, teachers prepare lessons, activities, and classroom-based assessments that support each child's specific attributes while ensuring that all students demonstrate mastery of the identified grade-level standards and benchmarks (Levy, 2008).

To differentiate instruction, teachers do not need to develop separate lessons for each and every student nor do they "dumb down" the curriculum. The teacher instead identifies ways to adapt the curriculum to fit the needs of all students in the classroom. All students, including those at-risk, can and do learn; therefore, it is the teacher's responsibility to be flexible in the methods of instruction and evaluation of children to meet the needs of every individual within the schools.

REALITIES OF DIFFERENTIATED INSTRUCTION

Differentiating instruction is just good teaching. When used well, in conjunction with identified standards, differentiated instruction affords every student the opportunity to succeed in the academic environment by presenting state mandated content in a way that works for that individual.

Content, Process, and Product

Differentiated instruction offers increased opportunities for both teachers and students to expand access to academic content as mandated by schools, districts, and state departments of education, and as measured by state assessment tools (Council of Chief State School Officers, and the National Governors Association Center for Best Practices, 2010b, National Governors Association, the Council of Chief State School Officers, and Achieve, Inc., 2008; Protheroe, 2007). Differentiated instruction, however, also illuminates the tensions between the standards-based movement, exemplified by NCLB (No Child Left Behind Act of 2001, 2001) and the student-centered approaches to education that better support students in the classroom (Kennedy, 2006). The standards movement identifies and measures "uniform benchmarks" for student achievement in each grade and within each specific content area (Sherman, 2009), thereby limiting the ability of the teacher to adequately identify students' individual learning, social, and pedagogical needs. At the same time, teachers incorporate other, informal assessment tools that help identify students' specific strengths and challenges. Thus, teachers continue to find ways to support students through a variety of differentiated approaches (Kennedy, 2006) even in the face of increasing standardization of academic goals and classroom expectations.

Whether using textbooks or other support materials to scaffold student learning, teachers are acutely aware of the different ways in which students internalize knowledge. All learning requires that learners have access to kinesthetic, aural, visual, and tactile approaches to the academic content. In fact, instructional differentiation suggests that even textbooks themselves may be differentiated, especially in terms of accessibility (e.g., hard copy, online, books-on-tape, video enhancement), in ways that offer students various ways to connect with the content. Johnson and Mastrion (2009, p. 8) explicitly suggest that the "mode of delivery means nothing as long as there's comprehension," suggesting that the onus is on the teacher to identify how to help students scaffold and structure the new knowledge. The integration of technological supports (such as video presentations, audio tools, and graphic displays) suggests that differentiated instruction is more than just the differentiation of the processes of teaching but includes the differentiation of accessibility of the material to be taught and learned.

Standards-based education articulates success through the assurance that all students have equitable access to appropriate content and pedagogical processes in order to produce similar outcomes. In other words, standards-based education focuses on the products of education, as measured by standardized assessment tools. Recall that in educational contexts, standardized assessments are tools, often characterized as "tests," that are validated across specific academic goals for specific grade levels, and are administered and scored in a consistent manner across all test takers. Students complete the test under the same set of conditions, hear the same set of directions, and answer the same set of questions (or questions that have been validated to assure similarity), thereby assuring that the students who complete the standardized assessment have "equal, unbiased opportunities to demonstrate what they know and can do" (Association of American Publishers, 2002, p. 5). Thus, classroom instruction can be differentiated to support different learning styles and specific content. Teaching methods can by individualized as long as the outcome of the classroom practices assures that all students can successfully display their knowledge when completing the standardized test.

CHALLENGES TO DIFFERENTIATED INSTRUCTION

Two issues raise specific concerns when differentiated instruction is incorporated into classroom practice. Careful attention must be paid to the standards and goals being addressed. At the same time, differentiated instruction must not be construed to be a tool for implicit tracking or ability grouping.

Differentiation and Standards

Many teachers associate differentiation with incorporation of "fun activities" that engage students in a variety of ways. Reliance on such activities, without maintaining a clear tie to the explicit standards, benchmarks, and key questions addressed in the curriculum, does little to support student success on standardized assessments (Levy, 2008; Wiggins & McTighe, 2005). The challenge here is to ensure that, regardless of the instructional activities that are embedded in the classroom practice, content mandates, standards, goals, and benchmarks are consistent for all students. Thus, differentiated instruction must clearly focus on student learning needs without unduly compromising student access to the academic content and skills that are measured by the standardized assessments.

While we may argue whether or not those assessment criteria are appropriate (Sherman, 2009), the reality in schools today is that those standardized assessments are used to evaluate student, teacher, and school success. It is therefore crucial that the assessment goals associated with the grade level and academic content are clearly embedded in all differentiated instructional activities. By doing so, teachers ensure that the differentiations not only meet the learning needs of all students but, simultaneously, prepare the students for success on the final standardized assessment.

Avoiding the Assumption of Tracking

Evidence suggests that well-organized classrooms that incorporate a variety of differentiated instructional techniques meet the academic needs of the various students in the classroom by engaging them in tasks and activities that support the co-creation of knowledge and collaborative skill development while increasing student confidence in learning how to learn (Mercier Smith, Fien, & Basaraba. 2009; Patterson, Conolly, & Ritter, 2009; Voltz, Sims, & Nelson, 2008). In such classrooms, teachers are attentive to the changing needs of students, as student confidence increases as they expand their knowledge and skills. Thus, individual students become more willing to explore different learning styles as supported by teacher pedagogical practices.

CONCLUDING THOUGHTS

Differentiated instruction, however, is often tacitly understood to support specialized learning and teaching needs in inclusive classrooms. That is, whether acknowledged or not, differentiated instruction becomes a tool for tracking in the classroom (Baglieri & Knopf, 2004; Dakarai, 2010; Hertberg-Davis, 2009). It is imperative that teachers who incorporate differentiated instructional strategies pay close attention to the specific students with whom they work. For example, by utilizing flexible grouping strategies that allow students to move to different groups as their learning needs evolve and by incorporating a variety of text-based, video-based, audio-based, and graphical learning tools, students are able to engage in learning processes across a variety of access points. At the same time, teachers cannot neglect how students prepare their responses and illustrate their new learnings and understandings. As suggested earlier, differentiated instructional strategies must directly allude to how the standards will be assessed. Assumptions of tracking often occur when one group of students (often the "advanced" group) focuses on varieties of learning processes while a second group (often the students struggling with the content and/or experiencing academic challenges) focuses solely on test-taking skills (Voltz, et al., 2008).

The goal of differentiated instruction is to support all students across both learning and assessment. Thus, well-structured classrooms that incorporate differentiated instruction offer all students opportunities to illustrate their learning through both standardized and idio-centric assessment possibilities.

REFERENCES

Arce, J., Luna, D., Borjian, A., & Conrad, M. (2005). No Child Left Behind: Who wins? Who loses? *Social Justice, 32* (3), 56-71.

Association of American Publishers. (2002). *Standardized assessment: A primer (Revised Edition)*. Washington, D.C.: Association of American Publishers. Retrieved April 17, 2010 from http://www.aapschool.org/pdf/Testing%20Primer%20Revised.pdf.

Baglieri, S. & Knopf, J.H. (2004). Normalizing difference in inclusive teaching. *Journal of Learning Disabilities, 37* (6), 525-529.

Bloomfield, D. C. & Cooper, B. C. (2003) NCLB: A new role for the federal government: An overview of the most sweeping federal education law since 1965. *T. H. E. Journal, 30* (10). Retrieved May, 10, 2010 from http://thejournal.com/articles/2003/05/01/nclb-a-new-role-for-the-federal-government.aspx?sc_lang=en.

Champagne, A. (2006). Then and now: Science assessment 1996 – 2006. *School Science and Mathematics, 106* (3), 113–123.

Council of Chief State School Officers, and the National Governors Association Center for Best Practices. (2010a). Common core state standards for English Language Arts and Literacy in History/Social Studies, Science, and Technical Subjects. *Common Core State Standards Initiative.* Retrieved August 30, 2011 from http://www.corestandards.org/assets/CCSSI_ELA%20Standards.pdf.

Council of Chief State School Officers, and the National Governors Association Center for Best Practices. (2010b). Common core state standards for Mathematics. *Common Core State*

Standards Initiative. Retrieved September 4, 2011 from http://www.corestandards.org/assets/CCSSI_Math%20Standards.pdf.

Council of Chief State School Officers, and the National Governors Association Center for Best Practices. (2011). *Common Core State Standards Initiatives.* Retrieved August 30, 2011 from http://www.corestandards.org/in-the-states.

Cox, S. G. (2008). Differentiated instruction in the elementary classroom. *Educational Digest, 73* (90), 52-54.

Dakarai, A. I. (2010). Focus on instruction turns around Chicago schools: Network gets results in 5 schools in Chicago without 'drastic' steps. *Education Week, 29* (16), 1, 14-15.

Harrison-Jones, L. (2007). No Child Left Behind and implications for Black students. *Journal of Negro Education, 76* (3), 346-356.

Hertberg-Davis, H. (2009). Myth 7: Differentiation in the regular classroom is equivalent to gifted programs and is sufficient. *Gifted Child Quarterly, 53* (4), 251-253.

Hoffman, J. (2003). Multiage teachers' beliefs and practices. *Journal of Research in Childhood Education, 18* (1), 5-15.

Holmes Group. (1995). *Tomorrow's schools of education: A report of the Holmes Group.* East Lansing, MI: The Holmes Group.

Hoover, J. J. & Patton, J. R. (2004). Differentiating standards-based education for students with diverse needs. *Remedial and Special Education, 25* (2), 74-78.

Johnson, D. & Mastrion, K. (2009). Do schools still need brick-and-mortar libraries? *Learning and Leading with Technology, 37* (3), 8-9.

Jorgensen, M. (2002). Can the testing industry meet growing demand? *Science and Technology, 19* (2), 59-62.

Kennedy, M. M. (2006). Knowledge and vision in teaching. *Journal of Teacher Education,* 57 (1), 1-7.

Kohl, F. M., McLaughlin, M. J., & Nagle, K. (2006). Alternate achievement standards and assessments: A descriptive investigation of 16 states. *Exceptional Children, 73* (1), 107–123.

Koppich, J. E. (2004). Using student tests to measure teacher quality. *CAESL Assessment Brief. Number 9.* San Francisco, CA: Center for Assessment and Evaluation of Student Leaning. Retrieved August 31, 2011 from http://www.caesl.org/briefs/Brief9.pdf.

Levy, H. M. (2008). Meeting the needs of all students through differentiated instruction: Helping every child reach and exceed standards. *The Clearing House, 81* (4), 161-164.

Liston, D., Whitcomb, J., & Borko, H. (2007). NCLB and scientifically-based research: Opportunities lost and found. *Journal of Teacher Education, 58* (2), 99–107.

Lombardi, T. P. & Burke, D. (1999). To test…or not to test? *Exceptional Children, 32* (1), 26-29.

Maag, J., & Katsiyannis, A. (1997). Ensuring appropriate education: Emerging remedies, litigation, compensation, and other legal considerations. *Exceptional Children, 63* (4), 451-462.

Mastropieri, M. A., Scruggs, T. E., Norland, J. J., Berkeley, S., McDuffie, K., Tornquist, E. H., & Connors, N. (2006). Differentiated curriculum enhancement in inclusive middle school science: Effects on classroom and high-stakes tests. *Journal of Special Education, 40* (3), 130-141.

Means, J. (2006). The Impact of IDEA 04 and NCLB on speech and language related services: How do we meet the challenges? *A Journal of the Oxford Round Table.* Fall, 2006 edition. Retrieved April 10, 2011 from http://www.forumonpublicpolicy.com/archive06/means.pdf .

Meier, D., & Finn, C. (2009). E pluribus unum? *Education Next, 9* (2), 50-57.

Mercier Smith, J. L., Fien, H., & Basaraba, D. (2009). Planning, evaluating and improving tiers of support in beginning reading. *Teaching Exceptional Children, 41* (5), 16-22.

Mirel, J. (2002). The decline of civic education. *Daedalus, 131* (3), 49-55.

Murnane, R. (2007). Improving the education of children living in poverty. *The Future of Children, 17* (2), 161-182.

National Council of Teachers of English [NCTE]. (1998-2011). *NCTE/IRA standards for the English Language Arts.* Urbana, IL: NCTE. Retrieved on August 31. 2011 from http://www.ncte.org/standards.

National Council of Teachers of Mathematics [NCTM]. (2011). *Standards and focal points.* Reston, VA: NCTM. Retrieved on August 31, 2011 from http://www.nctm.org/standards/.

National Council for the Social Studies [NCSS]. (2010). *Standards.* Silver Spring, MD: NCSS. Retrieved September 4, 2011 from http://www.socialstudies.org/standards.

National Governors Association, the Council of Chief State School Officers, and Achieve, Inc. (2008). *Benchmarking for success: Ensuring U.S. students receive a world-class education.* Washington, D.C.: National Governors Association. Retrieved August 30, 2011 from www.nga.org

No Child Left Behind Act of 2001. PL 107-110. 107th Congress. (2001). Retrieved April 16, 2010 from http://ed.gov/policy/elsec/leg/esea02/107-110.pdf.

Patterson, J. L., Conolly, M. C., & Ritter, S. A. (2009). Restructuring the inclusion classroom to facilitate differentiated instruction. *Middle School Journal, 41* (1), 46-52.

Philips, V. & Wong, C. (2010). Tying together the common core of standards, instruction, and assessments. *Phi Delta Kappan, 91* (5), 37-42.

Protheroe, N. (2007). Differentiating instruction in a standards-based environment. *Principal. 87* (2), 36-40.

Salomone, R. & Minow, M. (2010). *In Brown's wake: Legacies of America's educational landmark.* New York, NY: Oxford University Press.

Sherman, S. C. (2009). Haven't we seen this before?: Sustaining a vision in teacher education for progressive teaching practice. *Teacher Education Quarterly*, 36 (4), 41-60.

Thurlow, M. (2002). Positive educational results for all students: The promise of standards-based reform. *Remedial and Special Education, 23* (4), 195-202.

Townsend, B. L. (2002). 'Testing while Black': Standards-based reform and African American learners. *Remedial and Special Education, 23* (4), 222-230.

Voltz, D. L., Sims, M. J., & Nelson, B. (2008). Engineering successful inclusion in standards-based urban classrooms. *Middle School Journal, 39* (4), 24-30.

Wiggins, G. & McTighe, J. (2005). *Understanding by design: Expanded 2 nd edition.* Alexandria, VA: Association for Supervision and Curriculum Development.

Wormeli, R. (2006). *Fair isn't always equal: Assessment and grading in the differentiated classroom.* Portland, ME: Stenhouse Publishers.

Chapter Four

Assessment

A Guiding Force for Differentiation

Byung-In Seo & Deborah L. Smith

INTRODUCTION

Before any differentiated teaching can take place, teachers need to understand the learning abilities and skills of their students, so that the teachers know what and how to adapt their instructional methods. Ergo, teachers will give assessments in order to gather this information. The term "assessment" is commonly heard, but many people may not know its meaning. Assessment is an ongoing process, where the teacher gathers information about his/her students from a variety of sources. It includes a range of procedures to gain information on student learning (Miller, Linn, & Gronlund, 2009). Such procedures can be formal or informal. For example, assessments can include formal tests or informal teacher observations. "Testing," where teachers obtain a general idea of how the class is obtaining and retaining the material, is one form of assessment. In today's zeal for accountability, however, testing is often the only tool used to evaluate students' progress. "Evaluation" is when teachers make a judgment on the students' educational progress, based on the assessed information (Richardson, Morgan, & Fleener, 2009).

There are two purposes for assessing students. First, assessment provides information on how students are doing in the classroom and on the quality of their education. Second, assessment holds educational entities and the students accountable for the learning that takes place (Miller, et al., 2009). There are four categories of assessments: placement, formative, summative, and diagnostic. Placement assessments determine where the student is performing at the beginning of the learning process; diagnostic assessments identify learning difficulties that students may be having (Miller, et al.,

2009). Formative assessments are used to understand the students' strengths and weaknesses; with formative assessment data, teachers can understand what instructional methods work and do not work, to "form" or develop the student, and they are ongoing. Summative assessments, on the other hand, are used to understand all that the student learned or completed. Data from summative assessments will summarize all that the student knows about a particular topic (Alvermann, Phelps, & Ridgeway, 2007).

All assessments can be norm-referenced or criterion-referenced. Norm-referenced assessments, often known as standardized tests, assess students' academic abilities as compared to other students with similar characteristics. For example, scores on the Scholastic Aptitude Test (SAT) are measured against a norm or standard, and it is to measure how much students know about a particular subject or how well students have mastered an academic skill. These assessments need to have high measures of validity and reliability. High validity means that the assessment tests what it is supposed to assess. High reliability shows that when teachers use the assessment more than once, they will be testing the same intended skill or knowledge with consistent results (Miller, et al., 2009; Richardson, et al., 2009; Roe, Stoodt-Hill, & Burns, 2007). Therefore, when school districts report that their students performed at the 95th percentile, it means that the students took a norm-referenced assessment, and their scores were better than 95 percent of the students who also took the assessment.

The other kind of assessment is criterion-referenced assessments. Criterion-referenced assessments compare students to a predetermined set of skills or a body of knowledge that they are to know. These assessments help determine if students have mastered a particular skill, while norm-referenced assessments compare students to others who have also taken the same assessment (Miller, et al., 2009; Richardson, et al., 2009; Roe, et al., 2007).

Many educators see a disconnection between the emphasis on standardized assessments and differentiated instruction. Standardized testing is norm-referenced, so the student is compared to everyone else who also took the assessment. There is little emphasis on the individual student and his/her learning issues; students are compared en masse. With differentiation, however, teachers take each student's learning abilities into account, and they adjust their teaching methods to these different abilities. As a result, the emphasis is on the individual's learning process, not his/her product or grade.

UNDERSTANDING THE STUDENT

In the first act of Richard Rogers and Oscar Hammerstein's musical, *The King and I*, Anna, a new teacher hired by the king of Siam, sings "Getting to Know You," to the king's children. Here, Anna wants to initiate the process of learning the characteristics of her students. This process continues to take place with all teachers when they meet their students at the beginning of the year. For a differentiated classroom, this process is vital to the organization and teaching methods of the course. Differentiated instruction expects teachers to adapt their teaching methodologies so that all students have the opportunity to learn the material. Before any adaptation can take place, however, teachers need to learn and understand the nature of their students.

The Adolescent Brain

Many people believe that once children reach adolescence, their brains have grown to full maturation. This belief is not true. In infancy, mirror neurons are activated. Mirror neurons help create a mental template for individuals to associate tasks and situations. Throughout adolescence, these neurons continue to grow and mature. When teenagers see adults who they respect exhibit positive behaviors, then the adolescent will mirror or copy that behavior (Sylwester, 2007). Also, during adolescence, the frontal lobes of the brain undergo tremendous growth. As frontal lobes develop, adolescents become more aware of options and consequences, while learning to understand and relate to novel experiences (Sylwester, 2007).

Because the brain continues to grow throughout adolescence, it is unreasonable to treat teenagers as mini-adults. When treated as mini-adults, teachers assume that adolescents are capable of making adult decisions. Adolescent brains, however, are still maturing, growing, and changing within their learning and social environments. Brains do not grow at the same rate. Some adolescents may have more mature frontal lobes than others, while others may have more mirror neurons than others. In addition, adolescents' intellectual processes are heavily influenced by their social connections and interactions. Adolescents need to make personal connections to the material, be intellectually challenged as well as be emotionally engaged with the subject, within a supportive learning environment (Crawford, 2008). As a result, teachers need to differentiate their instruction and assessment tools for their students. Some students may need more direct instruction and can do well on objective assessments, while other students need a more creative means of assessment if teachers want a true measure of the students' understanding of the class material.

Learning Styles and Thinking Processes

Adolescents learn in different ways. One way to differentiate instruction is according to the students' thinking styles. Thinking styles are not the same as academic abilities. Instead, thinking styles focus on methods of self-governance. Sternberg and Zhang's (2005) theory of mental self-governance has five domains: functions, forms, levels, scope, and learnings. With each domain, there are sub-categories, and each sub-category has specific characteristics. For example, in the domain of function, there are three sub-categories: legislative, executive, and judicial. To Sternberg and Zhang, a legislative student is creative and works best as an independent creator. Legislative students will decide what he/she will do, not necessarily follow what another person told him/her to do. An executive student likes to have clear guidelines and boundaries, in regards to classroom activities and tasks. These students prefer traditional teaching methods. Finally, the judicial student likes the evaluative nature of a task. They are able to identify strengths and weaknesses in strategies, projects, and other people's ideas.

In addition to thinking styles, learning styles need to be taken into consideration. Cassidy (2004) examines 23 learning-styles models to determine students' learning styles. What is clear is that there is a tremendous variety of factors that can influence students' learning styles. For instance, some need to see the information visually while others learn best through auditory measures. There are those students who see only one "correct" answer to a problem (convergent thinking) as opposed to those who see the potential of having many solutions to a problem (divergent thinking). Also, for some students, the learning environment, like the amount of light in the classroom or the time of day, has an impact on how they learn. Hlawaty (2008-2009) studies learning styles of adolescents and finds that younger adolescents are primarily motivated by an authority figure, like a parent or teacher. As the adolescent becomes older, the motivation changes from being authority-based to being self-driven. Griggs and Dunn (1996) find that learning styles can differ among ethnic groups. For example, Asian-American students tend to learn best though auditory and visual methods, and Latino Americans learn best with auditory, visual, and kinesthetic methods.

Methods of Gathering Information about Students

In order to know how to differentiate instruction, teachers need to be aware of their students' current academic abilities in regards to their students' capabilities and interests within a specific content area. At the beginning of the school year, teachers need to first learn their students' prior knowledge about the subject. By understanding the students' prior knowledge, teachers can make specific connections between the new information and the students' existing knowledge (Lawrence-Brown, 2004). For example, a teacher may have two sections of Algebra I, but in one section, over half of the students either immensely dislike or are afraid of mathematics and can only perform basic arithmetic skills, and in the other section, most of the students have had Algebra in junior high school but do not test out of it to the next level.

Content in both classes will stay the same, yet the instructional delivery should differ.

There are various ways of getting to know students. One method is by using an Activity-Based Assessment (ABA) (Ferguson, Ralph, Meyer, et al., 2001). ABA is a list of activities in which the students participate on a regular basis. Teachers gather this information with each student individually through either oral or written interviews. By understanding their students' behaviors and routines, teachers learn about their students' abilities, interests, and preferences. With this information, teachers can make more informed curricular decisions. Students usually complete an ABA at the beginning of the school year.

Another data collection method is giving students an Interest Inventory (Kane 2007; Moore, Moore, Cunningham, & Cunningham, 2006; Tukey, 2002). An Interest Inventory is a set of written questions, in order to gain greater understanding of the students within a particular content area. Anyone can create his/her own inventory, asking specific questions. Questions on the Interest Inventory can be simple or detailed. Below are some examples of possible questions:

1. What is your favorite part about geometry class? Why is this your favorite part?
2. What part of English class do you try to avoid? What's so horrible about it?
3. When you come to chemistry class, how do you feel? Do you look forward to it? Is it your favorite class? Do you dread coming to class? Do you think it's a waste of time to be here?
4. If you like history, tell me why you like it. If you don't like history, tell me why you dislike it.
5. What is the best way for you to learn? Do you like to do group projects? Do you like to listen and take notes? Do you like to listen to books on tape? Do you like to watch videos? Tell me your favorite way to learn and why.
6. Write a list of everything that you know about plants. You can write anything from, "they're something that I eat," "they're green," to "trees are plants."

Sometimes, an assignment is given, and after grading the assignment, the teacher realizes that only 10 out of 30 students complete the assignment correctly. While 20 students do not complete the assignment correctly, there are no commonalities or trends in the errors. What is clear is that instruction needs to be differentiated so that the students can understand the material and future assignments. One way to determine the difficulties is by having a large group discussion. The teacher starts the discussion by telling the students that he/she is very concerned about the number of errors on the assignment. Next, he/she asks for possible reasons why there are so many errors. Finally, the teacher asks for suggestions on how he/she can better teach the material. Large-group discussion gives teachers the opportunity to understand the classroom community's interests. Adolescents are very perceptive about the presentation of class materials. As the teacher, it is necessary to keep an open mind about adolescents' comments, for such comments are insightful and valuable.

A large forum, however, may not be suitable. Instead of understanding the classroom community's interests, it may be more important to understand the individual's interests. On an individual level, another method of learning students' strengths and weaknesses is through tutorials and journals. Tutorials (or in-class conferences) can be used as a means of identifying students' weaknesses and strengths (Edwards & Pula, 2008; Tukey, 2002). These conferences are 10 to 15 minutes long, and the teacher meets with any student who wants to speak to the teacher. In these individual conferences, the teacher asks similar questions as in the group format, but individual responses can be given. If there is little time for tutorials, then teachers can use journaling to get student feedback (Werderich, 2002; Anonymous, 2000; Borasi & Rose, 1989). Journals are very useful because they provide a non-threatening medium for students to voice their opinions. Teachers get to know the students on an individual, more personal level, and teachers can get a sense of their students' academic skills. The student feedback helps the teacher to see what methodologies work, and students' feedback to the teacher gives information to make long term changes in the teaching methods used in the classroom.

DIAGNOSIS

Just as a doctor makes a diagnosis when treating a patient, teachers must constantly diagnose how the students in his or her classroom are learning and progressing. Also, just as doctors have many "tests" available for making a diagnosis, teachers have many possible avenues for determining students' progress. The key to successfully determining student needs is to practice assessment for the purpose of planning and guiding instruction. According to Zemelman, Daniels, and Hyde (2005), the best diagnostic tools for the classroom have the following traits. Diagnostic assessments:

- focus on complex whole outcomes rather than isolated sub-skills;
- are, most of the time, formative in nature so that data can be used to guide learning and adjust teaching;

- utilize methods that are descriptive and narrative rather than scored and numerical;
- involve students in the development process and self-assessment of their products;
- use triangulation principles, considering each student from several angles such as observations, conversations, portfolios, and performances over time;
- are an integral but moderated part of instruction;
- are non-competitive;
- are part of a program that includes community members and invites them to participate in the process.

The remainder of this chapter will focus upon assessment options that we believe meet Zemelman, et al.'s (2005) guidelines for effective assessment, once individual student diagnoses are complete. Making sure that a teacher's assessment practices meet these criteria can go a long way in guaranteeing that assessment is an embedded and valuable part of a teacher's curriculum rather than an interruption in the instructional process.

The key to appropriately differentiating instruction is accurate assessment of students. The following list of assessments is not panoptic, but it does provide many options for including formative assessments in the curriculum. Many of the assessments presented are interactive, meaning that they teach while testing or "focus on the ability of the learner to respond to interventions" (Brozo & Afflerbach, 2011, p. 10). These assessments have been selected based on their adherence to the traits of effective assessments and their ability to identify students' strengths as well as their needs. We recommend nine assessment practices that have been effective for us:

Assessment 1: Background Knowledge Check

Description:

A "background knowledge check" is a short questionnaire prepared by teachers to find out what a student already knows before introducing a new topic.

Purpose:

The purpose of a "background knowledge check" is to determine where to start in the lesson, which students need more help, and to focus students on the most important concepts being presented. Most prior knowledge assessments serve this dual purpose, (1) helping teachers learn about student preparation and (2) aiding students by focusing their attention on the key concepts. In addition, "with a "background knowledge check," teachers will be able to determine how well students can communicate what they know, and determine the students' ability to make connections to the new course subject.

Administration Guidelines:

Before introducing a new topic, think about what knowledge students are likely to already have. Think about what misconceptions students are likely to have as well. Try to determine an area where students are likely to have some connection with the content, and then use that area to lead into less familiar arenas. Write questions that guide students from the familiar to the less familiar and that probe into any of the possible misconceptions students are likely to have.

Assessment 2: Conferences

Description:

A "conference" is used to meet with students individually to talk about their progress in class and/or the course content. Using a "conference" as an assessment tool implies an organized approach where the "conference" is planned and monitored for the opportunity to learn about the student.

Purpose:

The purpose of individual "conferences" can be both academic and behavioral. These sessions can build rapport, unearth confusion, and provide students with the opportunity to demonstrate their understanding in a different venue.

Administration Guidelines:

For "conferences" there are some fairly simple guidelines, (1) tell students beforehand about the expectations for the conference and what will likely be discussed, and (2) let the student do the talking. The teacher jots notes and listens so that the student knows s/he is being heard. Sometimes it is amazing how much students enjoy talking when they are being recorded; it gives them a sense of importance.

Assessment 3: Double-Entry Journals

Description:

The "double-entry journal" is a tool that allows students to engage in a written conversation about the materials being presented. This Journal looks like a T-Chart on a page with the left and right side of the page split into separate columns. Table 4.1 is an example of a T-chart for a "double entry journal."

Purpose:

The purpose of a "double-entry journal" is to provide students with a format for selecting and responding to the main ideas in presented materials. This format then provides the teacher with a way to gauge what the students

Important Quotes or Passages	Your Response to the Quote or Passage

Table 4.1. Example of a T-chart for a Double-Entry Journal.

find important and to gain insight into students' viewpoints regarding the content.

Administration Guidelines:

Students begin a "double-entry journal" by writing, on the left-hand side of a page of paper, quotes from a text, video, discussion or lecture that they find intriguing. These quotes/passages could be selected for their profound or controversial nature, or their significance. The students then respond to the quotes on the corresponding right-hand side of the page. They can respond by elaborating on the passage, questioning the ideas, or making a real-world connection to the content.

Assessment 4: Observation

Description:

Similar to the section on "conferences," "observation" is something that teachers naturally perform each day. It is listed here as a reminder that "observation" can be a valuable assessment tool when the "observations" are planned and geared specifically toward learning about students. "Observation" differs from casual observation in that it is recorded and planned.

Purpose:

"Observations" of the students in a classroom can provide both academic and behavioral information. The purpose of formalizing the process can be for record keeping and for analyzing trends that might not be as evident without the written records.

Administration Guidelines:

The first step in administering an "observation" assessment is to plan the observation based on a specific purpose, e.g., I want to observe my science lab to assess students' skills in problem solving. Then, design an observation sheet that is formatted to make the "observations" focused on the task-at-hand; it may take some practice and revision to design an observation sheet that is convenient and thorough. A checklist, with room for comments, often works well for this.

Assessment 5: Performance Assessment

Description:

The concept behind a "performance assessment" is often synonymous with authentic assessment or alternative assessment. These vary from a content assessment in that it is designed to assess the students' ability to successfully perform a task based on their ability to master content; the task itself is more of a focus than the concepts.

Purpose:

The main purpose for a "performance assessment" is to allow teachers to assess students' skills at using their content knowledge to perform a task. A "performance assessment" allows teachers to gauge students' procedural knowledge in a natural setting.

Administration Guidelines:

A "performance assessment" can include anything from building a birdhouse, to giving a speech, to designing a webpage. The first step in designing an effective performance assessment is to determine which skills are to be assessed. For example, if the student is designing a birdhouse, will s/he be assessed on creativity, problem solving, the ability to work with power tools or all three? Once the performance skills to be assessed have been determined, the next step is to determine what level needs to be accomplished in order to succeed at the performance. For example, does a student need to incorporate humor for a successful speech? Does "the performance" need to make the audience at least chuckle? Determining the standards is an important step that must be deliberate and detailed. The next step is to share the performance criteria with students and then allow them to perform or practice for the performance before they are assessed. A rubric is often a clear way to determine students' proficiency on a performance assessment.

Assessment 6: Portfolio

Description:

A "portfolio" is sometimes mistakenly thought of as nothing more than a collection of student work. Given that models and artists present their "portfolios" as a collection of their best photographs or artwork, this misconception is understandable; however, a true portfolio involves the process of the student selecting the pieces to include in that portfolio. A "portfolio" also involves a chance for students to reflect on their own achievement and progress. Thus, while the end product can sometimes be presented as a collection of students' best works, the reflections and reflective process reveal the true value in portfolios.

Purpose:

"Portfolios" can be a valuable tool for determining students' learning processes. They are a great way to showcase students' achievements and for sharing their progress with parents and community members. Another purpose for including portfolios in a teacher's curriculum is that they provide a venue for asking students to set goals, reflect on progress, and learn about their own processes for learning. This self-analysis is an important skill for students in their journey to becoming independent learners.

Administration Guidelines:

There are 3 main processes ("collect," "select," and "reflect") involved with engaging students in portfolios. For each process it is important that the teacher consider these questions:

a. Collect. As part of the "collect" process a teacher should ask: What is my goal for asking students to collect pieces? Do I want pieces that show the process to be included or do I want just finished products? How much will students decide what to save and what input do I want to provide on how to create their collection? Where will the collection of student portfolios be housed? How can the collection process become an integrated part of the classroom without disturbing instruction time?

b. Select. As part of the "select" process a teacher should ask: What criteria will be used for the section process? What role will students play in determining the selection process? How can I engage students so that they understand the criteria that are important for their selection process? Who will make the selections, the students, teacher, or a mix of both? What skills do I want students to learn through the selection process?

c. Reflect. As part of the "reflect" process a teacher should ask: How formal do I want the reflection process to be? How often do I want students to reflect on their portfolios? What do I hope to accomplish through the reflection process? How can I connect student learning from the reflection process to other areas of the curriculum? Do I want others to reflect on the students' portfolios?

There are many considerations to take into account when implementing a "portfolio" system, and these questions should get a teacher thinking about what they want to accomplish with the portfolios.

Assessment 7: Self-Survey

Description:

A "self-survey" is a tool that asks students to examine their history, opinions, and values related to a certain content area. These are especially useful when introducing controversial content where students' prior beliefs may influence their success, e.g., cloning, genetics, the Holocaust, poetry, issues of race or diversity. This assessment can take many forms from a pie chart to short answer to essay writing, but the commonality is that it requires students to consider their own connections with a topic and evaluate the influence of their experiences and beliefs.

Purpose:

The purpose of asking students to complete a self-survey is to assess students' awareness of their attitudes and values as they relate to course content. This awareness can be valuable for teachers to know since it influences students' learning and can lead students to reflect on their attitudes and the impact these have on their achievement. Additionally, "self-surveys" can allow students the chance to see the connections between course content and societal issues, and develop a self-awareness related to how their values and attitudes influence their understanding of the content.

Administration Guidelines:

To administer a "self-survey," the teacher must determine how best to probe into students' past experiences and beliefs about the content being covered. For example, when teaching a poetry unit an English/Language Arts teacher may ask students to complete a pie chart where they fill in their attitudes and experiences related to poetry. This is often a good first step in a self-survey, since these connections are an effective means for determining students' attitudes and values. The next step is to evaluate students' experiences and connections and delve into how these might influence their understanding of content. A series of self-reflection questions based on what the teacher wants to learn about students can be developed. For example: Have your experiences with poetry been generally positive or negative? Why? What is your general attitude toward poetry? How can you make sure you are open-minded to our exploration of poetry in this course?

Assessment 8: Socratic Seminar

Description:

A "Socratic Seminar" is a discussion-based assessment that lends itself to measuring students' interaction skills as well as their mastery of particular content. This assessment is easiest to administer if students are seated in a circle and instructed to speak to each other rather than focusing on the teacher.

Purpose:

The purpose of a "Socratic Seminar" is to run an organized discussion, based on presented materials (via text, video, lecture, guest speaker) and measure students' clarity of thinking and their communication skills. "Socratic Seminars" provide teachers with information on how well their students can process materials and interact with the materials in an organized discussion. This assessment provides students the opportunity to participate in a discussion, and the teacher can gain feedback on their students' interaction skills. Having a dual purpose, the Socratic Seminar provides the teacher with information on students' discussion skills and mastery of content, while also providing additional learning opportunities for students as they discuss and analyze the materials.

Administration Guidelines:

Implementing a "Socratic Seminar" requires the following steps, (1) decide upon the material to be presented. It will be necessary that this material be deep/broad enough to elicit a discussion that allows students to reference the materials and also extrapolate and expand; (2) determine the criteria for assessing student participation, e.g., number of comments, reference to presented materials, quality of comments, and clarity of thinking. Clarity of thinking involves the following traits:

a. asking questions for clarity;
b. providing evidence/reasons;
c. referring to comments of classmates without repeating;
d. stating connections to other topics;
e. applying past knowledge to new situations;
f. finding humor (without hurting feelings);
g. stating the significance of what is being said;

(3) begin the discussion with a clear presentation of expectations and by sharing the criteria for assessing student participation so that students understand how to succeed; and (4) listen and moderate the discussion while assessing student participation. The teacher should try not to add her/his own input, thus allowing students the optimal response time.

Assessment 9: Vocabulary Analogies

Description:

A "vocabulary analogy" is a type of word problem that often appears on standardized tests. It is made up of two word pairs like this:

Graceful : Clumsy :: Late : _____

The goal in completing an analogy is to complete the second word pair based on the relationship of the first word pair. In this example "clumsy" is an antonym of "graceful" so a word that is an antonym of "late" should complete the equation, such as "early."

Purpose:

"Vocabulary analogy" assessments provide students with valuable vocabulary practice and teach students critical thinking skills as they determine the relationships between words. In addition, these assessments provide students with exposure to important vocabulary related to the topic of instruction and provide students the opportunity to connect new words to familiar concepts. When students create their own analogies, these analogies provide a tool for assessing students' understanding of the new concepts.

Administration Guidelines:

To administer a "vocabulary analogy" assessment it might help to begin by teaching students the most common kinds of relationships found in analogies, which are:

- synonyms, or words that have the same or similar meanings, as in WORK : LABOR
- descriptive, in which one word describes the other word, as in BLUE : SKY
- part to whole, in which one word is a part or a piece of the other, as in ARM : BODY
- item to category, in which one word names something that falls into the group named by the other word, as in MILK : BEVERAGE

Then, teach students to read analogies as a sentence. Such as "Milk is to beverage as Chocolate is to blank" and practice solving some vocabulary analogies together as a class.

The next step is to create analogies for students to complete using key vocabulary related to the content being presented. A final step may be to ask students to create their own vocabulary analogies, but this step should happen only after students have a clear grasp of the process.

The likely result of implementing some or all of these nine assessments in the classroom is that teachers will get a clearer picture of the variety of backgrounds, skill levels, attitudes, learning processes, academic levels, and behaviors that students bring with them to each lesson. This understanding may pose difficulties in many classrooms because the range of thinking styles and learning abilities can be extreme. The end result of using such assessments, though, is that differentiation will be made possible based on students' individual strengths and needs.

REMEDIATION

While some teachers consider assessment to be a culminating step where they measure what has been learned before moving on, most realize the value in using assessment as an initial step or as a way to check for students' progress along the way in lessons or units. Assessment is most valuable when the information gleaned from its analysis is used to plan and differentiate instruction to improve learning for students. Therefore, the steps necessary once you have collected assessment data are:

1. Analyze the data and interpret the results. This is where teachers determine how students are actually learning, feeling, thinking, and connecting based upon their assessment responses.
2. Formulate strategies, based on assessment results, to increase achievement. It is this step that guides teachers away from a teacher-centered approach toward a learner-centered approach as classroom learning experiences are based on students' strengths, weaknesses, attitudes, and prior knowledge.
3. Communicate assessment results with students. Student input can play a valuable role in this entire process. As students learn to set goals and analyze their own progress, it is important that their teachers guide this process with prompt feedback and assistance.

CONCLUDING THOUGHTS

It is important for schools to remember and act upon the knowledge that standardized tests are not the only measure of success that matters. Schools can collect and publish data on dropout rates, attendance figures, college success rates, community involvement, performance assessments, and other measures that show the parents and community how schools are improving.

Just as teachers should work in conjunction with parents and students to assess and diagnose areas for improvement, schools should work with their communities to evaluate programs and areas of need for their continued improvement. In this way assessment can be used to differentiate at the classroom-level and beyond for an education system that values the individual.

REFERENCES

Alvermann, D. E., Phelps, S. F., & Ridgeway, V. G. (2007). *Content area reading and literacy: Succeeding in today's diverse classrooms*. Boston, MA: Pearson Education.

Anonymous. (2000). Journal writing in the mathematics classroom: A beginner's approach. *Mathematics Teacher, 93* (2), 132-135.

Borasi, R. & Rose, B. J. (1989). Journal writing and mathematics instruction. *Educational Studies in Mathematics, 20* (4), 347-365.

Brozo, W. G. & Afflerbach, P. P. (2011). *Adolescent literacy inventory: Grades 6-12.* Boston, MA: Pearson Education.

Cassidy, S. (2004). Learning styles: An overview of theories, models, and measures. *Educational Psychology, 24* (4), 419-444.

Crawford, G. B. (2008). Differentiation *for the adolescent learner: Accommodating brain development, language, literacy, and special needs.* Thousand Oaks, CA: Corwin Press

Edwards, A. & Pula, J. (2008). In-class conferences as differentiated writing instruction: New uses for tutorials. *The Delta Kappa Gamma Bulletin, 74* (3), 10-14.

Ferguson, D. L., Ralph, G., Meyer, G., Lester, J., Droege, C., Guojonasdottir, H., Sampson, N. K., & Williams, J. (2001). *Designing personalized learning for every student.* Alexandria, VA: Association for Supervision and Curriculum Development.

Griggs, S. & Dunn, R. (1996). Learning styles of Asian-American adolescents. *Emergency Librarian, 24* (1), 8-13.

Hlawaty, H. (2008-2009). Learning and learning styles. *European Education, 40* (4), 23-45.

Kane, S. (2007). *Literacy & learning in the content areas.* Scottsdale, AZ: Holcomb Hathaway Publishers.

Lawrence-Brown, D. (2004). Differentiated instruction: Inclusive strategies for standard-based learning that benefit the whole class. *American Secondary Education, 32* (3), 34-62.

Miller, M. D., Linn, R. L., & Gronlund, N. E. (2009). *Measurement and assessment in teaching.* Upper Saddle River, NJ: Merrill-Pearson.

Moore, D., Moore, S. A., Cunningham, P. M., & Cunningham, J. W. (2006). *Developing readers and writers in the content areas, K-12.* Boston, MA: Pearson Education.

Richardson, J. S., Morgan, R. F., & Fleener, C. E. (2009). *Reading to learn in the content areas.* Belmont, CA: Wadsworth Cengage Learning.

Roe, B., Stoodt-Hill, B. D., & Burns, P. C. (2007). *Secondary school literacy instruction: The content areas.* Boston, MA: Houghton Mifflin.

Sternberg, R. J. & Zhang, L. (2005). Styles of thinking as a basis of differentiated instruction. *Theory into Practice, 44* (3), 245-253.

Sylwester, R. (2007). *The adolescent brain.* Thousand Oaks, CA: Corwin Press.

Tukey, L. (2002). Differentiated instruction and a game of golf. *Education Digest, 68* (3), 37-40.

Werderich, D. E. (2002). Individualized responses: Using journal letters as a vehicle for differentiated reading instruction. *Journal of Adolescent & Adult Literacy, 45* (8), 746-754.

Zemelman, S., Daniels, H., & Hyde, A. (2005). *Best practice: Today's standards for teaching and learning in America's schools.* Portsmouth, NH: Heinemann.

II

Differentiated Instruction and Content Area Applications

Chapter Five

Differentiating Instruction and Teaching the Middle School and High School English Language Arts

Shannon Pietras

INTRODUCTION

English has been called "the least subject-like of subjects, the least susceptible of definition" (Rosen, 1981, p. 5). Few educators choose to look at English as a whole due to the vast areas of skills that the term English covers. Teachers of English must cover the areas of writing, literature, and language, as well as the basic skills of language arts, i.e., reading, writing, listening, and speaking (Grossman & Shulman, 1994). English Language Arts (ELA) teachers cannot simply choose to teach one or two of the above areas. They must attempt to teach all of these curricular areas. Since it is difficult to cover all of these areas, teachers must select the purposes and areas they plan to emphasize in their classrooms (Grossman, 1990). In order to make informed decisions and exploit one aspect of the "curriculum potential" of English rather than another, teachers rely on their own understandings and beliefs about the nature of the discipline (Ben-Peretz, 1975). In most school districts, teachers are able to exercise considerable choice about additional texts to include, and about ways to approach those texts.

When teaching a text, teachers act upon the assumptions about the nature of the text, the nature of literature, what it means to read a text, how one rationalizes evidence to support a particular reading of a text, and the very nature of evidence itself. Through literature, students may adopt a critical stance to use in conjunction with a text (Grossman & Shulman, 1994). Students should be able to create theories and hypotheses of their own after observing how to create them in the classroom. All texts are human constructions rooted in particular time and knowledge. The particular pedagogical value of multiple interpretations lies in the diversity of the student readers (Grossman & Shulman, 1994). For example, Bevington (1990) explains that many new alternative readings to Shakespeare are feminist, historicist, and deconstructionist. Each sheds new light on an old text. The history of alternative interpretations becomes the beginning of a pedagogical repertoire, a set of alternative readings that can be used to transform the teachings of a particular text to diverse readers in diverse contexts (Grossman, 1990). If reading is a contract between a text and a reader, then teachers must believe there are multiple readings possible to any text. ELA teachers must not only guide their students through multiple interpretations of text, but must also recognize the multiple techniques of writing necessary for students to be effective outside of high school.

Another aspect of ELA that teachers must guide their students through is writing. Writing is an integral part of our society, and it is the job of the ELA teacher to assist students in the proper techniques of writing. The world is a very diverse place, and each student brings different experiences and dialects to the classroom (Grossman, 1990). A major problem that exists today is how teachers respond to students who bring to class different experiences with language, and different dialects. Teachers who grow up speaking standard or mainstream English, now must adapt their method of teaching in order to be effective in the changing environment (Schmoker & Graff, 2011).

Writing helps people properly communicate with one another. Students' writing gives teachers a clear picture of how well the students understand the concepts and how well they can communicate their learning (Schmoker & Graff, 2011). Writing is an important life skill that promotes clear thinking and deeper understanding even as computers and the Internet alter our means of communication. Students are not only expected to know, they are expected to communicate what they know both in school and in the world we imagine our students living in as adults (Van-Tassel-Baska, 2003). Writing is being taught in other subject areas; however, the responsibility of teaching writing still lies heavily in the ELA classroom. Student learning is enriched when they are taught to write well.

THE COMMON CORE STANDARDS FOR THE ENGLISH LANGUAGE ARTS

The Council of Chief State School Officers and the National Governors Association Center for Best Practices [CCSO and NGA] (2010, a, b) present the final Kindergarten through twelfth-grade Common Core State Standards documents for ELA and mathematics in June of 2010. These ELA and mathematics standards represent a set of expectations for student knowledge and skills that high school graduates need to master to succeed in college and careers.

To develop these standards, the CCSSO and the NGA have worked with representatives from participating states, a wide range of educators, content experts, researchers, national organizations, and community groups. These final standards reflect the invaluable feedback from the general public, teachers, parents, business leaders, states, and content area experts that are informed by the standards of other high-performing nations. The CCSO and the NGA believe that all students should be held to the same high expectations outlined in the Common Core State Standards. This includes students who are ELA learners.

Since so many states have signed on to the Common Core Standards, leaders and educators are collectively wondering how to make these standards a reality quickly, efficiently, and effectively. Successful implementation requires intensive professional development and training for teachers, principals, and district- and state-level staff. Strong leadership is also vital to implementing the standards. Many educators support the adoption of the common core standards. Smooth implementation requires clear communication and open discussion between policymakers, education leaders, teachers, staff, parents, and students. In order for schools to be able to answer questions regarding the common core, they must be properly informed. There are dozens of unanswered questions still lingering (Sloan, 2010). The ASCD (Association for Supervision and Curriculum Development) (The association, nd) supports high standards for student learning and achievement that are the result of a developmental process that is state-led, transparent, and implemented according to principles that:

- Educate the whole child through a broad and rich curriculum;
- Contain global competencies that develop the skills, knowledge, and attitudes to work effectively in an increasingly interdependent world;
- Provide equity in learning conditions for all students;
- Ensure effective instruction that results in increased learning for all students;
- Expand assessment options in measuring progress toward attaining the standards while maintaining accountability results;
- Rely on multiple indicators for assessing student performance and achievement;
- Develop coherent policies that support and align teacher preparation, licensure, and ongoing professional development requirements and activities;
- Include representation of educators at all levels and incorporate their input throughout the development, implementation, and evaluation process; and

- Maintain ongoing support among policymakers, educators, parents, and communities to secure necessary resources for the standards and their successful implementation.

In order for the common core to succeed, everyone must believe that all students can reach the standards. Standards alone do not address the in school and out-of-school influences that affect student achievement, but they do help provide guidance about where students should be in their skills and knowledge development. The common core standards are just the beginning of a brighter future for the nation's youth (Sloan, 2010).

IMPLEMENTATION OF THE COMMON CORE STANDARDS IN ENGLISH LANGUAGE ARTS

ELA will slowly change as the common core standards are implemented. The amount of informational texts (nonfiction) compared to literary texts (fiction) found in classrooms is now known, but the new standards place much more emphasis on informational texts. Even in kindergarten, the new ELA standards call for half of the texts to be informational and the other half literary. By the time students enter their senior year that could become seventy percent informational and thirty percent literary. Another change will be reflected in increasing the difficulty in the required texts.

Tightening the standards to become more focused on factual texts is also reflected in changes to writing expectations. Less emphasis will be placed on narrative and more on argumentative and explanatory writing. Many educators feel argument enlivens learning and is at the heart of inquiry. Education researchers have demonstrated that in-school opportunities to argue and debate about current issues, literary characters, and the pros and cons of mathematics solutions have an astonishing impact on learning and test scores. Argument not only makes subject matter more interesting, it also dramatically increases a learner's ability to retain, retrieve, apply, and synthesize knowledge (Schmoker & Graff, 2011). The Common Core Standards contain an endorsement of argument as the primary code for reading, talking, and writing about complex texts.

Many ELA educators are concerned about the possible removal of many literary (fiction) texts. ELA teachers believe fiction can take the learner anywhere, any time, and help them sense how it can feel to be a different gender, race, or nationality (Steiny, 2011). These experiences can prepare students for the uncertain future that lies ahead. Fiction often combines literacy skills with stories that broaden learners understanding of how and why different people, in different circumstances, make decisions, mistakes, and sacrifices. The common core ELA standards seem to say that students need to be exposed to more informational texts, more like what they will encounter in the real world (Sloan, 2010). Therefore, informational and expository texts will begin to work their way into the curriculum, and fictional texts may slowly begin to disappear.

The ELA Common Core Standards lay out a vision of what it means to be literate in the twenty-first century. The skills and understandings students are expected to demonstrate have wide applicability outside the reading that is at the heart of understanding and enjoying complex works of literature. Students who meet the standards will develop the skills in reading, writing, speaking, and listening that are the foundation for any creative and purposeful expression in language.

DIFFERENTIATING INSTRUCTION IN THE ENGLISH LANGUAGE ARTS

Even though most states are beginning to implement the ELA Common Core Standards, no one can debate that students learn differently. Therefore, teachers must be ready to engage students in instruction through different instructional strategies. In differentiated classrooms, teachers provide specific ways for each individual to learn as deeply as possible and as quickly as possible, without assuming one student's method of learning is identical to another student's (Tomlinson, 1999).

Teachers in differentiated classes use time flexibly, call upon a range of instructional strategies, and become partners with the students. Educators in differentiated classrooms accept, embrace, and plan for the fact that learners bring many different layers to school that make them all individuals.

The cornerstone of differentiation is active planning. The teacher plans instruction strategically to meet learners where they are and offer multiple avenues through which they can access, understand, and apply learning. In differentiating lessons to be effective to the needs of each learner, teachers must take into account not only the content, but also who they are teaching. Teachers need to know the varying readiness levels, interests, and learning profiles of each of their students and then design learning options to address these three factors (Corley, 2005). In adopting differentiated instruction, teachers must try to address student readiness, interest, and learning profiles.

When students enter middle school and high school ELA classes, many have a variety of reading and comprehension levels. Teachers must find a way to teach the curriculum with such a variety of reading and writing levels in their classes. Gifted children often achieve language competency at an earlier age than their peers. High-ability learners may excel in many language arts areas from reading and literary analysis to creative writing, poetry, and prose (Van Tassel-Baska, 2003). Typically, teaching in the ELA has emphasized reading skills and low-level questions over active learning and inquiry. With the adoption of the ELA Common Core Standards, this will slowly begin to change, but that does not delete the problem of multiple learning levels in the classroom. Low-level emphasis fails to challenge high-ability learners who have mastered the fundamental reading skills and are reading for higher application. Furthermore, only considering the higher-level learner leaves the average to below-average student behind. Therefore, there exists a real need to differentiate language arts experiences for learners at all stages of development.

DIFFERENTIATING INSTRUCTION AND LESSON PLANNING FOR THE ENGLISH LANGUAGE ARTS

In this section there are three lessons plans and one unit plan that provide a glimpse of how to differentiate instruction in a middle-level and high school ELA classroom. These lessons promote creativity and originality. A differentiated classroom is a dynamic environment where students move in and out of learning groups based on achievement data and interest. Students are sometimes permitted to choose activities or materials, and teachers move among groups to facilitate learning (Corley, 2005). The lesson plans provide multiple approaches to create learning experiences that complement the individual student's learning style. Each lesson links differentiated instruction to the ELA Common Core Standards.

Lesson Plan One. "Annabel Lee"

Lesson one can be used in an ELA seventh-grade classroom and involves the play by Edgar Allen Poe (2011), "Annabel Lee." The purpose of the lesson is for students to learn how to read metaphors and identify what an author is trying to say in their poetry. The students will also learn how to compare two separate pieces of literature and link common elements together. Lastly, students will be able to identify common threads and writing styles of a variety of authors. Using multiple intelligence strategies (Armstrong, 2009), students will be able to stretch their comprehension across two different mediums in order to link common mood and theme. Being able to make thematic and style connections is needed throughout the ELA. In addition state-mandated, standardized assessments rely heavily upon this skill.

The Lesson
  Essential Questions

  1. What is a metaphor?
  2. What is the author's message?

3. What common elements do a song and poem have?

4. What is the mood and theme?

Common Core Standards

Reading Standards for grades 6-12

RL.9-10.2. Determine a theme or central idea of a text and analyze in detail its development over the course of the text, including how it emerges and is shaped and refined by specific details; provide an objective summary of the text.

RL.9-10.10. Compare and contrast the experience of reading a story, drama, or poem to listening to or viewing an audio, video, or live version of the text, including contrasting what they "see" and "hear" when reading the text to what they perceive when they listen or watch.

1. Objective. Students will be able to make connections of similarities in theme and writing style, which are needed throughout the ELA.

2. Procedures

  a. Introduce reasons for reading

    i. To study Edgar Allan Poe's style

    ii. To understand themes

    iii. To compare and contrast theme and mood in different mediums

    iv. For enjoyment

    v. For mood

    vi. For expression

  b. Play audio of "Annabel Lee" (Poe, 2011). Discuss poem, characters, what happened, repetition.

  c. Pass out lyrics to class of My Immortal by Evanescence. While passing out the lyrics, discuss how the music can create even more of a mood and atmosphere.

  d. Play song, My Immortal. The song is chosen due to the lyrics talking about how the presence of a loved one still lingers with the singer.

  e. Multiple intelligences

    i. Interpersonal – Analysis of poem and song; have students break into groups to compare and contrast the song and poem.

    ii. Linguistic – Have students write a stanza of the poem from Annabel Lee's point of view. They must stay in the rhyme scheme and format of the original work. Poems must follow the rhyme scheme, stick with the mood created by Poe, and must stay within the original theme of lost love.

    iii. Spatial – Create a movie poster for "Annabel Lee" using one of the verses as the idea for the poster.

    iv. Musical (with a partner) – using the poem, "Annabel Lee," write a one verse song using repetitive lines as a chorus to go along with the instrumental beat.

3. Student materials

a. Textbook, writing utensil, paper

4. Formative Assessment. Through the first poem, "Annabel Lee," students will work together with the teacher to identify the key themes of the poem. Teacher can use a variety of methods to formatively assess the students as they work on this process, such as stopping and jotting their thoughts, the teacher walking around the room asking questions, and discussion overheard while working independently.

5. Summative Assessment. Students will be assessed at the completion of the unit based on the project they choose. Regardless of the option selected, students need to demonstrate the themes and writing styles of Poe's work. They need to also have made connections between the two pieces of literature used during this lesson.

Lesson Plan Two. The Harlem Renaissance

Another example of differentiating in a middle school ELA classroom involves a seventh- or eighth-grade ELA class that is learning about the Harlem Renaissance. Prior to this lesson, students need to have learned biographical information about the Harlem Renaissance, Langston Hughes, and Zora Neale Hurston. In order to be successful with the lesson, students need to be familiar with the time period and many of the issues that have occurred, such as racial discrimination and segregation.

This lesson incorporates the use of multiple intelligences (Armstrong, 2009) by allowing students to creatively represent a piece they read. Students will work in groups and have to critically analyze a piece, create a written poem, and create a visual image. Working in groups will allow students to use the multiple intelligences for the lesson's project.

The Lesson
Essential Questions

1. How are poems similar and different?
2. What tone does music create?
3. How do images and colors represent certain feelings and moods?

Common Core Standards

RL.9-10.2. Determine a theme or central idea of a text and analyze in detail its development over the course of the text, including how it emerges and is shaped and refined by specific details; provide an objective summary of the text.

SL.9-10.1. Initiate and participate effectively in a range of collaborative discussions (one- on-one, in groups, and teacher-led) with diverse partners on grades 9–10 topics, texts, and issues, building on others' ideas and expressing their own clearly and persuasively.

1. Objectives.

a. Students will be able to compare and contrast the poems "I, Too," "Harlem," and "The Weary Blues."

b. Students will be able to visually and orally interpret "The Weary Blues" by Langston Hughes

c. Students will be able to create a poem after listening to a blues or jazz song.

d. Students will be able to illustrate one of Hughes' poems using various colors and images to convey the emotions of the poem.

2. Procedures

a. Students are already familiar with the background information of the Harlem Renaissance. The students have read a couple poems by other Harlem Renaissance writers such as Zora Neale Hurston and James Weldon Johnson and discussed biographical information about the authors. To begin the lesson, students will listen to a jazz song. They are instructed to simply close their eyes and listen to the beat and melody. The song does not have any lyrics, but the students are asked to think about the feelings and emotions that are created when they listen to the music. The students have discussed how jazz creates a feeling or emotion and it is up to them how they interpret it during the lesson taught preceding this one. The students also have discussed during this lesson how the authors often discuss equality and racial discrimination in their poems and writing. (5 minutes)

b. After listening to the song once, play the song once more. Prior to playing the song the second time, ask the students to think of how they would put their emotions into words. Students are then placed into groups of three. Their task is to write a sixteen-line poem that discusses a Harlem Renaissance issue. Since the students have read Zora Neale Hurston two to three days prior, their poem must also include a male and female perspective. The poem is to be written in free verse so there should not be rhyme. (20 minutes)

c. After the students complete their poems, each group will read their poems out loud to the class. The class will also briefly discuss how these poems are their originals and someone else copying them now is unethical. That happens today when people illegally download songs that are not theirs. During the Harlem Renaissance, many of the artists are viewed live. There are no compact discs to listen to or download their music and poems online. (10 minutes)

d. Read Langston Hughes' "The Weary Blues" (2011). First read the poem without any music, and ask the students what type of feeling the poem has. The poem portrays the hard, working-class American and Hughes' admiration for the musicians who play the blues. It is supposed to be read to a blues beat. Next, the class hears the poem again, but an audio version being read to a blues beat. Students then can begin to understand the difference the music can make in the poem. (10 minutes)

  e. Spend the remainder of the class discussing discrimination, author's point-of-view, and mood, and have students respond to three questions (see below) in which they are asked to interpret components of the poem. (5 minutes)

    i. What vision of the musician did you develop as you read "The Weary Blues?"

    ii. How does the speaker seem to feel about the musician and blues music?

    iii. Is Hughes' response to racial discrimination effective?

3. Materials

Blues/Jazz CD

Textbook that includes "The Weary Blues," "I,Too," and "Harlem."

Paper

Pencil

Audio of "The Weary Blues"

4. Formative Assessment. As "The Weary Blues" is interpreted, students will respond to various teacher-directed questions, such as the ones listed above, in order to check for understanding. The questions at the end of the lesson also assist determining the students' knowledge of the poem.

5. Summative Assessment. After students read Hughes' other two poems, "I, Too," and "Harlem," (which takes place in the next two to three class periods) students will create an illustration to accompany one of the poems. The students should use colors and images to convey the mood of the poem. The size of the illustration should be at least on 8 ½" by 11" white paper. The title of the poem should be present. Each student will also provide a brief (1/2 page) explanation of their illustration. This half-page explanation should describe what thoughts and ideas the students are thinking as they designed their illustration. The teacher should develop an appropriate rubric for the illustration. Some key points in the rubric should be assessing whether the student is using appropriate colors and images to convey the meaning of the poem, creativity and imagination is evident, and an appropriate quote is chosen to represent the meaning of the poem.

Lesson 3. To Kill A Mockingbird

The following lesson is intended for a tenth-grade ELA classroom and has been created using the Thinking/Learning (T/L) System (Sparapani, 2000). The intent of the T/L System is to integrate the thinking skills with the teacher's regular classroom instruction. A thorough explanation of the T/L System can be found in Chapter 10.

After the class, participants will have an in-depth knowledge of prejudice in the novel *To Kill a Mockingbird* (Lee, 1995) and how prejudice currently affects the world. The lesson is a four-step process and in each process, students have a choice from three options.

In the first section, information gathering, students can perform one of the following tasks: cite an example of prejudice they have either encountered or know someone who encountered it. Then write a definition of prejudice, draw three illustrations to accompany three of the vocabulary words in *To Kill a Mockingbird* that reinforce stereotypes, or with a partner, describe four of the pictures taken during the 1930s (presented by the teacher) in 2-3 sentences. Imagine what the people are thinking and feeling.

In the second section, critical thinking, students can either compare examples of prejudice in the 1930s to the present, explain in three paragraphs how prejudice in society has either changed or remained the same, with two other people design a comic strip that depicts prejudice in the novel, or draw a plot diagram of the major prejudices in *To Kill a Mockingbird* and write two to three sentences explaining each one.

In the third section, decision making, students can write three paragraphs from the point of view of someone else in the courtroom during the Tom Robinson trial, find six examples of pictures displaying prejudice, or illustrate Atticus Finch and write two paragraphs describing the type of American and character he is.

For the final section, creative thinking, students can use their definition of prejudice (from section one) to write two paragraphs that explain the role prejudice plays in *To Kill a Mockingbird* (only one can be racism), with another student, revise the outcome of Tom Robinson's trial the way they believe it should end, and then perform a skit for the class portraying the new ending, or design the front headline in the newspaper that describes the outcome of Tom Robinson's trial. Write a five-sentence paragraph explaining the picture.

When doing a lesson using the T/L System, students should do all the activities in section one, information gathering. The teacher should then choose one activity from each of the other three sections, an "a" activity from one section, a "b" activity from the next section, and a "c" activity from the last section. Also, activities can be done in any order.

The Lesson
Essential Questions

1. What is prejudice?
2. How does prejudice affect society?
3. How is prejudice evident in *To Kill a Mockingbird?*

Common Core Standards

RL.9-10.1. Cite strong and thorough textual evidence to support analysis of what the text says explicitly as well as inferences drawn from the text.

W.9-10.1. Write arguments to support claims in an analysis of substantive topics or texts, using valid reasoning and relevant and sufficient evidence.

1. Objective

a. Students will be able to analyze and present in-depth knowledge of prejudice in *To Kill a Mockingbird* and how prejudice currently affects the world.

2. Procedures

a. Information Gathering (Knowledge/Comprehension)

i. Cite an example of prejudice you have either encountered or know someone who encountered it. Then write a definition of prejudice.

ii. Draw three illustrations to accompany three of the vocabulary words in *To Kill a Mockingbird* that reinforce stereotypes.

iii. With a partner, describe four of the pictures taken during the 1930s (presented by teacher) in 2-3 sentences. Imagine what the people are thinking and feeling.

3. Critical Thinking (Analysis)

a. Compare examples of prejudice in the 1930s to now. Explain in three paragraphs how things have either changed or remained the same.

b. With two other people, design a comic strip that depicts prejudice in the novel.

c. Draw a plot diagram of the major prejudices in the novel and write 2-3 sentences explaining each one.

4. Decision Making (Evaluation)

a. Write three paragraphs from the point of view of someone else in the courtroom during the Tom Robinson Trial.

b. Find six examples of pictures displaying prejudice.

c. Illustrate Atticus Finch and write two paragraphs describing the type of American and character he is.

5. Creative Thinking (Application/Synthesis)

a. Using your definition of prejudice, write two paragraphs that explain the role prejudice plays in *To Kill a Mockingbird* (only one can be racism).

b. With another student, revise the outcome of Tom Robinson's trial the way you believe it should end, and then perform a skit for the class portraying the new ending.

c. Design the front headline in the newspaper that describes the outcome of Tom Robinson's trial. Write one to two five-sentence paragraphs explaining the verdict, including two reactions from someone at the trial.

Materials

Paper
    Pencil
    To Kill a Mockingbird by Harper Lee

Formative Assessment

As students move through the process of the T/L System, students will either be reporting to the teacher or turning various assignments in after each step has been completed. If a concept is unclear, the teacher can direct students as needed to ensure understanding of the prejudice in *To Kill a Mockingbird* and in today's society. Groups and students will also be called on at random to report out their findings in various stages of the system.

Summative Assessment

The last step in the system provides for a final assessment on the lesson objectives. The final step, creative thinking, will be used as a final assessment and be graded as a writing assignment.

Unit. The Things They Carried

Educators can also differentiate in ELA using the 4MAT System (McCarthy, 1979), such as in this unit (see Table 5.1) that is created to coincide with the novel *The Things They Carried* (O'Brien, 1990). A 4MAT System unit has eight steps; each step is a complete lesson. The objectives for this unit is to interpret letters from soldiers, analyze war-inspired music, and discuss the emotions and meanings of war.

Essential Questions

1. What is the message in the letters written by the soldiers?
2. What is the purpose of war?
3. How are cultures different from one another?
4. What do the soldiers carry with them?

Common Core Standards

RI.9-10.3. Analyze how the author unfolds an analysis or series of ideas or events, including the order in which the points are made, how they are introduced and developed, and the connections that are drawn between them.

RI.9-10.7. Analyze various accounts of a subject told in different mediums (e.g., a person's life story in both print and multimedia), determining which details are emphasized in each account.

SL.9-10.1.Propel conversations by posing and responding to questions that relate the current discussion to broader themes or larger ideas; actively incorporate others into the discussion; and clarify, verify, or challenge ideas and conclusions.

1. Objectives. See Tables 5.1 to 5.4.

2. Procedures (This unit takes approximately 2-3 weeks to complete.). See Tables 5.1 to 5.4.

Quadrant 1. Integrating Experience

a. Lesson 1. Right Mode – Connect (See Table 5.1). In lesson 1, students, in groups, self-explore and examine letters written by soldiers and listen to music written during the 1960s and 1970s.

b. Lesson 2. Left Mode – Examine (See Table 5.1). Lesson 2 is a question/answer lesson in which students interact with a Vietnam War veteran.

Quadrant 2. Context

a. Lesson 3. Right Mode – Imagine (See Table 5.2). In lesson 3 students examine the difficulties faced during the Vietnam War by watching the documentary *Vietnam: We Were Heroes* (2002).

b. Lesson 4. Left Mode – Define (See Table 5.2). In lesson 4, students will be provided background information about the Vietnam War and the novel, *The Things They Carried* (1990) through lecture-based instruction.

Quadrant 3. Applications

a. Lesson 5. Left Mode – Try (See Table 5.3). In lesson 5, students will work on various worksheets, study guides, vocabulary sentences, and discussion questions based on the short story *The Things They Carried* (1990).

b. Lesson 6. Right Mode – Extend (See Table 5.3). Students have already examined letters (in Lesson 1). In this lesson, students will compose their own letter to a loved one, imagining that they are away at war and their death is a possibility. An example of a model letter can be found in Table 5.5.

Quadrant 4. Creation

a. Lesson 7. Left Mode – Refine (See Table 5.4). In this lesson, students will complete a unit examination and also create their own project, based on options provided by the teacher, that displays what they have learned in the unit.

b. Lesson 8. Right Mode – Integrate (See Table 5.4). In this lesson, students present their projects and "celebrate" the unit by having their own peace rally.

Lesson 1

Right Mode: Connect

Objectives:
1.   Students will be able to interpret letters from soldiers
2.   Students will be able to analyze war-inspired music
3.   Students will be able to discuss the emotions and meaning of "war"
Activity: The desks will be grouped into groups of 3 or 4 prior to the students entering the classroom. Students will sit at a designated area. The purpose of this lesson is for the students to be introduced to a war-time experience. The students are to self-explore and examine letters written by soldiers and listen to music written during the 1960s and 1970s. The role of the teacher is to motivate the students and help them stay involved. The teacher plays the music and has the students discuss the songs and identify war and peace concepts in the songs. Next, students will examine and read letters written by soldiers to loved ones at home. This again should be self-exploratory. Directions will be placed on each grouping of desks in order to keep the students on task. The directions will include having students highlight and discuss what is emotional about the letters and what the purposes of the letters are. Next, the teacher will provide background regarding the Vietnam War prior to moving into the next step. The students are also to record new information about "war" they are discovering.
Assessment
Participation in the activity

Table 5.1. Quadrant 1: Integrating Experience.

Lesson 2

Left Mode: Examine

Lesson Objectives:
1.   Students will be able to compose appropriate questions relating to the Vietnam War
2.   Students will be able to ask questions to a Vietnam Veteran
Activity: The purpose of this lesson is for students to be able to ask questions to a Vietnam War Veteran. Students are to compose a minimum of five questions prior to the question and answer session. A Vietnam Veteran will be visiting the classroom to discuss the Vietnam War with the students. Students are able to ask any questions they want, but are also told to research a couple questions prior to the session. The students are to lead the discussion by asking the Veteran questions and taking in all of his responses. Students may also use some of the knowledge acquired from the previous lesson and from knowledge acquired from their Social Studies class, therefore students will be well-equipped to construct thoughtful questions for the discussion.
Assessment
Participation in the activity

Table 5.1 continued.

Lesson 3

Right Mode: Image

Objectives:
1.   Students will be able to examine the difficulties faced during the Vietnam War
2.   Students will be able to observe the extremes the soldiers had to encounter and
persevere through
Documentary: *Vietnam: We Were Heroes (2002)*.
Activity: The purpose of the lesson is for students to observe the difficulties encountered
during the war. This is an in-class movie that is an account of the Vietnam War. This will
provide students with background information and also examine deeper accounts of the war.
Students must compose a 1-2 paragraph reflection of the documentary commenting on the
extremes the soldiers encountered.
Assessment
Successful completion of the journal reflection

Table 5.2. Quadrant 2: Context.

Lesson 4

Left Mode: Define

Lesson Objectives:
1.   Students will be able to analyze and evaluate the concepts of a short story
2.   Students will be able to read and listen to diverse texts
3.   Students will be able to determine the meaning of unfamiliar words or specialized
vocabulary
4.   Students will be able to demonstrate an understanding of the connections between the
short stories
Activity: Students will be provided background information about the Vietnam War and the
novel, *The Things They Carried* (1990) through lecture-based instruction. After completing
the background information, the class will begin to read several of the short stories in *The
Things They Carried*. The class will alternate between the teacher reading and students
reading out loud or silently. Each lesson will be teacher-driven and concepts such as grief,
denial, and the burdens the soldiers carry will be emphasized and directed by the teacher.
Students will be asked to respond verbally to questions being asked on the study guides and
complete the study guides while reading. During steps 4-5, students will read the stories, "The
Things They Carried," "Love," "Spin," "The Man I Killed," "In the Field," and "Ghost
Soldiers."
Assessment
Successful completion of the study guides

Table 5.2 continued.

Lesson 5

Left Mode: Try

Lesson Objectives:
1.   Students will be able to analyze concepts in the novel
2.   Students will be able to determine the meaning of unfamiliar words or specialized vocabulary
3.   Students will be able to demonstrate an understanding of the connections between the short stories
Activity: Students will work on various worksheets, study guides, vocabulary sentences, and discussion questions based on the short story read in class. The purpose is to reinforce the concepts and skills taught in Quadrant Two. This process provides reinforcement and encouragement for the previous lesson.
Assessment
Successful completion of the worksheets

Table 5.3. Quadrant 3: Applications.

Lesson 6

Right Mode: Extend

Objectives:
1.   Students will be able to apply personal and shared criteria to evaluate others work
2.   Students will be able to compose a personal letter to a loved one
Lesson Description: Students have examined actual letters from soldiers during the first lesson. Students have also read personal accounts of how the soldiers feel during the war and many of the difficulties they face during war time. Often times, thinking of something at home is the only thing that can keep the soldiers grounded and sane. During this lesson, students will compose their own letter to a loved one, imagining that they are away at war and that their death is possible. Students may include accounts of the Vietnamese culture, what keeps them sane, experimentation with drugs, and death. A model letter (see Table 5.5) will first be presented to students in order for them to see a quality example. The purpose of the lesson, however, is for them to design a letter to show what they have learned during the previous lessons. Students need to make it personal to them.
Assessment
Successful completion of a letter

Table 5.3 continued.

Lesson 7

Left Mode: Refine

Objectives:
1. Students will be able to design their own scoring rubric
2. Students will be able to construct a project best suited for them
3. Students will be able to present a project orally
4. Students will be able to apply personal meaning to their project
5. Students will be able to demonstrate an understanding of the text in the form of an assessment

Activity: The first part of the lesson is for students to complete an assessment based on the shorts stories read in *The Things They Carried*. The assessment should take approximately 25 minutes and be part multiple choice and short response. The next part of the lesson is for student to pick a project from the list below to complete, and also design a rubric for the teacher to grade the students on their project. The project and assessment are each worth 50 points. Some project ideas are:
1. Present the differences between the Vietnam War and another major war.
2. Present your findings in a PowerPoint Presentation with 10 slides, 3 points a slide. Presentation should be about 10 minutes.
3. Pick 2 items that, as a student, you carry in your backpack, and write one page each about why you carry them and what they mean to you. You must also include an illustration or collage to accompany your paper.
4. Pick one main character from *The Things They Carried* and write a character essay. The essay should be no less than 2 pages and no more than 3.
5. Interview a Vietnam Veteran and present your findings in a two-page paper. You should also include a transcript of your conversation and a picture.
6. Pick 1 of the stories from *The Things They Carried* not read and make a comic strip to illustrate the main points. You must have at least 6 main points and a sentence or two under each frame.
7. Pick 1 character from *The Things They Carried* and make a collage or illustration to represent the character. You must also include a half-page
8. explanation about why you chose the character and explain your illustration.
9. You may come up with your own project, but it must first be approved by the teacher.

Students will have 3 days to complete their project.
Assessment
Successful completion of one of the above projects

Table 5.4. Quadrant 4: Creation.

Lesson 8

Right Mode: Integrate

Objectives:
1. Students will be able to demonstrate knowledge of the material presented in lessons 1-7
2. Students will be able to develop personal meaning and appreciation for others work

Activity: The first part of the lesson is for students to present their projects to the class. Students are encouraged to "dress the part." The second part of the lesson is a celebration of their accomplishment. Students will have their own peace rally and listen to 70s music and hang their accomplishments.

Assessment

Participation in the activity

Table 5.4 continued.

25 May, 1968

Dear Roberta,

Today is probably the worst day I have ever lived in my entire, short life. Once again we were in contact with Charlie, and once again we suffered losses. The losses we had today hit home, as my best friend in this shit hole was killed. He was only 22 years old and was going on R&R on the first of June to meet his wife in Hawaii. I feel that if I was only a half second sooner in pulling the trigger, he would still be alive.

Strange how short a time a half of a second is—the difference between life and death. This morning we were talking about how we were only two years different in age and how we both had gotten married before coming to this place. You know, I can still feel his presence as I write this letter and hope that I am able to survive and leave this far behind me.

If there is a place called Hell this surely must be it, and we must be the Devil's disciples doing all his dirty work. I keep asking myself if there is a God, then how the hell some young men with so much to live for have to die. I just hope that his death is not in vain.

I look forward to the day when I will take my R&R. If I play my cards right, I should be able to get it for Hawaii so our anniversary will be in that time frame. The reason I say this is by Sept., I will have more than enough time in country to get my pick of places and dates. I promise I will do everything necessary to insure that I make that date, and I hope that tomorrow is quiet.

We will be going into base camp soon for our three-day stand down. I will try to write you a longer letter at that time. Please don't worry too much about me, as if you won't, for I will take care of myself and look forward to the day I am able to be with you again.

Love,

Stan

Table 5.5. Sample letter from a soldier in Vietnam.

CONCLUDING THOUGHTS

Differentiating instruction is based on a teaching philosophy that teachers should adapt instruction to student differences. Students in ELA classrooms are no different. They read, write, and comprehend at a variety of levels and have various ways in which they learn. Rather than making students march to one beat (the teacher's beat) teachers should modify their instruction to meet students' varying readiness levels, learning preferences, and interests. Educators have to continuously be accommodating the full diversity of their student's academic needs.

The ELA Common Core Standards help ensure that students gain adequate exposure to a range of texts and tasks. It is also vital for students to read increasingly complex texts through the grades. The ELA Common Core Standards work in tandem to define college and career readiness expectations. Each year in reading and writing, students should demonstrate increasing sophistication in all aspects of language use, and they should address increasingly demanding content and sources.

Teachers who can make the focus on concepts, emphasizing understanding and sense- making through differentiating instruction rather than through retention and regurgitation, will be better preparing students for college and the world beyond. The teacher, rather than an instructor, must become the facilitator (guiding students as they learn), the planner of activities, and the assessor based on growth and goal attainment.

It is important to carefully differentiate project work to meet the criterion of creativity in the classroom and coinciding with the ELA Common Core Standards. As students enter high school, more emphasis is placed on collaborative project work. It is critical that educators use a common set of standards (Common Core) to judge whether or not this type of work is sufficiently challenging all learners in the classroom. Providing multiple options for students enhances creativity and encourages students to push themselves.

REFERENCES

Armstrong, T. 2009). *Multiple intelligences in the classroom* (3rd ed.). Alexandria, VA: Association for Supervision and Curriculum Development.

Ben-Peretz, M. (1975). The concept of curriculum potential. *Curriculum Theory Network, 5* (2), 151-159.

Bevington, D. (1990, Spring). "Reconstructing Shakespeare." *University of Chicago Magazine* pp. 21-25.

Corley, M. (2005). Differentiated instruction: Adjusting to the needs of all learners. *National Center for the Study of Adult Learning and Literacy, 7* (C), 13-16.

Council of Chief State School Officers, and the National Governors Association Center for Best Practices. (2010a). Common core state standards for English Language Arts and Literacy in History/Social Studies, Science, and Technical Subjects. *Common Core State Standards Initiative.* Available at http://www.corestandards.org/assets/CCSSI_ELA%20Standards.pdf.

Council of Chief State School Officers, and the National Governors Association Center for Best Practices. (2010b). Common core state standards for Mathematics. *Common Core State Standards Initiative.* Available at http://www.corestandards.org/assets/CCSSI_Math%20Standards.pdf.

Grossman, P. (1990). *The making of a teacher: Teacher knowledge and teacher education.* New York, NY: Teachers College Press.

Grossman, P. & Shulman, P. (1994). Knowing, believing, and teaching of English. In T. Shanahan (Ed.). *Teachers thinking, teachers knowing* (pp. 3-21). Urbana, IL: National Council of Teachers of English.

Lee, H. (1995). *To kill a mockingbird*. New York, NY: Harper Collins.

Madacy Records. (2002). We were heroes [DVD].

McCarthy, B. (1979). *The 4MAT system: Teaching to learning styles using right/left mode techniques.* Oak Brooke, IL: EXCEL Publishing.

O'Brien, T. (1990). *The things they carried*. New York, NY: Houghton Mifflin Publishing Company.

Poe, E. A. (2011). *Poems of Edgar Allen Poe. Great literature online. 1997-2011.* Available athttp://poe.classicauthors.net/PoemsofEdgarAllenPoe/PoemsofEdgarAllenPoe9.html.

Rosen, H. (1981). *Neither Bleak House nor Liberty Hall.* London, UK: University of London Institute of Education.

Schmoker, M. & Graff, G. (2011). More argument, fewer standards. *Education Week, 30* (28), 31-33.

Sloan, W. (2010). Coming to terms with common core standards. *Educational Leadership, 16* (4), 1-9.

Sparapani, E. F. (2000). The effect of teaching for higher-level thinking: An analysis of teacher reactions. Education, *121* (1), 80-89.

Steiny, J. (2011). Fiction still holds real-life benefits for students. *The Providence Journal, 6* (1), 2-6.

The association for supervision and curriculum development. (n.d.). Available at http://www.ascd.org.

Tomlinson, C. (1999). *The differentiated classroom: Responding to the needs of all learners.* Alexandria, VA: Association for Supervision and Curriculum Development.

Van Tassel-Baska, J. (2003). *Differentiating the language arts for high ability learners, K-8.* Arlington, VA. (ERIC Document Reproduction Service No. ED 474306).

The Weary Blues. (2011). In Encyclopædia Britannica. Available athttp://www.britannica.com/EBchecked/topic/1003229/The-Weary-Blues.

Chapter Six

Differentiating Instruction for Teaching Middle School and High School Mathematics

Gary Malburg and David K. Pugalee

INTRODUCTION

The impact of the new Common Core State Standards [CCSS] (Common Core State Standards Initiative, 2010) initiative for mathematics on instruction is analyzed in this chapter. Specifically, how differentiated instruction promotes the CCSS goal of understanding mathematics is discussed. The need for differentiation by using rich-tasks to increase access to understanding of these standards for all students is presented. Descriptions of the CCSS and the history of the movement for mathematical standards are presented to offer insights into how mathematics instruction is intended to change with implementation of the standards.

Lesson plans are provided that illustrate the standards put forth in the CCSS. Designed for the middle and secondary levels, the three lessons are task-oriented for use with students of all abilities. Meant for seventh to ninth graders, representations of expressions in a problem-solving activity highlight the first lesson. The lesson is an introduction to communicating expressions in terms of variables. Building upon expressions and variables, the second lesson is appropriate for eighth or ninth graders and addresses problem solving in relationship to representations of linear functions. Quadratic functions, in relationship to real-life contexts, are the centerpiece of the third lesson for ninth to eleventh graders. All of the lessons are meant to be used at the beginning of a unit to bring context to the forefront (Wiggins & McTighe, 2006), but they can be modified to be used as enrichment of a unit, or as part of a summative performance assessment.

THE HISTORY OF STANDARDS-BASED EDUCATION AND MATHEMATICS

Educators hear of standards reform and think "been there, done that." In the past twenty years, educational reforms have struggled to address instruction or student understanding. First called for in 1983 in *A Nation at Risk* (National Commission on Excellence in Education, 1983) the standards-based education movement prompts states to increase the number of standards per grade level and the graduation requirements for mathematics. This greater number of standards at earlier and earlier ages with the goal of creating a more rigorous curriculum has had little effect on the United States international standing in mathematics (Fleischman, Hopstick, Pelczar, & Shelley, 2010), but has created a curriculum that is an "inch deep and mile wide." Further, while the proportion of twelfth graders taking advanced algebra has more than doubled in the past ten to fifteen years, proficient scores on the National Assessment of Educational Progress (NAEP) tests have hardly budged (Steen, 2007).

While national standards exist in many of the highest academically achieving countries, the default national standards in the United States exist in the form of a text-book curriculum (Wu, 2011). Researchers have found that there are no textbooks in the world with as many topics as U.S. textbooks, due in part because textbooks are marketed to states with different standards. Compared with books that cover few topics in more depth that are used in many high-performing countries (National Mathematics Advisory Panel, 2008), U.S. textbooks are less focused and coherent. When compared to international instructional approaches, this problem of poor curricular resources is compounded by the fact that mathematics instruction in the United States is textbook weighted and teacher-driven (On Course for Success, 2009; Trends in International Mathematics and Science Study [TIMMS], 1999). This mode of instruction results in limited success for students at both ends of the achievement spectrum. The PISA (Programme for International Student Achievement) report shows the percentage of fifteen-year-olds achieving at the highest levels is three to seven times lower than percentages for the top third of OECD (Organization for Economic Cooperation and Development) nations while instruction in the United States for low achievers is more likely to include only basic computation (National Governors Association, the Council of Chief State School Officers, and Achieve, Inc., 2008).The relative success in developing mathematical proficiency for U.S. students is about 30 percent (Steen, 2007).

The Common Core State Standards (CCSS) are meant to be a new way of doing business. Arising because of international competition in an ever-increasing global economy, the National Governors Association and the Council of Chief School Officers organized the CCSS movement to make education more rigorous, so students graduate from high school with college and career training readiness. Through engagement of educators across the nation, the creators have a document supported by nearly every state, the United States Department of Education, and such organizations as the ACT, NEA, AFT, and the College Board (Common Core State Standards Initiative, 2010). The resulting national curricular consistency should address financial and human resource issues through the need to develop assessments and support materials for teachers nation wide. Both will be needed to create a deeper, more personalized curriculum (National Governors Association, the Council of Chief State School Officers, and Achieve, Inc., 2008).

Considering educational reform movements in the top performing member nations of the OECD, the CCSS contains internationally benchmarked, concise standards, fewer in number than the conglomerate of state and textbook standards currently being implemented. While traditional U.S. students typically complete a specific topic driven lesson daily, instruction in other nations focuses on one thoroughly examined topic in a week (National Governors Association, the Council of Chief State School Officers, and Achieve, Inc., 2008). By eliminating the lesson-a-day paradigm, fewer guideposts create time to allow for brain-based practices, including elaboration on information and consolidation of principles (Wolfe, 2001).

WHAT THE CCSS SAYS ABOUT UNDERSTANDING IN MATHEMATICS

Unlike early reform movements, the CCSS focus on both content and cognitive skills. Because fewer standards are not a prescription for a concise, rigorous curriculum, these standards are intended to address what it means to understand mathematics. Understanding is substantiated through critical thinking, reflection, and communication of mathematical computations or proofs. No longer is it sufficient to be able to "do" mathematics. Computational skills or procedural fluency will progress with the conceptual fluency needed for problem solving where application of the mathematics is being stressed during instruction. The CCSS intends for procedural and conceptual fluency to proceed simultaneously (Common Core Standards Initiative, 2010).

Procedural skills and conceptual understanding of mathematics are attended to equally through two tiers of standards, the content standards and the mathematical practices standards. The content standards are made up of mathematical principles and content topics that are grade level appropriate. Meanwhile, the eight standards for mathematical practices describe thinking processes and the mental habits necessary to be mathematically proficient and demonstrate deep conceptual understanding. These mathematical practices standards are consistent from kindergarten through twelfth grade and address what it means for a student to understand, or be proficient in, mathematics (Common Core Standards Initiative, 2010). The CCSS focus on both conceptual and procedural fluency in an effort to define what it means for students to understand mathematics.

Based upon the best standards across states, the content standards will be familiar to most teachers. Extending the emphasis found in past standards, the CCSS content standards for mathematics are organized with trajectories across many grade levels to provide continuity. Based upon learning progressions, the logical progression of connected topics supports mathematical understanding and problem solving (Hiebert, Carpenter, Fennema, et al., 1997). The content standards are also connected to modeling or the application of mathematics and statistics to everyday life and decision-making (Common Core Standards Initiative, 2010).

The National Council of Supervisors of Mathematics [NCSM, 2010] warns that the first stage of implementation is not to align the content standards to current standards, but to focus on the mathematical practices. Conceptual fluency is shown in the demonstration of the practices. The eight mathematical practices state that mathematically proficient students, (1) Make sense of problems and persevere in solving them, (2) Reason abstractly and quantitatively, (3) Construct viable arguments and critique the reasoning of others, (4) Model with mathematics, (5) Use appropriate tools strategically, (6) Attend to precision, (7) Look for and make use of structure, and (8) Look for and express regularity in repeated reasoning (Common Core Standards Initiative, 2010).

The eight mathematical practices qualify the meaning of deep and flexible understanding of mathematics. Students communicate with mathematical precision, focusing on the relationships they have mapped out and the generalizations they have made in problem solving. Tools are used to justify their arguments and critique those of others (Common Core Standards Initiative, 2010). Evident is the call for greater commitment to the development of mathematical reasoning, student communication, and engagement in problem solving that involves more than work with "story" problems. Modeling standards that emphasize connections to the real world and these eight mathematical practices create the greatest impetus for changes in instruction because they simply cannot be met through traditional instruction.

Proficiency for all students can only be achieved through differentiating instruction. Instruction needs to be differentiated from traditional instruction with the application of context to the content, the use of 21st century skills including critical thinking and use of technological tools, and the communication involved in critiquing and justifying problem-solving pathways. Learning experiences that are real-life, more "hands on," and inquiry-based meet the needs of a wider range of students. Furthermore, the merging of content and context stimulates both the right and left hemispheres of the brain to increase understanding (Wolfe, 2001). Differentiated instruction with problem-solving tasks is the best way to inspire a student's spirit, increase emotional connectedness to the material, and to influence achievement at the same time (Armstrong, 2000; Mettetal, Jordan, & Harper, 1997; Wolfe, 2001). The CCSS, while not specifically addressing pedagogy, provide an impetus for differentiated instruction in mathematics and a commitment to improve fluency and achievement for students without tracking or separating students (Common Core Standards Initiative, 2010).

DIFFERENTIATION AND RICH LEARNING TASKS

Rich tasks accomplish the depth of problem solving needed for students to carry out the mathematical practices and to model or simulate real-life scenarios. Context increases engagement and reasons to seek solutions. For a learning task to be considered "rich," tasks need to have multiple entry points and solution paths to garner the math-talk and communication necessary for both depth and transfer of knowledge. Students must also be able to justify and support their solutions. As students persevere, reflect, and explore solutions to the tasks, the errors and re-evaluations deepen understanding (Martinez, 1998) and differentiate instruction of content. By using rich tasks with cooperative learning, the left- and right-brain needs and contexts are addressed, as suggested in the 4MAT system and Understanding by Design lesson formats as well as the interpersonal intelligence of the multiple intelligences theory (Armstrong, 2000; Huitt, 2009; Wiggins & McTighe, 2006).

With student choice of entry point and solution method, multiple intelligences are also easily incorporated within task-based instruction and can be used to differentiate the product used to demonstrate evidence of understanding. Through differentiation, engaging, rich tasks create a more personalized curriculum and can address student achievement by allowing students to use their intellectual strengths that are different from the linguistic and logical-mathematical intelligences typically associated with mathematics learning (Armstrong, 2000).

LESSON PLANNING AND TASKS

More diversity in learning opportunities through tasks creates more robust student learning (Kagan & Kagan, 1998). Yet, higher-level tasks often are implemented in ways that result in fractured student learning and lost opportunities for thinking and reasoning (Henningsen & Stein, 1997; Stein & Lane, 1996; Stein, Grover, & Henningsen, 1996). The Thinking Through a Lesson Protocol (TTLP) is a process designed to better guarantee greater reliability with task implementation and thus increase student understanding (Smith & Stein, 1998). TTLP helps teachers anticipate student sticking points and formulate leading questions that promote learning and refocus the students on the content (Smith, Bill, & Hughes, 2008). The questioning techniques in the TTLPs are adapted from work by Boerst, Sleep, and Ball (2011).

TTLP creates a three stage lesson. Stage 1 focuses on setting up the problem and can easily be used to incorporate differentiation of content assimilation. Student processing of information is addressed in stage 2, where the students explore the task at hand. Finally, stage 3 is presentation of student work (Smith, et al., 2008). The focus of the stage 3 presentation is on communicating the mathematics, and critiquing the thoughts of others. Here students have the choice of the product they present to the class to illustrate their understandings.

To set up stage 1, the teacher conducts a pre-assessment to make sure prior knowledge is sufficiently scaffolded. Often it is best to do this before the day of the task so as to not disrupt the flow of the lesson or create a time constraint for the reflections and closure of the lesson. The teacher chooses the task to match the standards that need to be addressed, and adjusts the context to best resonate with the uniqueness of the learners in the class. Stage 1 addresses differentiated instruction by modifying the presentation of the content. When initiated with the students, this stage should take about five minutes.

Of key importance is the launch of the exercise, as it creates the relevancy and emotional hook necessary for deeper engagement and greater retention (Wolfe, 2001). The launch could use any of Gardner's intelligences as a centerpiece (Armstrong,2000). The standards and expectations for student learning are defined in this section. Student thinking necessary for the task is analyzed and a student report form is developed. To do so, the teacher thinks of all possible solution paths and misconceptions that may arise. The teacher must choose how cooperative learning should be used in the lesson (Smith, et al., 2008).

Because of the multiple solution paths, ability grouping for tasks is usually preferred with the concrete and abstract learners placed in different groups. The open-ended nature that is critical to a successful task allows for solution paths that range from trial and error to equation-based algebra. The ability grouping allows students to gain confidence in their abilities as they become more successful, rather than feeling inadequate to the student who is already adept at abstract formula crunching (Paterson, 2007). Furthermore, students cannot just wait for the "smart" kid to get the answer for their group. The students get the opportunity to see value in their own concrete or intuitive skills as they relate to overall understanding.

Stage 2 centers mostly on monitoring student work and should take about fifteen to twenty minutes. To move the task along, the teacher is prepared with probing questions. "I wonder if that always works?" "What do you think would happen if we changed this factor to 25?" "How many other ways could you get the same answer?" Such questions lead students to gather supporting evidence, formulate justifications, and engage in reflection. Manipulatives that assist student exploration of the task should be available for tactile learners and students that may have difficulty with abstract thinking. Thinking through the multiple solutions and misconceptions prior to the lesson prepares the teacher for the non-starters, the groups that are struggling to make progress, and for the groups that finish quickly (Smith, et al., 2008). By virtue of multiple pathways, instruction is differentiated by the way students are allowed to process the information. Students achieve more because of the different ways orchestrated for them to express their understandings (Kornhaber, 2004).

Formative assessment is crucial in stage 2, as the teacher is listening for key communication addressing the essential questions and standards of the task. A formative assessment of student thinking form (see Table 6.1) is helpful to log evidence of understanding and to note the strategy used in problem-solving (table, graph, or algebraic). Furthermore, asking the students to not erase any of their thoughts or work as they attend to the problem also facilitates formative assessment. It is beneficial to allow students wrong answers, but to not allow erasing or crossing out multiple attempts because student misconceptions can then be more easily identified. The teacher walks around the room and makes notes on the student thinking form of the mathematical communication and strategies that students are using. By noting which groups or individuals attempt a certain strategy or encounter a common misconception, the teacher has a better idea for how to launch the discussion of the task in the final stage, and how to manage the remaining class time effectively.

Stage 3 is about bringing the mathematics in focus and managing the discussion. The classroom must be a safe environment that encourages and values all students, so discussion is elicited and student interactions are encouraged. Stage 3 needs about twenty minutes for the necessary communication and reflection to bring the focus of the task back to the goals of the lesson. Using the notes taken during stage 2, the effective teacher realizes that not every group's information needs to be shared. The key strategies and misconceptions are ordered and presented from most concrete to most abstract. It is ideal to start with any positive work from struggling students. The value of their contributions must be addressed before the "Cadillac" answer potentially shuts down all discussion. Starting in the concrete bridges the gap to the abstract for concrete learners (Caissy, 2002; Wolfe, 2001).

4: Exemplary. Proficient and explanation contains evidence with examples or extension to other contexts			
3: Proficient. Sufficient work OR explanation with only minor errors that do not detract from understanding of Big Ideas			
2: Progressing. Moderate understanding with a misconception that needs to be addressed			
1: Beginning. Student demonstrates merely an acquaintance or cursory knowledge of the topic			
0: Non-participant.			
Student	Understanding	Strategy	Evidence of understanding
	0—1—2—3—4		
	0—1—2—3—4		

Table 6.1. Form for Formative Assessment of Student Thinking Understanding the Rubric.

Multiple representations support reflection, communication, and greater understanding for a wider range of students (Kabiri & Smith, 2003). As students present their evidence and justify their conclusions, instruction is further differentiated in how the students get to process the information. Students also get the choice of what they produce as evidence for their claims. Pictures, tables, graphs, formulae, calculations, and even models can be used by students to show their understanding. During discussion, students are asked to repeat, agree, or add to the presentation. Asking students to generalize if their method will work for any number helps to bring the patterns and mathematical concepts to the center of the discussion. The lesson concludes with a review of the big ideas, an assessment of concepts still developing, and with a connection to future lessons. This can be done in discussion or with the use of exit slips, the latter of which has the benefit of providing the teacher immediate information on all students' understanding. One example is the 3-2-1 exit slip approach. Here students might make 3 statements involving big ideas, ask 2 questions they are still pondering, and make 1 evaluation, prediction, or generalization. Having exit slips ready as a time-saving alternative to discussion is extremely valuable for classroom management, as they can even be used after stage 2, if there is not sufficient time to have a class discussion on the task until day two. The three lesson plans that follow are all based on the TTLP process.

Lesson One. Developing Expressions

Essential Questions

1. How are numerical calculations related to generic expressions or functions?
2. How are repeated patterns in data related to expressions and applied to the task solution?
3. Why are certain expressions equivalent to each other?

Common Core State Standards

1. Mathematically proficient students construct viable arguments and critique the reasoning of others.
2. Mathematically proficient students look for and express regularity in repeated reasoning.
3. Mathematically proficient students see structure and relationships of equivalent expressions.
4. Mathematically proficient students can solve one variable equations and provide reasoning.

Lesson Objectives

1. Students will develop mathematical patterns numerically, physically, or algebraically in order to develop mathematical understanding of a problem.
2. Students will use repeated patterns in problem solving to develop mathematical expressions.
3. Students will communicate their understandings of repeated patterns with a verbal or written explanation and support their ideas numerically, algebraically, or visually.

Lesson one is formulated around a classic border problem task. Modifiable for seventh to ninth graders, representations of expressions in a problem-solving activity highlight the lesson. Students need prior knowledge of perimeter, area, and in defining numbers in relationship to distance on a number line (for example, 8 is 10-2). Understanding multiplication as repeated addition and the concept of substitution are essential to the task. Graph paper, tile manipulatives, and a t-chart for length and calculations will be needed for accommodations. A report form for students to organize their thoughts and visuals of borders from the internet atwww.texascurbnborders.com/before_and_after.phporhttp://www.czarfloors.com/borders.aspcomplete the list of needed resources.

Many content standards can be introduced or emphasized in this task. The focus in the TTLP is on expressions. Similarly, it is wise to focus on only two of the eight mathematical practices during any task. The choice here is on construction and critiquing of arguments and the use of regularity in repeated reasoning.

Launch

As part of the launch during Stage 1, presenting the visuals of borders, gardens, or tile mosaics can stimulate students in the visual, spatial, and naturalist intelligences while providing a catalyst for learning (Armstrong, 2000; Wolfe, 2001). The students are then shown a 10 by 10 square where the outside squares are a different color, creating a border (see Figure 6.1). Grouping will include think-pair-share, and then combining pairs to groups of four if needed. As students work independently, struggling students will be paired so the teacher can better provide necessary scaffolding.

Exploration

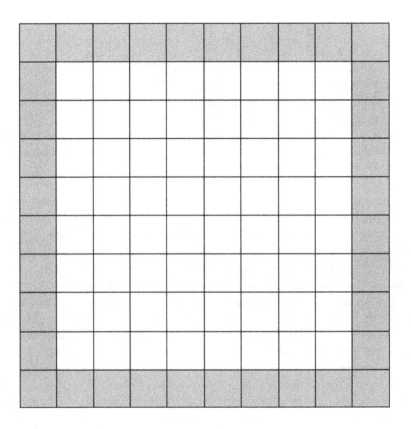

Figure 6.1. 10 by 10 Square with Border.

In stage 2, students get to choose how they gather and process the information. Students work on their own to calculate the number of tiles needed for a square with a length of 10. The most common misconception will be to multiply 4 sides by 10 tiles to get 40. This method counts the corners twice. Struggling students are given choices of tile manipulatives or graph paper to support or check their progress. Students then pair up and share their different methods. Students then work together to help each other write a description for the mathematics they use to solve the problem. Students are to attempt to write instructions in terms of any length to calculate the border. The challenge in stage 2 is to get students to speak in terms of "L" for length instead of the concrete number 10 for the 10 by 10 square. Staying in the concrete and creating written instructions for a 10 by 10 square may be an acceptable starting point for students struggling with the problem. A t-chart (see Figure 6.2) for a 9 x 9 and 8 x 8 grid should show enough structure to bridge student thinking to the abstract presentations of their classmates. Extensions create rigor for all students by asking some groups to find another way and to describe the mathematical processes in other ways, such as in terms of area.

Analysis of Solutions

During stage 3, or class discussion, the teacher starts with students sharing number calculations but not tables or variable expressions. Students look for patterns and similarities. Eventually the data are presented in a table so similarities become more evident. Misconceptions or situations where students change their calculation method from one square to the next inhibit identifying similarities or forming generalizations. These situations are critiqued by the students as they are presented. The bridge to the abstract comes by speaking in terms of length. For a 10 by 10 and then a 9 by 9 square, 10 + 10 + 8 + 8 and 9 + 9 + 7 + 7 will be written as length + length + length less two + length less two by the abstract thinkers as one example. This concept is

Length	calculation sample of student work
10	10 + 10 + 8 + 8
9	9 + 9 + 7 + 7
8	8 + 8 + 6 + 6

Figure 6.2. T-Chart of length vs. tiles calculation.

the big idea for the lesson and must be reached. A number line showing the distance from 10 to 8 and 9 to 7 aids the understanding for the concrete thinker when another number line is labeled with "L" (see Figure 6.3). For some classes, the leap to the abstract may have to be developed by the teacher during discussion.

Finally, the goal is to write the various computational strategies into a variety of expressions that the class analyzes for accuracy and equivalency. The class concludes by linking the task to future lessons such as how equivalency of expressions can be analyzed through mathematical principles like the distributive and associative properties or how to write expressions from contextual problems are likely associations.

For more details about this lesson see table 6.2.

Lesson Two. Representations of Rate of Change

Essential Questions

1. What information is essential in the problem and what information is redundant?
2. What is the repeated pattern in the table and/or graph?
3. How is the repeated pattern represented in the function/equation?
4. How is the constant rate of change used to solve the equation?

Common Core State Standards

1. Mathematically proficient students make sense of problems and persevere in solving them.
2. Mathematically proficient students model the mathematics with a table, graph, equation, or function and see correspondences between them.
3. Mathematically proficient students create equations that describe relationships.

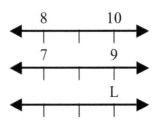

Figure 6.3. Number Line with Distances.

Stage 1: Launch the Problem	
Opening / Relevancy	Ask the students, "who is interested?" or "who has a parent that works in art, landscaping, architecture, or construction?" Show pictures of borders from those fields.
Statement / Questions	Bob the landscaper uses 1 ft by 1ft square pavers to border square garden beds for his customers without taking up more lawn space. He would like to have a general rule to know how many pavers to charge for based on the size of the bed but decides to start with a 10 ft by 10 ft bed first. Tell how many pavers he needs for the border and then create a way for Bob to know the number of tiles quickly for any length square garden. You will work on your own and then share with a partner in 5 minutes.
Anticipated Strategies / Misconceptions	$4 \times 10 = 40 \ldots 10 + 10 + 8 + 8 \ldots 2 \times 10 + 2 \times 8 \ldots 10 + 9 + 9 + 8 \ldots 10 + 10 + 8(2)$ Total area / area unshaded … Perimeter = 4 Defining length will be easy substituting L for 10 but defining 8 or 9 will be hard. (8 is Length-2) (9 is L -1) … $2L + 2$ (L-2) … 4(L-1) … $L^2 - (L-2)^2$

Stage 2: Student Exploration	
Who to address	Questions
Off-task students	Where could you begin? Could you work it out another way? With graph paper or tiles? Draw and Count?
Struggling students	1. Can you give instructions using as few numbers as possible for a 10 by 10? (only use #s 1-4 and 10) 2. Can you define your numbers in the calculation in terms of the number 10? 3. What does the operations or numbers represent? (Multiplier, repeated addition, etc) 4. Can you explain your thinking? What does L or X represent? 5. Can you show what the math would look like for a ____ ft long square garden? Is there a pattern you can describe? 6. Can you make a table for multiple lengths of square gardens in column 1 and work in column 2? Are calculating the same way for every new length?
Extensions	1. Can you make written instructions for someone to find the answer for any random length square garden in general? 2. Can you create an expression related to perimeter? Related to area? 3. How many other ways could you get the same answer?

Table 6.2. TTLP for Border Task.

Stage 3: Analysis of the Solutions	
Parts of discussion	Questions / statements
Initiating the discussion	1. What did you do first when trying to solve the problem? 2. Will someone share an expression they think works for any length square? (Strategically start from most concrete to most abstract…Present the Cadillac without mistakes last!)
Eliciting strategies	1. Walk us through your steps. 2. Can you show us what you mean? 3. Can you repeat that?
Focusing on mathematical ideas	1. Does this method work for any length? Can you explain why? 2. What would happen for a square of length 4?
Encouraging interactions	1. Does everyone agree with this strategy? 2. What are you concerned with? 3. How is this similar to the last strategy? 4. How is it different from last strategy? 5. Does this method relate to perimeter? 6. Does it relate to area?
Concluding the discussion	1. Some of the key points in our discussion today were expressions. What are expressions? 2. Can anyone give an example of equivalent expressions? 3. Why are they equivalent?

Table 6.2 continued.

4. Mathematically proficient students can write a function that recognizes a constant rate of change.

Lesson Objectives

1. Students will identify important variables and patterns in order to develop mathematical understanding of a problem.
2. Students will use repeated patterns in problem solving to develop algebraic equations involving a constant rate of change.
3. Students will communicate their understandings with verbal or written explanation and support their ideas numerically, algebraically, or visually.

Lesson 2 involves the nesting of objects and the effect nesting has on total height. Building upon expressions and variables, the second lesson is appropriate for eighth or ninth graders and addresses problem-solving in relationship to multiple representations of linear functions and constant rate of change. Prior knowledge of representing relationships between proportional quantities in tables, graphs, and functions is preferred, and is addressed by common core standards in grades six and seven. Provide a table labeled number of containers and height for the students who cannot easily access an entry point for the activity. In this task, students calculate the number of nested containers that can be stored under a given height restriction. If quantities for height and gap between containers are carefully selected, advanced topics in rounding can be addressed. A 40 cm container with a 1.5 cm gap when two containers are nested and a height restriction of 74 cm per stack is a great example. The calculation of 23.667 containers would have to be rounded down to fit under the height restriction.

Launch

As part of the launch, two containers in the classroom nested one inside the other provide the visual imperative to the success of the concrete learners. The problem is to analyze the relationship between height of a stack of containers and the number of containers in the stack. Students think-pair-share before offering their suggestions in a classroom discussion. By not giving the information to the students immediately, they have to make sense of the problem and analyze the quantities that are needed and those that are redundant. This stage should take no more than fifteen minutes.

Exploration

As in lesson 1, students get to choose how they gather and process the information in this stage. Students work in groups of 3 or 4 and can use repeated addition, a table, or an equation to solve the problem. The most common misconception is in dividing the maximum height by the total height of one or two nested containers or in applying order of operations. Sometimes students solve for "x" as the number of containers added to the first one and are therefore one container short in their answer. Others will round incorrectly and have an answer that is one more container than the desired result. The challenge and extension arises from providing justification and multiple pieces of evidence for the solution. This stage could be completely modified to the concrete level by using styrofoam cups that students can manipulate to solve a similar problem.

Analysis of Solutions

Start with two concrete representations and calculations that end with different answers [40+1.5+1.5+1.5…..+1.5= 73 (22 repeated additions of 1.5) and (74-40)/1.5 = 22.67] are great examples. Use them to discuss similarities in the repeated pattern and highlight the constant rate of change. Discussion clears up misconceptions, and the multiple representations of the rate of change connect the concrete to the abstract equation or function. An abstract concept that can be addressed is the meaning of the y-intercept and what "x" represents for the equation. The latter can be accomplished by showing that the rate of change is repeatedly added one time less than the number of bins. Conclude the lesson with the distributive property and discussing the equivalency of $y = 1.5x + 38.5$ and $y = 1.5(x - 1) + 40$. This is used to clarify the y-intercept discussion and can be a precursor to future lessons on the point slope form of a function by using $y - 40 = 1.5(x-1)$.

For more details about this lesson see table 6.3.

Lesson Three. Quadratic functions

Essential Questions

1. Why is area an important measurement for a dog kennel?
2. How is the maximum area of a dog kennel supported with evidence visually, graphically, or algebraically?
3. How do the data from this task compare to linear data sets?
4. How are the features of a quadratic function in a table or graph applicable to the real-life context of maximizing the area of a dog kennel?

Common Core State Standards

1. Mathematically proficient students reason abstractly and quantitatively.
2. Mathematically proficient students attend to precision in their mathematical communication.
3. Mathematically proficient students interpret functions that arise in applications in terms of the context.
4. Mathematically proficient students interpret key features of graphs and tables and sketch graphs showing key features in application to context.

Lesson Objectives

1. Students will organize mathematical data in order to develop mathematical understanding of a problem.
2. Students will develop equations based upon key features from tables and graphs.
3. Students will accurately communicate the relationship of the numerical and graphical evidence to the real-life solution to a problem

Lesson three involves maximizing the area given a set perimeter value for a rectangular shape. This lesson is typical for algebra I classes but can be modified for a review of x-intercepts, their connection to the factors of quad-

Stage 1: Launch the Problem	
Opening / Relevancy	Anybody involved in the school recycling program or watch those shows about hoarders? Today's lesson is about solving a storage problem we had last summer with the recycling bins. (have 3 bins nested in the classroom)
Statement / Questions	Mr. Smith, our principal, needs to store the recycling bins in our classroom for summer. Mr. Smith would like a general rule for how tall a certain number of bins would be but wants us to figure out how many bins would be in a stack that does not pass the ledge of the chalkboard. Justify your answer with as many pieces of mathematical evidence as you can. Turn to a person near you and discuss what you need to know from me to solve the problem. Use class discussion to bring all thoughts forward and then focus on essential information. Students will need the height of one bin, and the average gap between two bins and the height of the window sill.
Anticipated Strategies / Misconceptions	Students will think they need perimeter, area, the number of containers and possibly even the volume. Students may use the height of two containers and divide into the height of the sill. Students may simply divide the height of the sill by the height of 1 or 2 containers. Students may make a table, graph of data, or an equation. $40cm + 1.5cm(x) = 74$ finds the number of bins added to first bin or students may work table backwards to find y intercept $1.5x + 38.5 = 74$ cm. Best answer is $1.5(x-1) + 40 = 74$. Students may round 23.6 to 24 containers when rounding up is wrong here because of situation.
Stage 2: Student Exploration	
Who to address	Questions
Off-task students	1. How tall would 1 container be? 2 containers? 3 containers? 2. Where could you begin? 3. Could you draw or repeatedly add?
Struggling students	1. Do we consider the full height of each container every time? 2. Is there a pattern? 3. Have you tried using a graph or table? 4. Can you explain your thinking? 5. Will this always work?
Extensions	1. Can you provide evidence with a table? A graph? An equation? 2. Can you do this a different way? Create another equation? 3. What does the x represent? 4. What does the 40 represent? 5. What does the 38.5 represent? 6. What is the function that shows height from a number of containers?

Table 6.3. TTLP for Stacking Containers Task.

Stage 3: Analysis of the Solutions	
Parts of discussion	Questions / statements
Initiating the discussion	1. What did you do first when trying to solve the problem? 2. Will someone share their method?
Eliciting strategies	1. Walk us through your steps 2. Can you show us what you mean? 3. Can you repeat that?
Focusing on mathematical ideas	1. Does this method always work? 2. Is this similar to any problem solving we have done before? 3. Can you explain why this is true? 4. Can you show what the math would look like for a bin ___ tall, for a nest ___ big, to fit under a ledge ___ tall?
Encouraging interaction	1. Does everyone agree with this strategy? 2. What are you concerned with? 3. How is this similar to the last strategy? 4. How is it different from last strategy?
Concluding the discussion	1. One of the key points in our discussion today was rate of change. What is the rate of change? 2. What is the relationship between height of a stack and number of bins? 3. How is the rate of change represented in the table, graph, or solution?

Table 6.3 continued.

ratics, and vertex form in algebra II. Prior knowledge of linear functions supports the exploration of the quadratic function in this task. Students also need to know the formula for area of a rectangle and understand symmetry. Graph paper, 30 cm of pipe cleaners, and a report form with tables provide accommodations for struggling students and concrete learners. The focus of the lesson is on interpreting key features of a quadratic function in application to a real-world context. The lesson works well when done over two days.

The goal of day one is to gather data and finish with a square, triangle, and circle exit slip that has students make three comments. One statement is focused on what they are square with (what they understand), a triangle statement that includes three related points on a topic from the task, and one concept that is still circling around in their heads. On day two, students will share their results through discussion on the features of the graph, table, and function for area.

Launch

After the class is surveyed for dog ownership, students are challenged to build a three-sided structure that butts up to a house for a dog kennel. The students are given a set amount of material (30 m) and asked to design the best dog kennel they can. Students are placed into small groups by their level of abstract thinking to attack the problem.

Exploration

Students can process the information by drawing or modeling the possible kennels on graph paper or with pipe cleaners. Drawings are very important for the students that do not easily make the connection to the importance of area in the problem. The next challenge is to get students to organize their evidence in tables. Some may skip right to organizing length, width, and area combinations in table format.

The most common error is when students run fence on the house side, thus wasting the house as an edge of the kennel. Most students will think of only whole number combinations. Push the abstract thinkers to formulate a function for width as 30 minus twice the length and to substitute that into the formula for area to find $A = L(30 - 2L)$.

Analysis of Solutions

Start the discussion with one of the groups that have drawn all of the possible kennels. Emphasize why area is the defining quantity for the best kennel. Next, share the group work that ended with the best length for the side of the structure as 7 or 8 feet. This leads to a discussion about symmetry. The symmetrical features of the graph and table will be related to the solution of the real-world problem. Next, attention to the highest values in the table and the graph are related to the best design for the kennel in terms of area. In closing, the function that models the graph will be discovered as a class and the future lessons on patterns in the table will be noted.

For more details about this lesson see Table 6.4.

CONCLUDING THOUGHTS

The CCSS for mathematics creates a guide for a more coherent, rigorous curriculum focused on developing a deeper understanding of mathematics content and practices. The depth of understanding to be proficient in the eight mathematical practices of the CCSS requires more than traditional instruction. Differentiated instruction fosters thinking that may not be the sequential, linear thinking rewarded through more traditional mathematics instruction and deepens the understanding for a greater number of students (Casey & Tucker, 1994). More robust learning results from differentiated classroom instruction that includes a balance of instructional methods (Kagan & Kagan, 1998).

Stage 1: Launch the Problem	
Opening / Relevancy	How many people in here have a dog? How many want a dog? What is one of the first things you need if you have a dog? A fenced in yard is needed.
Statement / Questions	Today, you are going to design an area for a dog to play by making a kennel off the back door of a house. (Show diagram) What is the advantage to building the kennel this way? You have enough money to buy 30 meters of fence. Design the most effective dog kennel under the given restraints. Summarize your findings and support with evidence.
Anticipated Strategies / Misconceptions	Students may need to draw or build the possibilities. Students may not make the connection that area is the important issue in kennel design. Drawings or models may be four sides equal to a perimeter of 30 instead of 3 sides equal to 30. Students may calculate area incorrectly. Students need to put evidence into a table and a graph. Students may not choose a consistent unit for the graph axis. Students will define area as length times width but will not be able to define it only in terms of length where $A = L(30 - 2L)$. Most students will not see 7.5 ft as best answer and will report 7 or 8 feet as creating the best area. Students may fail to make the connection that long and skinny rectangles are not better for the dog because area is the most important feature.
Stage 2: Student Exploration	
Who to address	Questions
Off-task students	1. Where could you begin? 2. Can you draw an example of a kennel on graph paper? 3. Would you like 30 cm of toothpicks to layout a model?
Struggling students	1. What are you trying to do here? 2. What are you finding troubling? 3. Can you create a kennel with a length of ___? 4. Can you organize data in a table by length and width? and area?
Extensions	1. Can you write a function for width using L? 2. Can you substitute that function into A= L x W? 3. What would happen if there were ____ meters of fence? If the kennel was 4 sided?

Table 6.4. TTLP for Dog Kennels Task.

The lessons presented in this chapter differentiate instruction and allow students to use multiple solution pathways, communication, and reflection (Caulfield, Sheats-Harkness, & Riley, 2003). Tasks also can be used to add context to the procedural techniques that are effectively delivered through teacher modeling (National Mathematics Advisory Panel, 2008). A task-

Stage 3: Analysis of the Solutions	
Parts of discussion	Questions / statements
Initiating the discussion	Looking at the drawings, why is one of these kennels better than another?
Eliciting strategies	1. Can you walk us through your steps? 2. Can you repeat that? 3. Is there a length that might be better than 7 or 8ft? 4. Could you explain that to a fifth grader?
Focusing on mathematical ideas	1. How is symmetry related to this problem? 2. What is the importance of a maximum and its relationship in the data and the context of the problem? 3. What is the function for width? for area?
Encouraging interactions	1. Does everyone agree with this? 2. What are you concerned with? 3. Is the width function linear? 4. The area function linear? 5. What evidence can you share?
Concluding the discussion	1. Can anyone summarize the difference between this parabolic function and linear functions? 2. Can anyone modify that with mathematical vocabulary? 3. Tomorrow we will continue exploration of parabolas by looking at the patterns in the tables closer.

Table 6.4 continued.

oriented mathematics classroom fosters an active learning environment needed for greater success in mathematics (Knuth & Jones, 1991). Whether the tasks are differentiated through the use of Gardner's Multiple Intelligences (Gardner, 1983), McCarthy's 4MAT system (McCarthy, 1980), or Edwards and Sparapani's Thinking/Learning System (Edwards and Sparapani, 1996), the development of human inquiry aids understanding and creates a richer curriculum for all (Costa & Liebmann, 1995).

REFERENCES

Armstrong, T. (2000). *Multiple intelligences in the classroom*. (2nd ed.). Alexandria, VA: Association for Supervision and Curriculum Development.

Boerst, T., Sleep, L., & Ball, D. (2011). Preparing teachers to lead mathematics discussions. *Teachers College Record, 113* (12), 2844-2877.

Caissy, G. A. (2002). *Early Adolescence: Understanding the 10 to 15 year old*. Cambridge, MA: Perseus Publishing.

Casey, M. B. & Tucker, E. C. (1994). Problem-centered classrooms: Creating lifelong learning. *Phi Delta Kappan, 76* (2), 139-143.

Caulfield, R., Sheats-Harkness, S., & Riley, R. (2003). Surprise! Turn routine problems into worthwhile tasks. *Mathematics Teaching in the Middle School.* Retrieved online November 27, 2011 fromwww.nctm.org.

Common Core State Standards Initiative. (2010). *Common Core State Standards for mathematics.* Retrieved from http://www.corestandards.org/assets/CCSSI_Math%20Standards.pdf .

Costa, A. L. & Liebmann, R. (1995). Process is as important as content. *Educational Leadership, 56* (6), 58.

Edwards, P., & Sparapani, E. F. 1996). The thinking/learning system: A teaching strategy for the management of diverse learning styles and abilities. *Educational Studies and Research, 14* (2), 2-12.

Fleischman, H. L., Hopstock, P. J., Pelczar, M. P., & Shelley, B. E. (2010). *Highlights from PISA 2009: Performance of U.S. 15-year-old students in reading, mathematics, and science literacy in an international contex*t. (NCES 2011-004). U.S. Department of Education, National Center for Education Statistics. Washington, D.C.: U.S. Government Printing Office. Retrieved online November 21 2011 fromhttp://nces.ed.gov/pubs2011/2011004.pdf.

Gardner, H. (1983). *Frames of mind: The theory of multiple intelligences.* New York, NY: Basic Books.

Henningsen, M. & Stein, M. K. (1997). Mathematical tasks and student cognition: Classroom-based factors that support and inhibit high-level mathematical thinking and reasoning. *Journal for Research in Mathematics Education, 29*, 524-549.

Hiebert, J., Carpenter, T., Fennema, E., Fuson, K. C., Wearne, D., Murray, H., Olivier, A., & Human, P. (1997). *Making Sense: Teaching and learning mathematics with understanding.* Portsmouth, NH: Heinemann.

Huitt, W. (2009). I*ndividual differences: The 4MAT system. Educational Psychology Interactive.* Valdosta, GA. Valdosta State University. Retrieved online November, 21, 2011 fromhttp://www.edpsycinteractive.org/topics/instruct/4mat.html.

Kabiri, M. S. & Smith, N. L. (2003). Turning traditional textbook problems into open-ended problems. *Mathematics Teaching in the Middle School.* Retrieved online November 27, 2011 fromwww.nctm.org.

Kagan, S. & Kagan, M. (1998). *Multiple intelligences: The complete MI book.* San Clemente, CA: Kagan Cooperative Learning.

Knuth, R. A. & Jones, B. F. (1991). *What does research say about mathematics?* Oak Brook, IL: North Central Regional Educational Laboratory. Available online athttp://www.ncrel.org.

Kornhaber, M. L. (2004). Multiple intelligences: From the ivory tower to the dusty classroom – But why? *Teachers College Record, 106* (1), 67-76.

Martinez, M. E. (1998). What is Problem Solving?. *Phi Delta Kappan, 79*, 605-609.

McCarthy, B. (1980). *The 4MAT system.* Oakbrook, IL: Excel.

Mettetal, G., Jordan, C., & Harper, S. (1997). Attitudes towards a multiple intelligences curriculum. *Journal of Educational Research, 91* (2), 115-122.

National Commission on Excellence in Education. (1983). *A Nation at Risk.* Retrieved on November 28, 2011 fromhttp://www2.ed.gov/pubs/NatAtRisk/risk.html.

National Council of Supervisors of Mathematics (2011). *Illustrating the standards for mathematical practices: Getting started.* Retrieved online fromhttp://www.mathedleadership.org/ccss/materials.html.

National Governors Association, the Council of Chief State School Officers, and Achieve, Inc. (2008). *Benchmarking for success: Ensuring U.S. students receive a world-class education.* Washington, D.C.: National Governors Association. Retrieved online November 21, 2011 fromhttp://www.corestandards.org/assets/0812BENCHMARKING.pdf.

National Mathematics Advisory Panel. (2008). *Foundations for success: The final report of the National Mathematics Advisory Panel.* U.S. Department of Education: Washington, DC. Available at http://www2.ed.gov/about/bdscomm/list/mathpanel/report/final-report.pdf.

On course for success: A close look at high school courses that prepare all students for college and work. (2009). Retrieved online November 21, 2011 fromhttp://www.act.org/research/policymakers/pdf/success_report.pdf.

Paterson, J. (2007). The power of self-esteem: Build it and they will flourish. *Middle Ground*, *11* (2), 8-10.

Smith, M. S., Bill, V., & Hughes, E. K. (2008). Thinking through a lesson: Successfully implementing high-level tasks. *Mathematics Teaching in the Middle School*, *14*, (3), 132-138.

Smith, M. S. & Stein, M. K. (1998). Selecting and creating mathematical tasks: From research to practice. *Mathematics Teaching in the Middle School*, *3*, 344-350.

Steen, L. (2007). Every teacher is a teacher of mathematics. *Principal Leadership*, *7* (5), 16-20.

Stein, M. K., Grover, B. W., & Henningsen, M. (1996). Building student capacity for mathematical thinking and reasoning: An analysis of mathematical tasks used in reform classrooms. *American Educational Research Journal*, *33*, 455-488.

Stein, M. K. & Lane, S. (1996). Instructional tasks and the development of student capacity to think and reason: An analysis of the relationship between teaching and learning in a reform mathematics project. *Educational Research and Evaluation*, 2, 50-80.

Trends in International Mathematics and Science Study [TIMMS]. (1999). Retrieved online athttp://nces.ed.gov/timss/results99_2.asp.

Wiggins, D. & McTighe, J. (2006). *Understanding by design* (expanded 2nd edition). Alexandria, VA: Association for Supervision and Curriculum Development.

Wolfe, P. (2001). *Brain matters: Translating research into classroom practice*. Alexandria, VA: Association for Supervision and Curriculum Development.

Wu, H. (2011). Phoenix rising: Bringing the common core state mathematics standards to life. *American Educator*, *35* (3), 3-13.

Chapter Seven

Differentiating Instruction and Teaching in Middle-School and High-School Science

Jonathon A. Gould & Betsy L. Diegel

INTRODUCTION

The relationship between differentiated instruction and the National Science Education Standards is explored in this chapter. An overview of the national science standards, with benefits highlighted, is shared, providing teachers with insight into the larger picture of science education, and exposing connections to students' learning preferences through differentiated instruction. Connections between learner choice regarding the process and the products of conceptual understanding are also examined. Through dialog between teacher and student, student and student, and student and the curriculum, insights are gained, and learning is made visible and tangible.

Three lesson plans are provided for use in the middle-level and high-school level classrooms. The first lesson plan can be employed in a single lesson, or over multiple days, and is appropriate for the beginning teacher (1-3 years of teaching experience), at the middle-level grades, in the area of Earth and space/science education. The second lesson plan is appropriate for an intermediate-level teacher (4-6 years of teaching experience), at the upper, middle-level or lower, high-school level, in the area of biology. The third lesson plan is for a veteran teacher (7 or more years of teaching experience), at the high-school level, in the area of chemistry. The lessons vary with respect to the level of difficulty surrounding content, teacher competence, or both. A veteran teacher may be better-prepared to embrace constructivist teaching methods or higher-level content, when compared to a novice teacher. However, both the beginning teacher and the veteran teacher, and all of their students, will benefit from flexible teaching practices, embracing both constructivist and brain-based learning practices.

OVERVIEW OF THE NATIONAL SCIENCE STANDARDS

The National Science Education Standards are initially created to guide our nation toward a scientifically literate society. The standards provide a vision and definition for scientific literacy. A framework for science education, and a forum for stakeholders to engage in rich, scientific discourse, is facilitated through the standards. In addition, the national science standards offer a coherent vision of what all students need to understand and be able to demonstrate in science.

In 1989, the first national standards were proposed by the NCTM (National Council of Teachers of Mathematics, 1989). The mathematics proposal spawned conversation towards the development of other education standards, including standards for science. The science standards were initially drafted in response to the American Association for the Advancement of Science Project 2061 (American Association for the Advancement of Science, 1993). The project defined scientific literacy for all high school graduates. In 1991, the National Science Teachers Association proposed the National Science Education Standards (National Science Teachers Association, 1992).

Teachers benefit from the national science standards through increased-student comprehension and demonstration of the standards by students. Students benefit from the national science standards through enhanced conceptual understanding of scientific concepts. Overall, the manifestations lend themselves to the upward mobility of the scientific community. The interactions between researchers, practitioners in the field, and members of commerce enable our nation to collectively share in the decision-making processes, which in turn fuel a global society. The national science standards provide an objective lens to view the scientific world, and a unique vantage point to evaluate the abilities of its constituents. In addition, the science standards provide a necessary vehicle for the evaluation and support of students, teachers, programs, and processes.

Embracing a set of national science standards encourages coherence between each state, and between a state and its local governing bodies. Improvements in science education complement an increase in the ability of students to compete in an ever-changing global economy. National science standards foster a level of consistency between state-level curricula, while remaining cognizant of current research and best practices at the local level (American Association for the Advancement of Science, 1993). The science standards provide a means to scaffold from existing school structures to a shared vision for all involved in the pursuit of academic excellence.

Schools implementing the science standards showcase student learning in science, through direct and inquiry-based lessons, which challenge students at their unique levels of understanding. The knowledge base students construct is specific, measurable, and observable. Teachers share in the discussion, which students initiate. The science standards maintain focus for all involved in the scientific conversation.

The National Science Education Standards articulate the mission statement of scientific accountability, while offering a tangible description of the components needed in creating a scientifically literate society. As the needed medium, for an intentionally-scientific conversation, the science standards create the impetus for discourse in the scientific community. The science standards speak to the need for all teachers to embrace data-driven pedagogical decisions, learner choice, and differentiated-science instruction.

DIFFERENTIATING INSTRUCTION AND TEACHING SCIENCE

The differentiated-science classroom embraces a myriad of learning styles to achieve its goal of conceptual understanding for all. Within the mindset of remaining flexible, many goals are obtained. As a teacher, one goal is to understand students' backgrounds, interests, likes, dislikes, and the style by which each student learns. In science classrooms, as in most classrooms, two specific types of learners exist. There are students who struggle to master the science concepts and students who master conceptual understanding with a reduced level of effort. Ironically, both types of learners need additional academic assistance to grasp concepts. The advanced learners are often ahead of classmates' academic abilities. Lost interest in school, however, may impede learning for the advanced students. Struggling students grapple with concepts, attempting to connect each to their lives. Science teachers embracing differentiated instruction offer a vehicle for students to navigate this dilemma. Employing the concept of learner choice regarding the process of learning, in addition to the final student products, can stimulate student interest in science and school for the more advanced students, while assisting struggling students with connections to the content.

To this end, the veteran teacher possesses many arrows in her/his quiver, affording the ability to transition from the concrete to the abstract, and back with ease. This practice complements the 4MAT System (McCarthy, 1990) in which a lesson begins with a real-world application, employs simulated practice in the classroom, and concludes with a real-world/student-created product. These practices help define differentiated instruction, embracing flexibility and brain-based learning, while addressing all levels of student interest and/or ability levels. In addition, differentiated instruction provides a framework for the scaffolding of knowledge and increasing conceptual understanding of topics.

The novice teacher may spend more time in the arena of a behaviorist teaching style, due to the increased level of prediction surrounding classroom activities, student outcomes, and the time involved for each. Although differentiated instruction may initially appear to increase the amount of time needed to obtain objectives in the scope-and-sequence (timeline) of a school district's calendar, when the amount of time invested in re-teaching concepts is calculated, differentiated instruction actually provides increased levels of conceptual understanding at a reduced level of time on topics, with dialog between students and the content, peers, and teacher encouraged throughout the learning process. As with all academic conversations, a link must be created, supported, and strengthened over time.

In order to have an effective differentiated-science classroom, the teacher must have a good relationship with the students, and understand how students learn science. Students learn through symbolic-thought processes, concrete examples, and through visual and/or auditory understanding (Sizer & Sizer, 1999). Teachers equipped with the theoretical knowledge of their learners, and, armed with a practical understanding of science standards, are setting-the-stage for success for their students.

ADDRESSING THE NATIONAL SCIENCE STANDARDS BY DIFFERENTIATING INSTRUCTION IN SCIENCE

Differentiated Instruction and Lesson Planning

Differentiated instruction emphasizes creating learning experiences which complement each individual student's learning style. This can be accomplished in unique formats. This section provides three lesson plan examples which highlight these formats and link differentiated instruction to the national science standards. The first lesson plan focuses on differentiation of the process (choice of task and/or grouping configuration) and final products (choice of visual representation, narrative description, physical demonstration) of teaching and learning. The second and third lesson plans embrace all components of differentiated instruction. The formatting of all lesson plans utilizes a modification of a direct instruction plan (Sparks-Langer, Starko, Pasch, Burke, Moody, & Gardner, 2004), embracing both flexibility and brain-based learning.

Each lesson employs a pre-assessment and a post-assessment. The pre-assessment is offered at the onset of the lesson, to activate and assess prior knowledge. The pre-assessment is scored, but not returned to the student until the results of the post-assessment are available. This practice maintains the self-esteem of the student, and offers an authentic manner in which the conceptual understanding and growth of a student can be measured.

Although the lesson plans provide a direction for teaching and appear very structured/linear (which should appeal to most administrators, attempting to balance both the quality and quantity of information addressed, for a given school year), the focus is on the specific needs of the learners, the content, and the instructional practices (in that order) needed to sync all components of learning. The needs of the teacher take a distant fourth place in the line-up.

In the following lesson plan (Lesson Plan 1) the scientific concepts of "Cycles of the Earth" are explored. The lesson is designed to last for a single, fifty-five minute session, in a middle-level classroom. The lesson, however, may span multiple days, employing both a pre-assessment and multiple post-assessments. In the lesson, common science standards (NSTA Standards B.3.22-26) are taught from unique perspectives. Lesson plan 1 complements the beginning teacher's skill level and acts as a spring-board for the veteran teacher's pedagogical repertoire. The lesson is more effective if taught over multiple days, with a pre-assessment (short pre-test, questioning session, checklists of knowns/unknowns) offered at the onset of the lessons, and two post-assessments (possibly a written assessment and a performance assessment) at the conclusion of the lesson.

Lesson Plan 1 – Differentiation of Process and Product for Cycles of the Earth

Lesson 1 differentiates the task, or learning objective, offering a choice in the selection of the cycle of the Earth the student is to understand. The lesson also differentiates the setting in which students learn the material, with students choosing to work individually, in groups of two, or in groups of three. In addition, the lesson differentiates the final product employing Gardner's Multiple Intelligences (Gardner, 1993). For final products, students choose to complete a poster (Naturalistic/Spatial-Visual Intelligences), a written paper (Naturalistic/Linguistic/Intrapersonal Intelligences), a demonstration of a scientific experiment (Naturalistic/Bodily-Kinesthetic/Interpersonal/ Logical-Mathematical Intelligences), a conceptual model (Naturalistic/Spatial-Visual Intelligences), a poem/song (Naturalistic/Musical Intelligences), or another pre-approved method for showcasing a student's conceptual understanding of concepts learned. In addition, all students write a written exam over the concepts of cycles of the Earth, and the rock, water, or nitrogen cycle. This form of differentiated instruction appeals to middle-level students because learners are given a choice of task, grouping configuration, and final product.

Key Questions

    a. Who benefits from knowing about the rock, water, or nitrogen cycle?
    b. What are the rock, water, and nitrogen cycles?
    c. Where do the rock, water, and nitrogen cycles occur?
    d. When is knowledge of the rock, water, or nitrogen cycle beneficial?
    e. Why should all students learn about the rock, water, and nitrogen cycles?

1. Content Focus/Grade Level/Content Standards & Benchmarks. Cycles of the Earth / Middle Level / Characteristics and importance of cycles of matter such as water, rock, and nitrogen (NSTA Standards B.3.22-26)

2. Purpose/Relevancy. An understanding of the different cycles of the Earth provides students with insight into their world, and the cycles they interact with. Students will benefit from knowledge about Earth's cycles by making predictions regarding the sequence of events following a typical rain shower (water cycle), a recent eruption of a volcano (rock cycle), or the creation of a compost center (nitrogen cycle).

3. Special Needs Considerations/Accommodations. Students are provided with a Peer-Review Partner, a copy of the teacher's notes (employing a modified Cloze Procedure), notes with a larger font, or an audio version of any printed material. Additional time to complete in-class assignments (and/ or assessments) will be made available.

4. Resources. Microsoft Office 2007 Power Point presentations on the rock cycle, the water cycle, and the nitrogen cycle; colored pencils, magazine pictures, scissors, glue sticks, and 3 separate tables (for cycle-centers). For the final project, students may use poster-board (for posters), Microsoft Office 2007 Power Point and/or Word (for written paper), assorted scientific equipment (for demonstration of a scientific experiment), modeling clay or construction paper (for conceptual model), or various musical instruments and/or pre-recorded music (for poem/song).

5. Performance Objective ABCD (Learning Outcome). The student (A) will be able to demonstrate conceptual understanding of the Rock Cycle, the Water Cycle, or the Nitrogen Cycle (B) on a written exam and the creation of a project (including, but not limited to, a poster, a written paper, a demonstration of a scientific experiment, a conceptual model, a poem/song, or another pre-approved method of showcasing a student's conceptual understanding of concepts learned) (C), with 90% + proficiency on both the project and the written exam (D).

6. Content-Literacy Strategy. The KWL chart (Kane, 2007; Tovani, 2004) is a content-literacy strategy which complements and frames students' writ-

ing abilities, while activating and assessing students' prior knowledge and interest levels.

7. "Bell-Work." Students copy the KWL chart from the board, and begin to record two things they "Know" about the rock cycle, the water cycle, or the nitrogen cycle, and two things they "Wonder" about each cycle. Students are instructed to save what they have "Learned" about the cycles until the middle and end of the lesson.

8. Opening/Anticipatory Set. The teacher asks students the following questions:

a. "When you hear the word "Cycle," what do you think of?" (Students are given a chance to respond).

b. "Can anyone describe what they know about the rock cycle?" (Students respond).

c. "How about the water cycle?" (Students respond). "Can anyone explain what the nitrogen cycle is?" (Students respond).

d. "Today, we will explore all three cycles, giving YOU the choice of which cycle to explore, working individually or in groups of 2 or 3, and a choice of final products!"

9. Instructional Method

a. Students are provided with an overview of each "cycle-center," and where textbooks and materials are located to explore each cycle. A looping power point presentation, offering insight for all three cycles, will be made available for all students via a video projector and/or individual laptop computer.

b. Students are reminded of their ability to work individually (the student must complete at least one poster), or in a group of two students (the two students must share the responsibility of creating two different cycle posters), or in a group of three students (the three students must share the responsibility of creating three posters – one for each cycle).

c. Students are asked to group-up in groups of one, two, or three students, and then to move to one of the cycle-centers.

d. One member from each cycle-center is asked to clarify the task, and (if a correct response was given) to oversee the cycle-center for the rest of the lesson. Each power point presentation is then initiated.

e. A rubric for each final project students create as an individual or group project is provided, and students are reminded of the requirement to also pass a written exam over the concept of cycles. Choices for the final project include (but are not limited to):

i. A visual representation of the rock cycle, the water cycle, or the nitrogen cycle, in the form of a poster.

ii. A written narrative (2-3 page paper) explaining the concept of cycles, and the rock, water, or nitrogen cycle.

iii. A demonstration of a scientific experiment regarding the rock, water, or nitrogen cycle.

iv. A conceptual model of the rock, water, or nitrogen cycle.

v. A pre-approved final project/product, which showcases student understanding of cycles of the Earth and one of the cycles learned in class. An example could be the actual creation of the written exam the class will take, embracing all levels of Bloom's Cognitive Taxonomy (Bloom, 1956), for one or more cycles learned in class, or the creation and presentation of a poem or song about one or more of the cycles.

10. Guided Practice

a. As the teacher moves around the room, student conversations are facilitated, while students explore cycles of the Earth.

b. Every 10-15 minutes, students are asked to record an additional "L" on their KWL chart, and volunteers share responses with the entire class.

c. As students complete their final products, the teacher assesses each according to the rubric.

11. Lesson Closure. The teacher asks students the following questions:

a. "Now when you hear the word cycle, what do you think of?" (Students are given a chance to respond).

b. "Can anyone describe what they have learned about the rock cycle?" (Students respond).

c. "How about the water cycle?" (Students respond). "Can anyone explain what the nitrogen cycle is now?" (Students respond).

d. "As you leave today, please remember to complete your exit ticket (recording three main concepts learned and one question you still have), hand it to me when leaving, and share one thing which surprised/challenged you today – nice job everyone!"

12. Formative Assessment / Questioning Strategies. The teacher uses a "Thumbs-Up/Thumbs-Down" assessment approach, and instructs students to record one new thing learned, about the cycle chosen by the student, every 15 minutes, and on their "Exit Ticket" (Sparks-Langer, et al, 2004). After discussion, surrounding the exit tickets, students take a quiz, addressing the concepts of "Cycles of the Earth," and the rock cycle, the water cycle, or the nitrogen cycle, during the next class session.

13. Re-teaching Plan / Independent Practice / Extension Activity

a. Re-teaching Plan: Teacher uses results from the exit tickets and/or formative assessment to re-teach concepts that 20% (or more) of the class "missed" on the quiz.

b. Independent Practice: Teacher instructs students to complete their final products at home.

c. Extension Activity: Teacher instructs students to complete a final product for a second cycle of her or his choice.

14. Summative Assessment. Two end-of-unit assessments inform the teacher of strengths in instructional design – a written assessment and a performance assessment.

15. Reflection Notes (Teacher records thoughts, reflections, and reactions in this space after each time lesson is conducted.)

Lesson Plan 1 differentiates the task, grouping configuration, and final product regarding concepts learned for cycles of the Earth. This lesson plan embraces flexibility, learner choice, inquiry-based instruction, collaboration, physical movement, and cooperative learning strategies. In addition, employing multiple assessments at varying skill-levels and at different times complements the philosophy of differentiated instruction.

Lesson Plan 2 – Teaching Organic Molecules Through Learner Choice

Lesson Plan 2, explores concepts in biology (organic molecules, NSTA Standard B.2.16), and is designed for an upper, middle-level classroom or a lower, high school level classroom. The lesson is designed to last a single, fifty-five minute session. The lesson requires dialog between students, and acknowledges the importance of learner choice for the type of organic molecule (substance) to explore, a choice in grouping configuration, and a choice in final product. To minimize redundancy, duplicated components ask the reader to refer back to Lesson Plan 1.

Key Questions

    a. Who benefits from knowing about organic molecules?
    b. What are carbohydrates, fats, lipids, proteins, and nucleic acids?
    c. Where does digestion occur?
    d. When is knowledge of organic molecules beneficial?
    e. Why should all students learn about organic molecules and their connection to eating habits?

1. Content Focus/Grade Level/Content Standards & Benchmarks. Organic Molecules / Upper Middle Level, Lower High School Level / Solvents (especially water) and solutions (NSTA Standard B.2.16).

2. Purpose/Relevancy. An understanding of organic molecules provides students with insight into the worlds of living organisms, eating habits, and biology. Students will benefit from knowledge about organic molecules as increased understanding of carbohydrates, fats, proteins, and nucleic acids are explored.

3. Special Needs Considerations/Accommodations: See Lesson Plan 1

4. Resources: Water, eye-droppers, sugar, vegetable oil, starch, egg white, Petri dishes, and safety glasses.

5. Performance Objective ABCD (Learning Outcome): The student (A) will be able to demonstrate conceptual understanding of organic molecules (B) on a written exam and the creation of a project (including, but not limited to, a poster, a written paper, a demonstration of a scientific experiment) (C), with 90% + proficiency on both the project and the written exam (D).

6. Content Literacy Strategy: KWL Chart. See Lesson Plan 1

7. "Bell-Work:" Copy KWL Chart. See Lesson Plan 1

8. Opening / Anticipatory Set (?). The teacher says to the students,

    a. "Does everything you eat dissolve in water?" (Students are given a chance to respond).

    b. "Can anyone describe a protein, lipid, or carbohydrate?" (Students respond).

    c. "Today, we will unpack some of the mysteries of the human body!"

9. Instructional Method

    a. The teacher reviews proteins,

    b. The teacher reviews carbohydrates, (Teacher asks students to record one fact learned during the last ten minutes, on the "L" portion of their KWL chart).

    c. The teacher reviews lipids,

    d. The teacher reviews nucleic acids,

    e. The teacher leads a discussion, encouraging student dialog, regarding food choices (diet) people make, (Teacher asks students to record one additional fact learned during the last 15 minutes, on the "L" portion of their KWL chart.

    f. The teacher reviews procedures for lab safety.

10. Guided Practice

    a. The teacher demonstrates each step, one at a time, with students immediately completing each step, while working individually, or in groups of two to four:

        i. Sugar, vegetable oil, egg white, and starch are placed into separate Petri dishes.

        ii. Students are allowed to choose which substance she/he will experiment with.

        iii. Students record initial observations of substance in their Petri dish, and then share responses with a peer.

        iv. Students record how their substance feels.

        v. Students are instructed to add water to their substance and gently stir.

        vi. Students are asked to describe physical changes (if observed) to their substance with a peer. Each peer then paraphrases what she/he heard, to check for accuracy.

vii. Students are asked to predict other substances from their diet which will dissolve in water, sharing first with a peer, and then with the whole class.

b. The teacher provides an overview of each final project which students can create on an individual basis, and the requirement to also take a written exam over the concept of organic molecules. Choices for the final project include (but are not limited to):

i. A visual representation of substances from students' diets which dissolve in water, and those which do not.

ii. A written narrative (2-3 page paper) explaining which substances from their diet dissolve in water, and which do not, providing a rationale.

iii. A demonstration of a scientific experiment regarding other substances from students' diets which dissolve in water.

11. Lesson Closure. Teacher asks students to record one additional fact learned during the last 20-30 minutes on the "L" portion of their KWL chart. The teacher asks students the following questions:

a. "Does everything dissolve in water?" (Students are given a chance to respond).

b. "Can anyone describe what they have learned about organic molecules?" (Students respond).

c. "As you leave today, please hand me your KWL chart and be prepared to share one more thing you learned about electron dot structures – remember, you may not say the same thing as the person in front of you, so please have at least two ideas in your mind – nice job today!"

12. Formative Assessment / Questioning Strategies: See Lesson Plan 1

13. Re-teaching Plan / Independent Practice / Extension Activity

a. Re-teaching Plan: Teacher uses results from the KWL Charts and/or formative assessment to re-teach concepts that 20% (or more) of the class "missed" on the quiz.

b. Independent Practice: Teacher instructs students to complete their final project.

c. Extension Activity: Students are asked to apply what she/he has learned to her/his choices for diet by making a diet brochure for an elementary-level student.

14. Summative Assessment: See Lesson Plan 1

15. Reflection Notes: See Lesson Plan 1

Lesson Plan 2 is an effective, differentiated-instruction lesson because it requires dialog between students, and acknowledges the importance of learner choice for the type of organic molecule (substance) to explore, a choice in grouping configuration, and a choice in the final product the student chooses to provide evidence regarding concepts learned. In this lesson plan, the teacher uses Gardner's Multiple Intelligences (Gardner, 1993), allowing the student to choose between a poster (Naturalistic/Visual-Spatial Intelligences), a

written paper (Naturalistic/Linguistic/Intrapersonal Intelligences), or a demonstration of a scientific experiment (Naturalistic/Bodily-Kinesthetic/Inter-
personal/ Mathematical-Logistic Intelligences). In addition, all students write
a written exam over the concepts of organic molecules. This form of differentiated instruction appeals to middle-level and high-school level students
because learner choice of organic molecule (substance), choice in grouping
configuration, and choice of final product are acknowledged as important
aspects of learning.

Lesson Plan 3 – Teaching Electron-Dot Structures Through Learner Choice

The third lesson plan, Lesson Plan 3, explores concepts in chemistry (electron dot structures, NSTA Standards C.3.a.2-3), and is designed for a high-
school level classroom. The lesson is designed to last a single, fifty-five-
minute class session. The lesson requires dialog between students, includes
physical movement throughout the lesson, and acknowledges the importance
of learner choice for the type of element to explore, a choice in grouping
configuration, and a choice in final product.

Key Questions:

   a. Who benefits from knowing about electron dot structures?
   b. What are the basic principles of ionic, covalent, and metallic bonding?
   c. Where do electrons occur in the structure of an atom?
   d. When is knowledge of the physical and chemical properties and clas-
      sification of elements beneficial?
   e. Why should all students learn about electron dot structures?

1. Content Focus/Grade Level/Content Standards & Benchmarks. Electron
Dot Structures / High-School Level / Basic principles of ionic, covalent, and
metallic bonding, and physical and chemical properties and classification of
elements including periodicity (NSTA Standards C.3.a.2-3).
   2. Purpose/Relevancy. An understanding of electron dot structure provides students with insight into the world of atoms, elements, and chemistry.
Students will benefit from knowledge about electron dot structures as increased understanding of ionic and covalent bonding is explored.
   3. Special Needs Considerations/Accommodations: See Lesson Plan 1
   4. Resources. Individual dry-erase boards and dry-erase markers
   5. Performance Objective ABCD (Learning Outcome). The student (A)
will be able to demonstrate conceptual understanding of electron dot structures (B) on a written exam and the creation of a project (including, but not
limited to, a poster, a written paper, a demonstration of a scientific experi-

ment, a conceptual model, or another pre-approved method of showcasing a student's conceptual understanding of concepts learned) (C), with 90% + proficiency on both the project and the written exam (D).

6. Content Literacy Strategy: KWL Chart. See Lesson Plan 1

7. "Bell-Work": Copy KWL Chart. See Lesson Plan 1

8. Opening / Anticipatory Set. The teacher says to the students,

a. "A picture is worth a thousand words. What does that mean?" (Students are given a chance to respond).

b. "What types of pictures make chemistry easier to see and understand?" (Students respond).

c. "Today, we will unpack some of the mysteries of the atom, focusing primarily on electron dot structures!"

9. Instructional Method

a. The teacher reviews the process of finding the number of valence electrons,

b. The teacher reviews electron dot structures with the class, (Teacher asks students to record one fact learned during the last ten minutes on the "L" portion of their KWL chart, and then share that fact with a peer),

c. The teacher reviews cations with the class,

d. The teacher reviews anions with the class,

e. The teacher reviews the octet rule with the class, and

f. The teacher reviews the nomenclature of ions with the class, (Teacher asks students to record three additional fact learned during the last fifteen minutes on the "L" portion of their KWL chart, and then share two of the three facts with a peer).

10. Guided Practice

a. Students practice, working individually or in groups of two, three or four, on individual dry-erase boards:

i. finding the number of valence electrons,

ii. creating electron dot structures,

iii. drawing cations,

iv. drawing anions,

v. students then stand-up, moving into physical representations of the electron dot structures for assigned atoms.

Begin by modeling the Helium atom, requiring six students, and following these steps: (a) Four students stand near each other, in the center of the room, labeled (sticky notes work well) as two protons and two neutrons; (b) A fifth and sixth student is needed to walk around the first four students, labeled as electrons, equally spaced, "zooming" around in their shell.

Next, model the Carbon Atom, requiring 18 students, and following these steps: (a) 12 students stand near each other, in the center of the room, with six students labeled as protons and six students labeled as neutrons; (b) Six more students are needed to walk around the first 12 students, labeled as electrons, in the following manner: 2 students walk around the protons and neutrons, equally spaced, in the first shell, and then the remaining 4 students walk around the protons, neutrons and the first two electrons, again equally spaced, to form the second shell.

Ask students how many students would be needed to model electron dot structures for Hydrogen and Oxygen.

Ask students to pick an atom, and share the number of students required to model it (and the approximate space – would a classroom work, or would the gymnasium or a football field be better?)

b. The teacher provides an overview of each final project which students can create on an individual basis, and the requirement to also take a written exam over the concept of electron dot structures. Choices for the final project include (but are not limited to):

i. a visual representation of an electron dot structure, in the form of a poster.

ii. A written narrative (2-3 page paper) explaining the concept of electron dot structures.

iii. A demonstration of a scientific experiment regarding an electron dot structure.

iv. A three-dimensional model of an electron dot structure.

v. A pre-approved final project/product, which showcases student understanding of electron dot structures. An example could be the actual creation of the written exam the class will take, embracing all levels of Bloom's Cognitive Taxonomy (Bloom, 1956), for one or more cycles learned in class.

11. Lesson Closure. Teacher asks students to record one additional fact learned during the last 20-30 minutes on the "L" portion of their KWL chart. The teacher asks students the following questions:

a. "Now when you hear the phrase, "electron dot structures," what do you think of?" (Students are given a chance to respond).

b. "Can anyone describe what they have learned about electron dot structures?" (Students respond).

c. "As you leave today, please hand me your KWL chart and be prepared to share one more thing you learned about electron dot structures – remember, you may not say the same thing as the person in front of you, so please have at least two ideas in your mind – nice job today!"

12. Formative Assessments: See Lesson Plan 1

13. Re-teaching Plan / Independent Practice / Extension Activity

a. Re-teaching Plan. Teacher uses results from the KWL Chart and/or formative assessment to re-teach concepts that 20% (or more) of the class "missed" on the quiz.

b. Independent Practice. Teacher instructs students to complete their final project.

c. Extension Activity. Teacher instructs students to compare and contrast electron dot structures and the solar system.

14. Summative Assessment: See Lesson Plan 1

15. Reflection Notes: See Lesson Plan 1

Lesson Plan 3 is an effective, differentiated-instruction lesson because it requires dialog between students, physical movement, and acknowledges the importance of learner choice for the type of element to explore, a choice in grouping configuration, and a choice in the final product the student chooses to provide evidence regarding concepts learned. In this lesson plan, the teacher uses Gardner's Multiple Intelligences (Gardner, 1993), allowing the student to choose between a poster (Naturalistic/Visual-Spatial Intelligences), a written paper (Naturalistic/Linguistic/Intrapersonal Intelligences), a demonstration of a scientific experiment (Naturalistic/Bodily-Kinesthetic/Interpersonal/ Logical-Mathematical Intelligences), a three-dimensional model (Naturalistic/Visual-Spatial Intelligences), or another pre-approved method for showcasing a student's conceptual understanding of concepts learned. In addition, all students write a written exam over the concepts of electron dot structures. This form of differentiated instruction appeals to high school students because learner choice, embracing multiple forms of process, and final product are acknowledged as important aspects of learning.

CONCLUSION

The National Science Education Standards guide our nation toward a scientifically literate society, providing a definition for scientific literacy. The national science standards create a vision of what all students need to understand and be able to demonstrate in science. Differentiating instruction in science affects student interest in science through acknowledgment of the importance of dialog between students, physical movement, and learner choice. Teachers who make learning relevant, by assessing prior knowledge and activating student interest, encouraging dialog between students, embracing movement during lessons, and offering choices for learners' process (the act of learning new information) and product (the act of showcasing information learned) will witness increased results on the high-stakes assessments (Sparks-Langer, et al, 2004) used by states to measure the standards and benchmarks in science, and attain adequate yearly progress.

REFERENCES

American Association for the Advancement of Science (1993). *Benchmarks for science Literacy*. New York, NY: Oxford University Press.

Bloom, B. S. Ed. (1956). *Taxonomy of educational objectives: Book I. Cognitive domain*. New York, NY: Longman, Inc.

Gardner, H. (1993). Creating minds: An anatomy of creativity as seen through the eyes of Freud, Einstein, Picasso, Stravinsky, Eliot, Graham, and Ghandi. New York, NY: Basic Books.

Gunter, M. A., Estes, T. H., & Mintz, S. L. (2007). *Instruction: A models approach*. Boston, MA: Pearson Education.

Kane, S. (2007). *Literacy and learning in the content area* (2nd ed.). Scottsdale, AZ: Holcomb Hathaway Publishers.

McCarthy, B. (1990). Using the 4MAT system to bring learning styles to schools. *Educational Leadership, 48* (2), 31-37.

National Council of Teachers of Mathematics. (1989). *Curriculum and evaluation standards for school mathematics*. Reston, VA: NCTM.

National Science Teachers Association (1992). *Scope, sequence and coordination of secondary school science. Vol.1. The content core: A guide for curriculum developers*. Washington, DC: NSTA. Available at http://www.nsta.org/publications/nses.aspx.

Sizer, T. R., & Sizer, N. F. (1999). *The students are watching: Schools and the moral contract*. Boston, MA: Beacon Press.

Sparks-Langer, G. M., Starko, A. J., Pasch, M, Burke, W, Moody, C. D., & Gardner, T. G., 2004). *Teaching as decision making: Successful practices for the secondary teacher*. Upper Saddle River, NJ: Pearson Education, Inc.

Tovani, C. (2004). *Do I really have to teach reading?: Content comprehension, grades 6 – 12*. Portland, ME: Stenhouse Publishers.

Chapter Eight

Differentiated Instruction and Inquiry-Based Learning in Middle School and High School Social Studies

C. Rodney Williams

"History and geography ... are the information studies par excellence of the schools"
—(Dewey, 1916, p. 107).

INTRODUCTION

The National Council for the Social Studies (NCSS) in its definition of social studies states that "The primary purpose of social studies is to help young people develop the ability to make informed and reasoned decisions for the public good as citizens of a culturally diverse, democratic society in an interdependent world" (National curriculum standards for social studies: A framework for teaching, learning, and assessment, 2010). These standards are thematic (e.g., "people, places, and environment") and focus on developing higher-level thinking skills rather than focusing on the accumulation of facts and basic comprehension that are typical in a direct instruction approach to learning social studies where lectures, whole group instruction, and worksheets are the norm.

Philosophical beliefs embedded in the concept of differentiated instruction can be applied to a variety of approaches to teaching and learning and especially to almost any type of inquiry-based or active learning approach to social studies. Differentiated instruction aims to connect learning with learner interests by providing learners with multiple ways to access subject matter and multiple ways to demonstrate learning that correspond to students' learning readiness, learning preferences, and interests and life experiences (Tomlinson, 2000). A key principle of differentiated instruction is that learners learn best when learning environments and opportunities are natural and authentic (Tomlinson, 2000); a principle that, for social studies, can be more naturally incorporated into an inquiry based approach than in a direct instruction approach.

The term "inquiry-based instruction" is defined broadly in this chapter and refers to any model of teaching that is not direct instruction and that requires the active involvement of students in their own learning. Inquiry-based approaches include, among others, project-based learning, issues-centered social studies, document-based social studies, cooperative learning, and problem-based social studies.

This chapter argues that a refined approach to inquiry-based teaching and learning that takes into account the principles of differentiated instruction can help teachers foster the development of higher-level thinking skills among all their students, and move them toward the goal of becoming informed citizens in a democratic society in a challenging and exciting learning environment. This can be accomplished by attending to learners' individual needs, abilities, learning preferences, and interests and life experiences, key principles of differentiated instruction (Tomlinson, 2000).

Differentiated instruction is a relatively new term used in education, but the concept has been around for some time. There have been advocates for differentiating instruction in the social studies for at least the past one hundred years. The American philosopher, John Dewey, argues for an approach that connects learning to the learners' experiences in his chapter on geography and history in *Democracy and Education*, his best known work (Dewey, 1916). Alan J. Singer, a contemporary author, argues in his book on teaching middle and high school social studies, that "…structured experiential learning is the most effective way to teach social studies on every level" (Singer, 2009, p. 83). Like Singer, this writer agrees that this conception of teaching and learning can apply to both middle and high school socials studies, differing only in the levels of difficulty in skill development and conceptual sophistication (Singer, 2009).

Recent research (Bransford, Brown, & Cocking, 2000) on how people learn suggests that an inquiry-based approach to social studies may be the most effective way to help students learn. The field of cognitive psychology has more or less validated Dewey's ideas about inquiry-based teaching and learning through decades of rigorous study (Bransford, et al., 2000). This research suggests that helping student make connections between what they already know and new material that teachers want students to learn is best achieved in classrooms where the learning connects to students' life experiences in ways that allow them to construct their own individual meanings about the world, a view which complements the concept of differentiated instruction. Lecturing, the most ubiquitous method of teaching social studies, especially in high schools, is perhaps the least effective way to help *all* students learn social studies, a major goal of those who advocate for differentiated learning environments for students.

It is important to recognize, however, some of the obstacles that may be encountered as teachers learn to incorporate the inquiry-based approach into their social studies teaching. First of all, designing quality inquiry-based instruction is often difficult, time-consuming, and complex, which perhaps accounts for why teachers do not learn how to do this in their teacher education programs (Seixas, 2001) or see it modeled in their university content area courses (Feiman-Nemser & Remillard, 1996). Another closely related reason for lack of knowledge and understanding of this approach is that schools do not provide the kinds of sustained professional development that teachers need to help them learn this complex way of teaching (Ball & Cohen, 1999). Finally, learning how to use primary sources in social studies instruction is a relatively complex process, and most social studies teachers have not been trained to use them. Incorporating principles of differentiated instruction adds another layer of complexity to this approach.

With all of the above in mind, it is important to also note that most standards for the social studies call for using inquiry-based approaches to learning social studies (National curriculum standards for social studies: A framework for teaching, learning, and assessment, 2010; National standards for civics and government, 1995; National standards for social studies teachers, 1997; National standards for United States history, 1998; National standards for world history, 1998; U.S. national geography standards, 1998). In addition, the new Common Core Standards for Literacy in History/Social Studies require students, among other expectations, to be able to "Write arguments focused on discipline specific content," and "Conduct short as well as more sustained research projects to answer a question (including a self-generated question) or solve a problem; narrow or broaden the inquiry when appropriate; synthesize multiple sources on the subject, demonstrating understanding of the subject under investigation" (Common core state standards for English language arts & literacy in history/social studies, science, and technical subjects: 6-12, 2010). Clearly, these standards require that social studies teachers must learn how to incorporate an inquiry-based approach to teaching and learning (whatever model they choose) along with principles of differentiated instruction into their classrooms in order that standards are met (Tomlinson, 2000). It is the goal of this chapter to help social studies teachers to begin to think about how to do this.

Some social studies teachers claim that they use inquiry-based approaches labeling them "hands on" social studies. Some "hands on" approaches, however, do not always satisfy one criterion that is critically important in teaching social studies, namely that "hands on" approaches to teaching social studies must also be "minds on." To ensure that all students have access to "minds-on" approaches in inquiry-based social studies, teachers must incorporate principles of differentiated instruction that lead to the development of higher levels of thinking among all students, not just select groups of students.

There are many ways to achieve a "hands on – minds on" inquiry-based approach to teaching social studies in which the instruction is also differentiated. This chapter will not attempt to address all the models of inquiry-based learning in the social studies, but instead will present "vignettes" of actual teaching that illustrate some attributes of some of these models. Vignettes demonstrate where differentiated instruction is evident in lessons. These vignettes illustrate how teachers can begin to learn (with effort and persistence) how to develop their own personal models of inquiry-based teaching and learning that incorporate principles of differentiated instruction. And, despite their imperfections the vignettes also illustrate how "active" learning in the social studies can excite and motivate students to learn in the subject area they historically disdain and often perform poorly on in high-stakes standardized tests.

VIGNETTES OF INQUIRY TEACHING AND LEARNING IN THE SOCIAL STUDIES

As previously discussed, despite the difficulties and lack of opportunities to learn about inquiry-based teaching and learning that incorporate principles of differentiated instruction it is still possible for social studies teachers to develop expertise in this teaching methodology through personal determination and collaboration with colleagues. Suggestions for how teachers can take charge of their own learning to incorporate principles of differentiated instruction into inquiry-based teaching and learning are offered below in the context of the descriptions of lessons implemented by teachers in middle and high school settings. Resources and other materials, including those that are technology-based, that can help teachers learn how to design and implement their own approach to inquiry-based learning in the social studies are also included with each vignette. All of the vignettes involve teachers who are either students or former students enrolled at universities where the writer has worked or who are volunteers who are recruited to participate in various projects for social studies teachers.

VIGNETTE 1. DIFFERENTIATED INSTRUCTION IN HIGH SCHOOL ECONOMICS: SIMULATIONS, ROLE-PLAYING, COOPERATIVE LEARNING, AND RESEARCH

The inquiry-based teaching and learning activities and differentiated instruction strategies described here were derived from a research project the writer directed when he was a faculty member at a large Midwestern university. The project involved four high school economics teachers who taught in school settings in a large metropolitan area that reflected a wide range of socio-economic conditions. The unit that teachers and university personnel planned collaboratively, and that teachers implemented in their classrooms, was an "issues-centered" approach to teaching social studies (Evans & Saxe, 1996) that also incorporated features of WebQuests (Dodge, 2007), simulations and role-playing (Joyce & Weil, 1996), and cooperative learning (Johnson, Johnson, & Holubec, 1994).

The unit is designed to help students learn basic concepts in economics such as "supply and demand." This vignette describes activities that take place in the course of implementing a series of lessons on economics and the electricity market.

Teachers, along with project staff, who designed the unit in which the activities described below were situated, collaborated on using a "Teaching for Understanding" approach (Wiske, 1998) to unit design and implementation. "Throughlines" or "essential questions" that teachers and project staff developed to frame students' inquiries during the unit included(1) "How do we solve problems of scarcity?" (2) "How do we hold informed decisions about economic conditions?" and (3) "How do we present, research, collaborate, and communicate about economic issues?" (Williams, 2003). The unit addressed "Content Standard 4" in the *Michigan Curriculum Framework for Social Studies*: "All students will explain how a free market economic system works, as well as other economic systems, to coordinate and facilitate the exchange, production, distribution and consumption of goods and services" (Michigan curriculum framework, 1996). Although there were several related "understanding goals" for the unit, one goal focused on a desired learning outcome for the entire unit: "Students will understand the positive and negative elements of a market system to promote better decision making" (Williams, 2003). The activity where students demonstrated their overall learning in the unit (a culminating performance of understanding) was also included in the plan: "Students will demonstrate their understanding of how learned concepts relate to real-life issues in their group presentations" (Williams, 2003).

The issue that framed the unit was the California electricity crisis of 2000, deregulation of the electricity market, and the related Enron scandal. Regulation of the electricity market was also a current issue in the state where these schools were located and was under consideration by the state legislature. Students were introduced to the unit and told how it would unfold. Subsequently, a series of lessons were enacted to help students understand principles of supply and demand. Finally, toward the end of the unit students were assigned in groups to research the issue using articles and primary sources. After engaging in group discussions about their research, each group was assigned the role of a particular interest group. These were role-groups that were likely to have had an interest in whether electricity markets were regulated or deregulated, i.e., small business owners, homeowners, large corporations, senior citizens, etc. Each group was assigned the task of developing a position on regulation or deregulation of the electricity market that would be presented and argued before a "mock" committee of the legislature. Teachers and some parents played the role of the committee. Groups were required to include concepts like "supply and demand" in their arguments in ways that demonstrated an understanding of these concepts as well as cite evidence from their research that bolstered their argument. The culminating activity for this unit was a legislative "committee hearing" where groups argued their cases. Committee members provided feedback to students about the quality and persuasiveness of their arguments using a rubric designed by teachers.

Almost all of the students involved, including those in low income and high-income areas, were excited and enthusiastic as they engaged in their discussions and research. Despite sometimes being befuddled about what it was that they were expected to do, their final presentations to the "legislative committee" were well informed and argued passionately. And, despite the complexities, and occasional frustrations, involved in implementing this inquiry-based unit, after the project had concluded teachers enthusiastically endorsed this model of instruction and vowed to use it again.

The project team observed and videotaped, in their classrooms, almost all of the lessons implemented by the four teachers. The team was not looking for instances of practice where differentiated instruction was used; rather, it was looking to see how the inquiry-based unit on economics unfolded in each classroom and how closely it adhered to the "Teaching for Understanding" framework (Wiske, 1998). In reflecting on the lessons, however, it was evident that some, but not all, teachers used some principles of differentiated instruction as they taught the unit.

For instance, one teacher designed her groups according to their perceived "readiness" level to conduct research and engage in discussions about the articles they were assigned to read and discuss. She then provided extra support for students in groups that she perceived to be less ready to engage in the task while letting other groups work more independently. While she did not vary content (all groups read the same articles) that addressed varying levels of difficulty and abstractness by using a differentiated strategy called "tiered learning experiences," (Chick, 2010), she did make an effort to scaffold students' learning in these groups that she perceived as struggling with the content by providing extra support as they read and discussed the material. Other teachers who did not configure groups this way found that many students were at times "lost and confused" as they engaged in the research task.

All teachers used the principle of differentiated instruction that addressed learners' interests by designing the activities so that students could choose which particular interest group most closely matched their own perspectives on market regulation. Motivation, empowerment, and achievement were strongly linked to student interests (Chick, 2010). Students' enthusiasm for the issues they studied was evident throughout the unit and especially in the culminating activity, where they argued passionately for their position on regulation of the electricity market to the mock legislative committee.

To a degree, teachers also addressed students' learning preferences, another important principle of differentiated instruction, by providing a variety of activities that included conducting research on the internet, discussion, writing, role-playing, simulations, and presentation. Graphs and charts also were used as teachers taught students about "supply and demand" as they prepared students to conduct research. Students created their own graphs using special software installed on graphing calculators. One teacher also had students' do "pushups" to illustrate attributes of "supply and demand." Employing students' "kinesthetic intelligence" in this activity enlivened what might have been a boring teacher-led lecture on "supply and demand." Providing a variety of ways to learn and demonstrate learning complemented ideas found in Howard Gardner's research on "multiple intelligences" (Gardner, 2011).

VIGNETTES 2 & 3. DIFFERENTIATED INSTRUCTION IN HIGH SCHOOL AND MIDDLE SCHOOL SOCIAL STUDIES: DOCUMENT-BASED & DISCUSSION-BASED SOCIAL STUDIES

The lessons in the two vignettes described below were taught in the context of the development of an online project at a large Midwestern university in which the writer participated (Civics online, 2001). The site provides teachers with materials and strategies to help them develop units and lessons designed around the theme of "Core Democratic Values," which was a component of the social studies standards in the state where the project took place (Michigan curriculum framework, 1996).

Teachers were recruited from a list of teachers who had been identified as "excellent" social studies teachers. The writer designed multimedia case studies of each teacher's lessons including interviews with each teacher and with some students. The case studies could be found on the site (Civics

Online, 2001) by clicking on the "Teachers" tab located on the site home page.

VIGNETTE 2. DIFFERENTIATED INSTRUCTION IN AP HIGH SCHOOL U.S. HISTORY: DOCUMENT-BASED SOCIAL STUDIES

John Andrews (not his real name), a social studies teacher at a suburban high school, taught a lesson focused on the integration of "Core Democratic Values" into the social studies curriculum. The lesson was designed to help students develop a better understanding of the issues surrounding the post revolutionary, pre-Constitutional era leading into the actual study of the Constitution. Mr. Andrews' activity required students to move from station to station where they read and collaboratively interpreted primary sources from the Articles of Confederation period. The lesson was designed to help students develop a better understanding of the issues surrounding the post revolutionary, pre-Constitutional era leading into the actual study of the Constitution. Mr. Andrews first previewed the assignment with his students, linking it to future assignments, lessons, and units.

Although Mr. Andrews used lecture as his primary teaching methodology in the class (12th-grade Advanced Placement U. S. History), he incorporated one inquiry-based strategy, document analysis, to help students gain a better understanding of primary sources that he deemed important to the study of this period in U. S. history. Mr. Andrews' students were serious and attentive as they participated in this document analysis activity. Mr. Andrews suggested, in an interview with the writer after the lesson, that he was attuned to one principle of differentiated instruction, differentiating according to learner preferences and abilities. In the interview, he acknowledged differences between the ways the station activity might be designed for his AP students and for a different group of learners. Mr. Andrews said,

> The discussion at each station seemed to be particularly valuable. In hindsight, I might accompany each station with specific questions to be answered and discussed by the group, although I believe this would depend on the age level. While such a support would be necessary for some more concrete learners, at the AP level for which this lesson was designed, this lesson became an important experience at individual analysis. The use of direct questions at that level might inhibit the students' abilities to critically take apart historical documents and analyze/interpret them on their own (Civics online, 2001).

For more information on how to use primary and secondary sources in social studies teaching visit two excellent resources, the *Library of Congress: American Memory* at http://www.loc.gov/teachers/ and the *National Archives* at http://www.archives.gov/education/. Both sites have step-by-step lessons designed to help students critically examine primary sources as well as access to a plethora of primary source material. Another resource for teachers who might want to emulate Mr. Andrews' approach to teaching history is the *National Center for History in the Schools (NCHS)* (National center for history in the schools, UCLA, 2012). NCHS offers units designed by teachers and scholars that provide background material for teachers as well as lessons that contain primary sources.

VIGNETTE 3. DIFFERENTIATED INSTRUCTION IN MIDDLE SCHOOL SOCIAL STUDIES: DISCUSSION

One method for differentiating instruction in social studies is through the use of questioning strategies (Troxclair, 2000). Raising the level of questioning and using "provocative questioning" ("what if" types of questions) is the most appropriate way to accomplish this in social studies classrooms (Troxclair, 2000). These questions encourage students to extend their thinking and motivate them to acquire more knowledge or engage in new activities (Troxclair, 2000).

Charles Smith (not his real name) taught social studies at the middle level in a midsized urban district. He served on an advisory board for the web-based project described above (Civics Online) and also allowed project personnel to observe and videotape his teaching in an eighth-grade social studies (U. S. History) class. At the time of the project, Mr. Smith was a new teacher who was somewhat hesitant and unsure about how to incorporate "Core Democratic Values" into his social studies lessons. Mr. Smith was also a novice at facilitating classroom discussion, a critically important skill that all social studies teachers should strive to master (Parker & Hess, 2001). During the lesson that project personnel observed Mr. Smith led a discussion with his students about Core Democratic Values. Mr. Smith wrote some of the Core Democratic Values (liberty, justice, the common good) on the board and asked students to define them. He recorded their responses on the board. Students had a hard time, however, determining how to respond, and midway through the discussion Mr. Smith abruptly shifted gears and went on to another component of the lesson, abandoning the discussion entirely.

During a follow-up interview with project personnel, Mr. Smith acknowledged his frustration with facilitating this discussion and blamed the ambiguous and highly abstract nature of Core Democratic Values and students' limited subject matter knowledge for the students' poor responses. Mr. Smith also, however, acknowledged his relative inexperience in facilitating discussion as a reason for the lack of success he had with this lesson.

In the same interview, Mr. Smith recounted how he recognized how important discussion was in social studies to scaffold students' understanding of complex subject matter and related issues. He told the interviewer about a lesson he taught subsequent to the lesson that was observed in which he had a good measure of success in facilitating discussion. The discussion focused on the rights of gay and lesbian citizens. Many social studies teachers would no doubt regard this as an extremely controversial issue and would avoid it. Mr. Smith recognized the nature of the controversy, especially for middle school students, but thoughtfully planned how he would facilitate the discussion so as to avoid controversy. He prefaced the discussion by laying down some ground rules for his students about "civil discourse." During the discussion, he also made sure his own opinions on the subject were not revealed. In gauging the discussion's success, Mr. Smith related how many students' opinions had changed as a result of the discussion and how he now felt empowered to facilitate more discussion in his lessons.

Discussion-based strategies that can play a part in fostering successful discussions and differentiating instruction include "think-pair-share" and "Socratic Circles." For more information on "Socratic Circles" see http://www.edutopia.org/blog/socratic-seminar-john-suralik-blake-wiggs.   These strategies can even be used in mostly lecture-based instruction in ways that broaden and deepen students' understanding and motivation to learn important subject matter.

VIGNETTE 4. DIFFERENTIATED INSTRUCTION IN GEOGRAPHY: PROJECT-BASED LEARNING, COOPERATIVE LEARNING, AND RESEARCH

As part of a professional development program designed to help social studies teachers learn inquiry-based strategies, which the writer directed, participating geography and history teachers were asked to teach a lesson using strategies introduced and modeled in workshops by project personnel. The lesson described and discussed here (titled "Geo-Diary") was adapted by a retired social studies teacher, and member of the program staff, from a much longer lesson titled "Geo-History" (Gersmehl, 2008). The lesson was designed to develop both students' geographic content knowledge and spatial perspective.

Goals for student learning include the following, (1) Read and interpret maps, (2) Create and evaluate regions and regional data, (3) Explain the significance of location, (4) Describe geographic analogies, (5) Interpret and predict change over space through movement, diffusion, routes, barriers, and hierarchies, (6) Compare places and regions, (7) Explain the possible causes and consequences of different patterns, and (8) Explain ecological and spatial interrelationships and associations.

The adapted "Geo-Diary" lesson asked students to create a poster based on the task requirements, which involved describing where they lived, including their local community, in as many ways, and as creatively and complexly, as possible, e.g., "What are some identifiable neighborhood areas, features, stereotypes, facts, and well-known places in your locale?" Students were to share descriptions in pairs, small groups, or whole groups. Then using a "Thinking Routine" called "What Makes You Say That?" (Visible thinking, 2008) students were to relate their summary descriptions, value judgments, and viewpoints, and were asked to explain and evaluate their impressions and knowledge of their community.

Two teachers (one a middle school teacher, the other a high school teacher) participating in the project shared a videotape of their lessons with the rest of the project participants. In both cases, it was clear that students were deeply engaged in the project and that they had "fun" while they were completing it. Their lessons reflected careful planning and skillful implementation. Both teachers incorporated principles of differentiated instruction into their lessons. They allowed students choices, and multiple ways of presenting their project (poster board, PowerPoint, video). The two teachers also demonstrated the principle of differentiated instruction that attended to the connection between curriculum and students' interests and life experiences (Tomlinson, 2000).

For more information on teaching inquiry-based geography see http://www.cst.cmich.edu/mga/ (Michigan Geographic Alliance).

CONCLUDING THOUGHTS

Despite the dearth of opportunities for social studies teachers to learn about inquiry-based teaching and learning and differentiated instruction, it is still possible for teachers who are motivated to improve their teaching and students' learning to accomplish professional learning goals. There are numerous resources, including those mentioned in this chapter, that foster the knowledge and skills needed to teach inquiry-based social studies. One of the best online resources is Annenberg Learner (Annenberg learner: Teacher professional development and classroom resources across the curriculum, 2012). This site offers comprehensive online workshops on a variety of topics related to teaching social studies. Workshops include text, materials, and video, and are self-paced. One workshop deals with using primary sources in social studies. Workshops can be completed individually or in teams.

Standards now require that teachers use an inquiry-based approach to teaching social studies. In addition, what we know from research on learning and motivation strongly suggests that inquiry-based learning results in deeper and more meaningful learning for students. Research also suggests that incorporating principles of differentiated instruction into an inquiry-based learning strategy can increase the probability that all students can learn from this approach. As the teaching vignettes (cases) described in this chapter illustrate, students are engaged and excited when they are taught with inquiry-based methods.

Social studies teachers may not be able to teach this way all the time, considering the amount of time required for their own learning and for preparation, but it is possible to start in small ways to teach social studies using inquiry-based approaches that also incorporate principles of differentiated instruction. Teachers need to transform social studies teaching from presenting endless lists of facts (Wilson, 1991) to rich, project-based learning environments where what students learn actually fosters the goal of the social studies, an informed citizenry that makes choices that improve the common good in a democratic society.

REFERENCES

Annenberg learner: Teacher professional development and classroom resources across the curriculum. (2012). Retrieved February 4, 2012, from http://www.learner.org/.

Ball, D. L. & Cohen, D. K. (1999). Developing practice, developing practitioners: Toward a practice-based theory of professional education. In L. Darling-Hammond & G. Sykes (Eds.), *Teaching as the learning profession: Handbook of policy and practice* (pp. 3-32). San Francisco, CA: Jossey-Bass Inc.

Bransford, J., Brown, A. L., & Cocking, R. R. (2000). *How people learn:Brain, mind, experience, and school* (Expanded ed.). Washington, D.C.: National Academy Press.

Chick, K. A. (2010). Highlights in history: Differentiated instruction in the social studies classroom. *Middle Level Learning, 38* (May/June), 6-10.

Civics online. (2001). Retrieved September 15, 2003, from http://www.civics-online.org.

Common core state standards for English language arts & literacy in history/social studies, science, and technical subjects: 6-12. (2010). Retrieved January 6, 2012, from http://www.corestandards.org/assets/CCSSI_ELA%20Standards.pdf.

Dewey, J. (1916). *Democracy and education.* New York, NY: The Free Press.

Dodge, B. (2007). *Webquest.org* Retrieved March 6, 2012, from http://webquest.org/.

Evans, R. W. & Saxe, D. W. (1996). *Handbook on teaching social issues.* Washington, D.C.: National Council for the Social Studies.

Feiman-Nemser, S. & Remillard, J. (1996). Perspectives on learning to teach. In J. Sikula (Ed.), *The teacher educator's handbook* (2nd ed., pp. 63-91). New York, NY: Macmillan.

Gardner, H. (2011). *Frames of mind: The theory of mutliple intelligences* New York, NY: Basic Books.

Gersmehl, P. (2008). *Teaching geography* (2nd ed.). New York, NY: The Guilford Press.

Johnson, D. W., Johnson, R. T., & Holubec, E. J. (1994). *Cooperative learning in the classroom.* Alexandria, VA: Association for Supervision and Curriculum Development.

Joyce, B. & Weil, M. (1996). *Models of teaching* Boston, MA: Allyn and Bacon.

Michigan curriculum framework. (1996). Retrieved April 24, 2012, from http://www.michigan.gov/documents/MichiganCurriculumFramework_8172_7.pdf.

National center for history in the schools, UCLA. (2012). Retrieved March 7, 2012, from http://www.nchs.ucla.edu/.

National curriculum standards for social studies: A framework for teaching, learning, and assessment. (2010). Retrieved from http://www.ncss.org/standards/stitle.html.

National standards for civics and government. (1995). Retrieved March 14, 2012, from http://www.civiced.org/index.php?page=stds.

National standards for social studies teachers. (1997). Retrieved May 5, 2002, from http://www.socialstudies.org/standards/teachers/vol1/home.shtml.

National standards for United States history. (1998). Retrieved March 1, 2012, from http://www.sscnet.ucla.edu/nchs/us-toc.htm.

National standards for world history. (1998). Retrieved March 3, 2012, from http://www.sscnet.ucla.edu/nchs/wrldtoc.html.

Parker, W. C. & Hess, D. (2001). Teaching with and for discussion. *Teaching and Teacher Education, 17*, 273-289.

Seixas, P. (2001). Review of research on social studies. In V. Richardson (Ed.), *Handbook of research on teaching* (pp. 545-565). Washington, D.C.: American Educational Research Association.

Singer, A. J. (2009). *Social studies for secondary schools; Teaching to learn, learning to teach* (3rd ed.). New York, NY: Taylor & Francis.

Tomlinson, C. A. (2000). Reconcilable differences? Standards-based teaching and differentiation. *Educational Leadership, 58* (1), 6-11.

Troxclair, D. A. (2000). Differentiating instruction for gifted students in regular education social studies classes. *Roeper Review, 22* (3), 195-198.

U. S. national geography standards. (1998). Retrieved March 14, 2012, from *http://www.nationalgeographic.com/xpeditions/standards/matrix.html* .

Visible thinking. (2008). Retrieved March 6, 2012, from http://pzweb.harvard.edu/vt/VisibleThinking_html_files/VisibleThinking1.html.

Williams, C. R. (2003). *High school economics unit. Curriculum unit design*. Ann Arbor, MI: University of Michigan, School of Education.

Wilson, S. M. (1991). Parade of facts, stories of the past: What do novice history teachers need to know? In M. M. Kennedy (Ed.), *Teaching academic subjects to diverse learners* (pp. 97-116). New York, NY: Teachers College Press.

Wiske, M. S. (Ed.). (1998). *Teaching for understanding: Linking research with practice*. San Francisco, CA: Jossey-Bass Publishers.

Chapter Nine

Differentiating Instruction and Teaching the Middle School and High School Arts

Carolyn J. Schaeffer & Scott R. Kirst

INTRODUCTION

In this chapter, the relationship between differentiated instruction and the impact it has teaching the National Standards for Arts Education are explored. The main goal of differentiation is teaching according to students' needs. If students are at different levels of knowledge or skills, teachers must find a way to teach all the levels present. In the arts, differentiated instruction must push the most talented to their fullest potential while helping less accomplished students reach their highest level of creativity. The arts are inherently open-ended subjects that make differentiation less obvious to the students; however, arts in the classroom can be used more readily than the other subjects taught in the content area classroom. A powerful effect of learning the arts is that students are less aware of the practice of differentiation. This sensitive and encouraging approach to each individual student's talents is essential to create a classroom environment for optimum learning (Tomlinson, 1995).

Analysis of research (see, for example, Cornett, 2003; Cornett, 1999; Goldberg, 2006; Tomlinson, 2000, 1999; Worley, 2006) provides evidence that three main overarching concepts must be consciously integrated into the arts when differentiating instruction. First, the teacher must expect common outcomes of the students by using differentiated tasks that are linked to ability and talents. The changing of the outcome based on perceived talents or deficiencies may not only alienate certain students, but also provide a divergence of interests in the arts and music. Second, the teacher must engage the students by designing the lesson to be relevant and interesting. The student must be an active participant in the learning process and, by actively engaging the student in their own learning, the teacher is best able to direct their energy into designing appropriate objectives and assessments. Third, the teacher must take into account prior knowledge so that he/she can build on pre-existing knowledge. Knowing the students is essential if teachers are to comprehend what the students should know, understand, and be able to do.

OVERVIEW OF THE NATIONAL STANDARDS FOR ARTS EDUCATION

With the passing of *Goals 2000: Educate America Act,* arts education is at the core of educational reform. The arts are written into federal law, and that law acknowledges the arts as core subjects. The arts are just as important to education as English language arts, mathematics, history, science, and foreign languages. The goal of arts education is to connect people and experience directly, to build the bridge between verbal and nonverbal communication, and between logical thinking and emotional thinking, to better gain an understanding of the whole.

The National Standards for Arts Education (Consortium of National Arts Education, 2007) provide the value and importance of the arts for the educational well- being of our young people and our country. These standards provide a crucial foundation for helping students learn the characteristics of each of the arts. The national standards provide a framework for arts education, including dance, visual arts, theater, and music.

The standards are a framework for helping students learn the characteristics of the arts by using a wide range of subject matter, symbols, meaningful images, and expressions, to reflect the students' ideas, feelings, and emotions. The students grow more sophisticated in their need to use the arts to reflect their feelings and emotions, and in their abilities to evaluate the merits of their efforts. The standards provide that framework in a way that promotes the students' thinking, working, communicating, reasoning, and investigating skills, and provide for their growing familiarity with the ideas, concepts, issues, dilemmas, and knowledge important in the arts. As students gain this knowledge and these skills, they gain in their ability to apply the knowledge and skills in the visual arts to their widening personal worlds.

The standards provide a vision of competence and educational effectiveness, but without creating a mold into which all arts programs must fit (Protheroe, 2007). The arts standards are focused on the results of student learning that comes from a basic education in the arts and builds upon each other each year so that a child advances to a new level of understanding. The standards provide educational goals, not a curriculum. Their purpose is to help improve all types of art instruction.

Using the arts standards benefits the student, teacher, and society. Using the arts standards benefits the student and teacher because it cultivates the whole child, gradually building many kinds of literacy while developing intuition, reasoning, imagination, and dexterity into unique forms of expression and communication. The students learn to respect the often very different ways others have of thinking, working, and expressing themselves. Teachers also benefit through increased student awareness and comprehension of the arts.

Using the National Standards for Arts Education in schools benefits society because students of the arts disciplines gain powerful tools for understanding human experiences, learning problem solving, respect for others and their way of thinking, and gaining experience in communication to be able to more clearly express themselves. The students learn to make decisions in situations where there are no standard answers. By studying the arts, students stimulate their natural creativity and learn to develop it to meet the needs of a complex and competitive society (Brinkman, 2010; Landsberger 2007).

The arts are unique because the arts borrow their content from other disciplines and then apply that content to an expressive, aesthetic form. The arts also teach broader learning concepts than the core content standards. Additionally, the 21st century skills of critical thinking, problem solving, working with others, communication skills, and decision-making are integral to every element of the arts, and carry over into all of the other subject areas.

DIFFERENTIATING INSTRUCTION AND TEACHING THE ARTS

The arts (art, drama, and music) have, historically, a legitimate place at the core of quality education for students. The arts are academic, not just entertainment, enrichment, or special events, and they possess substantive content that both demands and merits rigorous exploration. The arts have value in their own right through a complement and partnership with the other disciplines. The arts are a way of reaching and engaging students with diverse learning styles, of fostering and supporting social growth, of unifying content, and of powerfully communicating meaning. Through differentiating instruction in art, drama, and music, children better understand themselves and others. In addition, the arts are in all races, ethnicities, and cultures; the arts are an intrinsic part of the human experience.

When children are exposed to different art forms the "whole child" is being taught. The teacher is not only teaching in one or two specific ways but is actively engaging and meeting the whole needs of the student. The students are being educated in the knowledge and skills using different methods of instruction. When students are exposed to information in different means they are apt to learn in multiple ways (Heacox, 2002). If a student is familiar with what is being talked about, they are more likely to be motivated and willing to learn.

In a world where students are often asked to find the "right" answer, which can cause an undo amount of stress for perfection, the nature of education in the arts asks students to look for many different answers. Instead of assuming that there is only one answer to be found, one of the main goals of the arts is to foster the search for possible answers. It is through this multi-faceted search that students are encouraged to explore and use their own gifts to come up with a possible answer that also helps promote decision-making and critical thinking. The knowledge that there is not necessarily a "right" or "wrong" answer promotes an atmosphere in which students feel comfortable to contribute.

The teaching of the arts is as concerned with skills and a process as with the outcomes. The dominant teaching methodology usually involves all of the students involved in a set task, with differentiation of the outcome being the primary focus. There are some occasions when teaching the arts should challenge the specific needs of the student. This is called differentiation by task. Differentiation by task allows a student to complete a lesson that matches their ability (Hollingsworth, 2009). The tasks may be differentiated on the basis of inherent difficulty, the amount of structure, the amount of guidance given, or a combination of all three. This approach to teaching in the arts avoids pre-judging the students' potential in the specific arts lesson and allows a task to be matched to the ability of the student so that all levels of ability experience success.

LESSON PLANS FOR DIFFERENTIATING INSTRUCTION IN THE ARTS

In this section there are three lessons plans that provide a snap shot of how to differentiate instruction in a middle-level and high school arts classroom. These lessons enhance creativity through the arts and link differentiated instruction to the national arts standards. The lesson plans provide multiple approaches to create learning experiences that complement the individual student's learning style.

Lesson Plan One: Understanding and Drawing Perspective in the 5-8 Classroom

The first lesson plan is designed for understanding and drawing perspectives in the middle level (5-8) classroom. The lesson plan expects the same outcomes from the students, but it allows the teacher to vary the task for the students by providing ample opportunities for more complex shapes and pictures. Additionally, by having the students create their own pictures, they are able to provide material they find engaging and exciting. Also, the teacher provides a detailed pre-assessment for the students to assist in identifying the knowledge and skills the students already have and can be built upon.

This is a tiered lesson, with various cognitive levels and formative assessments available to assess those levels. As there are many types of students in the class as well as many steps involved in the lesson, the teacher should provide something akin to a checklist of these steps for the students so they are better able to follow along and self-assess where they are. Examples of criteria that could be included would be to draw the object, identify where the artist was positioned when drawing, and whether or not they label the horizon, vanishing point, and convergence lines. Within the work time, the teacher needs to make sure students can walk around and articulate their thoughts and questions with each other as they develop their ideas of perspective.

The Lesson Plan
    Content area: Visual Arts
    Grade level: 5-8
    Lesson Overview-Overarching Goal: Students are able to connect the idea of perspective and position in space within a piece of art.
    Lesson Outcomes
    Students will:

- draw an object, using a ruler, in space, using one-point perspective
- identify where the artist was positioned in space when drawing
- label where the horizon, vanishing point, and convergence lines are in a drawing

Key question
    How does the perspective of an artist affect what art looks like?
    The National Standards For Arts Education
    Visual Arts 5-8
    Standard 3. Choosing and evaluating a range of subject matter, symbols, and ideas
    Visual Arts 5-8
    Standard 5. Reflecting upon and assessing the characteristics and merits of their work and work of others.
    Uniqueness of the Learner
    The 5-8 learner is just beginning to developmentally understand the idea of perspective. This lesson engages the learner by taking the role of someone else to identify with his or her observations and thoughts. This developmen-

tal stage is intrigued that not everyone sees life the same way they do; this is imperative to develop creative and critical thinking skills.

Materials Needed

9½" x 11" White paper with front faces of blocks on it and unique vanishing point (see Figure 9.1)

Post it notes, three equal-sized, table-top blocks (6 x 8 inch per side), Pencils, Rulers, Digital Camera, Computer, and Projector

Procedures

Pre-Assessment: Have students interact with the computer/SMART board/pictures and ask the students regarding their idea of perspective in art. Why do the students think perspective is important in art and life?

Engage: The teacher will take different pictures of the same scene from different perspectives and, in front of the class, project the pictures using the computer.

Discussion

1. Ask the students where they believe the artist/photographer is standing at the time the art/photo is created. Ask what visual cues they use to determine where the person is.
2. Talk about the idea of horizon, vanishing point, and convergence helping to determine the perspective.
3. Show Vincent van Gogh's "Café Terrace at Night" or other painting/ picture/photo and discuss where the artist is and what visual cues help to identify where they are.
4. Write these ideas on the board and facilitate discussion on what each of the terms mean.
5. Have the students take pictures of each other from the left, right, and center, and project examples through the computer and projector to discuss where the photographer is at the time the picture is taken.
6. Hand out the paper with the blocks on it (Figure 9.1) and discuss where the vanishing point, horizon line, and convergence lines would be if the student stands to the left, center, or right (see Figure 9.1) of the blocks. Use actual tabletop blocks in the room and have the students walk around to see what sides and faces they can see. If students are having difficulty, label the faces of the blocks to easily identify what they can and cannot see.
7. Instruct the students, using the white board or software, as to how to draw the horizon, vanishing point, and orthogonal (convergence) lines.
8. Separate the students into groups of three. One student will have the vanishing point to the right of the blocks, left of the blocks, and behind the blocks.
9. The students will then draw the pictures on the model.

10. After the pictures are finished, the students will vote (using voting software or by hand) as to where the artist is when drawing the picture. Separate them and place on three separate areas.
11. Using a gallery walk, have the students walk around and label four separate drawings of their colleagues with individually identified and numbered/coded post-it notes. They will identify on each of the four drawings the convergence, horizon, and vanishing point using three post-it notes for each picture.
12. After the gallery walk, the teacher will facilitate a discussion on what is difficult and what is easy with this activity.

Differentiation

Instruction: This is a tiered assignment, with various levels and formative assessments to develop the thoughts and ideas of the students. Provide a checklist of these steps to the students so they are better able to follow along. Make sure students can walk around and vocalize their thoughts with each other as they develop their ideas of perspective.

Assessment: Instead of a gallery walk, the teacher may provide a web page with the student pictures or have voting software to ask the class, as a whole, their thoughts on the various perspectives. The teacher should identify which students make correct and incorrect identifications in the gallery walk, based on the codes, to differentiate future lessons and activities.

Assessment

Formative: Each of the procedural steps should be given to the students as a checklist so that the students can self-assess themselves formatively. Provide feedback, both verbal and written, regarding their thoughts of the process.

Summative: Assessment will be on the post-it notes the teacher creates and places on the student's drawings. A common checklist may be created to help the students know and understand what should be shown. Criteria for the checklist include the correct identification of horizon, vanishing point, and convergence lines, and the accuracy of the students' individual drawings.

REFERENCE FOR THE LESSON

N. A. (2010). *Café Terrace at Night*. Available at http://www.artquotes.net/masters/vangogh/vangogh_nightcafe.htm.

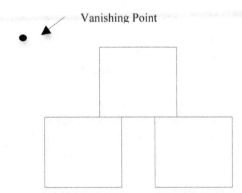

Artist's perception while standing to the left of the bricks

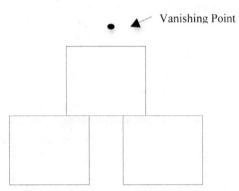

Artist's perception while standing in the center of the bricks

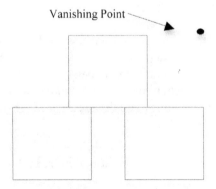

Artist's perception while standing to the right of the bricks

Figure 9.1. Artist's Perception While Standing to the Left, Center, and Right of Bricks.

Lesson Plan Two: An Introduction to Genre of Folk Tales and the Study of Russian Folk Tales in a 9-12 Classroom

The second lesson plan focuses on folktales and drama in the high school (9-12) classroom. The lesson plan expects the same outcomes from the students, but it allows the teacher to vary the task for the students by providing ample opportunities for more complex analysis, moral questioning, technology, and dialogue. Additionally, by having the students choose their own version of a modern fairy tale, they are able to provide material they find appealing and interesting. Also, the teacher provides a detailed pre-assessment for the students to assist in identifying the knowledge and skills the students already have and can be built upon within the discourse and subsequent analysis.

Planning for these overarching differentiation facets will take some effort. The teacher should have multiple ways for the students to hear/read the folktales. For example, the teacher should use technologies such as speech-to-text software, audio books, and recording devices to assure the students understand the folktales in context. There are also ways to vary instruction by using the Internet, such as giving access to a wiki or a discussion board to assure each student has a fair voice in the analysis of the folktales. It is also noteworthy to match the students to folktales in regards to their reading level and comfort with literacy.

As always, assessment planning is also important. Students may elect to record their analysis rather than write it, as the criteria are the same for both. The students may also show a presentation or draw a picture regarding the similarities and differences in the folktales.

The Lesson Plan
   Content area: Drama Theater
   Grade level: 9-12
   Lesson Overview-Overarching Goal: An introduction to genre of folktales and the study of Russian Folktales.
   Lesson Outcomes
   Students will:

• Find the elements of the tale that identify with Russian culture
• Organize their answers into a chart
• Analyze their answers
• Compare their answers with other students
• Adapt Russian folktales to New American folktales

Key question
   What is the importance of folktales in culture?
   The National Standards For Arts Education

Theater (9-12)

Standard 1. Script writing through improvising, writing, and refining scripts based on personal experience and heritage, imagination, literature, and history

Theater (9-12)

Standard 3. Designing and producing by conceptualizing and realizing artistic interpretations for informal or formal productions

Theater (9-12)

Standard 5. Researching by evaluating and synthesizing cultural and historical information to support artistic choices

Theater (9-12)

Standard 6. Comparing and integrating art forms by analyzing traditional theatre, dance, music, visual arts, and new art forms

Materials Needed

A variety of Russian Folktales

Russian Folktale chart (see Table 9.1)

Writing a folktale outline (see Table 9.3)

Uniqueness of the 9-12 learner

The 9-12 learner has three characteristics that this lesson addresses:

1. The students are excited about and already know how to use technology to express their ideas in creative thinking in integrative arts.
2. The students are intrigued at this stage regarding the morals and ethics they are dealing with at their developmental level.
3. The students are engaged in social development, critical thinking, and dialogue to compare and contrast their thoughts with the thoughts of others.

Procedures

Russian Folk Tale Title:	
Characters	Setting
Russian words used	Food or drink mentions
Conflict of the story	Additional cultural references

Table 9.1. Russian Folk Tale Chart.

Pre-Assessment: Have the students write the words and phrases that come to mind when they hear "folktale." The students can then share the words and create a concept map on the white board. The teacher should watch for misconceptions or issues that come up in the understanding of the idea of "folktale."

Engage: Read part of a folktale out loud to the class to engage student interest.

Discussion

1. Allow the students to give examples of folktales, e.g., Paul Bunyan, Pecos Bill, Johnny Appleseed.
2. What are folktales? (Folktales are short, fictional stories that may be set in any time and place, and often teach a moral).
3. Russian Folktales originated among peasants and in the villages. They were part of the oral tradition passed down from generation to generation. Many of the tales were gathered in serial form (from 1855 to 1864) by an ethnographer named Afanas'ev.
4. Have students read at least three Russian folktales. Available online at: Russian-crafts.com/tales.html. (read together out loud, to oneself, or using audio books).
5. Fill out the folktale charts (see Tables 9.1 & 9.2) alone and together as a group (examples can include concept mapping ideas or voting software). The students can have either two copies of each table, or the teacher can have the students create a class one on the board or computer/projector. Have the student select one Russian folktale and one Modern folktale to compare. Formatively assess the accuracy of the charts as the students complete them.
6. Ask students to compare findings of charts.

Probing Questions

- What can be learned from Russia through its folktales?
- How did Russians live in the past?
- What did they eat and drink?
- What were their fears and joys?
- Did the tales have exaggerations, or characters with special abilities?
- Did the stories have morals?
- Did they refer to any historical occurrences?

Culminating Activity

Option 1:

Modern Folk Tale Title:	
Characters	Setting
Russian words used	Food or drink mentions
Conflict of the story	Additional cultural references

Table 9.2. Modern Folk Tale Chart.

Select one Russian folktale that was read. Adapt the folktale to a new American folktale. Look at the elements that are typically "Russian" and think about how students could adapt the tale with typically "American" elements. Use the handout "Outline for Writing A Folktale" (see Table 9.3) to assist in this task.

Option 2:
Break students into groups and have them collaborate to write a script based on one of the folktales studied in class. Act out the folktale to the class using criteria developed by the teacher and students (time, props, costumes, scripts, etc.)

Option 3:
Students use own life experiences to script, plan, and collaborate in a group video or live presentation of a current moral dilemma that would be solved by the moral of the folk tale. The criteria for the scripts and plans will be developed by the teacher and students.

Assessments
Formative: During the discussion and observation of the students reading and interpreting the folk tales, the teacher will make sure they understand the various ideas presented and guide if necessary. The teacher will meet with each group and document the option chosen for assignment and include notes of their progress of the required criteria on the project. Each group will be provided feedback from the teacher based on their progress and team collaboration. The teacher should assess how the workload for each team is being allocated and suggest that the teams review the probing questions at the beginning of the lesson.

Outline for Writing a Folk Tale	
Beginning	1. Introduce the main character 2. Describe the setting 3. Begin the plot
Middle	1. Introduce the character's problem 2. Introduce the minor characters 3. Build toward the point of highest interest
Ending	1. Reach the point of highest interest 2. Wind down the action and give the final outcome

Table 9.3. Outline for Writing a Folk Tale.

Summative: Using the tables (see Tables 9.1 and 9.2) developed during the discussion, students will write 2-3 paragraphs detailing aspects of Russian folktales. The essays should discuss the extent to which Russian folktales reveal elements of Russian culture. The paragraphs are graded on three criteria, identification of morals/ethics in the folktale, comparing and contrasting the folktale to American folktales, and the correct interpretation of the folktales.

Differentiation

Instruction: Have multiple ways for the students to hear/read the folktales. Use technologies such as speech-to-text software, audiobooks, and recording devices to assure the students are understanding the folktales in context. Provide multiple ways and means for instruction. If students are shy or reserved, provide access to a wiki or discussion board to assure each student has a fair voice in the analysis of the folktales. This may require more time for the lesson. Match the students to folktales in regards to their reading level and comfort with literacy.

Assessment: Students may elect to record their analysis rather than write it, as the criteria are the same for both. The student may also show a presentation or draw a picture regarding the similarities and differences in the folktales. When formatively assessing students, the teacher must be able to provide variety to the feedback given to the students (auditory, written, or visual)

REFERENCES FOR LESSON PLAN TWO

Afanasev, A. (1945). *Russian fairy tales.* New York, NY: Pantheon Books.
Chandler, R. (1980). *Russian folk tales*. New York, NY: Random House.
Onassis, J. (Ed.). (1978). *The Firebird and other Russian fairy tales.* New York, NY: Viking Press.
Russian craft tales. (n.d.). Available at http://russian-crafts.com/tales.html.

Lesson Plan Three: A Comparison of Classical and Contemporary Music for Grades 5-8

The third lesson plan focuses on comparing classical and contemporary music in the middle level (5-8) classroom. The lesson plan expects the same outcomes from the students, but it allows the teacher to vary the task for the students by providing ample opportunities for more variance in the depth of analysis due to the types of classical and contemporary music the students pick and are exposed to. Additionally, by having the students choose their own modern music measures, they are able to provide material they find engaging and intriguing. Finally, the teacher provides a detailed pre-assessment for the students to assist in identifying the knowledge and skills the students already have and can be built upon within the discourse and subsequent analysis.

Planning for a lesson like this will need some time and resources. For example, the teacher may provide samples of billboard hits to analyze, rather than make components of the lesson open-ended, to assist struggling students. For the students who can read music, the teacher may also provide sheet music as well. Utilization of drumming or percussion instruments may also help learners with the tempo and pattern of the music, and other students can use music software on the computers to present their interpretations of the assignments. Teachers may also provide opportunities to use appropriate music videos that may be incorporated into the music clips to support the mastery of the material.

Teachers should also vary the type of assessments of the lesson based on the pre-assessment of the students. For example, the students may record their own thoughts for assessment tools and incorporate sounds and music into them to express their ideas. The teacher may also wish to utilize peer assessment strategies within the audio clip presentations and the journals. Criteria for these types of assessments may be created as a class so that each student can understand how to evaluate the work presented.

The Lesson Plan
     Content area: Music
     Grade level: 5-8
     Lesson Overview-Overarching Goal: Students will compare current and classical music to recognize the major and minor keys by sound and identify Italian terms that relate to music tempo
     Lesson Outcomes
     Students will:

- Compare current and classical music as they relate to tempo (allegro and adagio), dynamics (piano and forte) and patterns.

- Discuss tempi and identify the Italian terms that relate to musical tempo.
- Analyze patterns and form in the music given and the music they select.

Key question

What makes music timeless?

The National Standards For Arts Education

Music (5-8)

Standard 6. Listening to, analyzing, and describing music.

Music (5-8)

Standard 9. Understanding music in relation to history and culture.

Materials Needed

Classical music (Vivaldi – The Four Seasons)

Recording devices

Two 11" x 14" cards per student (one with "Piano" and "Forte" on the front and back and one with "Allegro" and "Adagio" on the front and back)

Uniqueness of the Learner

The 5-8 learner, developmentally, is engaged in musical thinking and thoughts. As this lesson engages the learner to compare and contrast their own music with classical music, the teacher is able to connect with the learner's affective network.

Procedure

Pre-Assessment: Group discussion and dialogue regarding students' thoughts on music (both contemporary and classical) and the structures and patterns related to each. Formatively assess the discussion by asking questions of the students to see if there are any issues that may need to be addressed in the lesson.

Engage: Play a piece of contemporary music (Billboard top 10 hit) and ask the students to describe what they have heard.

Discussion:

1. Play the music again and ask the students to listen and describe what they have heard. Have them look for the elements of the music (tempo, dynamics, and patterns)
2. Now listen to Vivaldi (The Four Seasons – Spring) and identify the tempos, dynamics and patterns heard. Put "piano" and "forte" on the board and identify how these relate to the dynamics of music.
3. Write the words "adagio" and "allegro" on the board. Have the students, as they listen to the classical music, read the musical notations of Vivaldi's music and ask if "adagio" is slower or faster then "allegro"
4. Have the students listen to the contemporary music again and have them visually show, using the "adagio" and "allegro" cards, when they believe the tempo and the dynamics are heard.

5. Showing stanzas from the classical music, ask the students if there are patterns that they can see that are similar to the contemporary music.
6. Have students identify a current song to analyze. Each individual student will look for tempo, dynamics, and patterns that are similar to the classical.
7. In small groups, listen to each other's analysis and pick the portions to share with the entire group for each characteristic. Using recording devices, the students will create a two-minute synopsis of the clips of the music to share with the entire class.
8. In the entire group, share the two-minute synopsis that shows similarities in tempo, dynamics, and patterns. The teacher will listen for accuracy and facilitate dialogue with the class.
9. Students will self-assess in journal writing how well they are able to identify tempo, dynamics, and patterns as well as reflect how they collaborated with their group. This journal writing is an open-ended reflection based on directions from the teacher.

Assessment

Formative: Each step outlined in the procedure should be observed based on student understanding. Provide written or verbal feedback during the development of the students' clips of music. Additional practice time or discussion may be needed after formatively assessing the journal. To assess the journal, teachers will read and identify incorrect or misunderstood reflections of the class.

Summative: Students will receive group and individual feedback from the teacher after reading their journal reflections and listening to the clips in class. The journal will be graded based on three criteria, i.e., accuracy of the analysis of the tempo, dynamics, and patterns.

Differentiation

Instruction: The teacher may provide samples of billboard hits to analyze, rather than make the instruction open-ended, to assist struggling students. The teacher may provide sheet music, as well, for the students who can read music. Utilization of drumming or percussion instruments will, if needed, also help learners with the tempo and pattern of the music. Students can use music software on the computers to present the clips. For visual learners, the use of appropriate music videos may also be incorporated into the clips to show mastery of the material.

Assessment: Students may record their own verbal thoughts for the journal and incorporate sounds and music into a digital recording to express their ideas. Peer assessment can also be integrated within the audio-clip presentations and the journals. Criteria would need to be created as a class so that each student can understand how to evaluate the work presented.

REFERENCE FOR LESSON PLAN THREE

Vivaldi, A. (1723). *Vivaldi: Concerto No. 1 in E major, Op. 8, RV 269, "La primavera".*

CONCLUDING THOUGHTS

The National Standards for Arts Education are a framework to understand the characteristics of the arts and create a vision of what students need to understand and be able to demonstrate in the arts. Differentiating instruction in the arts classroom allows students to be challenged to strive to find success in the arts through a variety of classroom learning experiences.

The educational success of adolescents in the U.S. depends on creating a society that is literate, imaginative, competent, and creative. The arts provide adolescents with the tools not only for understanding the world but also for contributing to it and making it their own. The teacher, of course, is the final expert about how to differentiate in their own personal classroom. Knowing the students and their desire to learn is the first step in overcoming the grand chasm between teaching material and learning material.

In the end, truly successful implementation of differentiation in the arts can only come about when students and their learning are at the center, which means motivating and enabling them to meet the standards. With a steady focus on the learning goals teachers can use the standards to empower students to be successful.

REFERENCES

Brinkman, D. J. (2010). Teaching creatively and teaching for creativity. *Arts Education Policy Review, 111* (2), 48-50.

Consortium of National Arts Education. (2007). *National standards for art education: Dance, music, theatre, and visual arts. What every young American should know and be able to do in the arts.* Reston, VA: Author.

Cornett, C.E. (2003). *Creating meaning through literature and the arts: An integration resource for classroom teachers* (2nd ed.). Upper Saddle River, NJ: Merrill Prentice Hall.

Cornett, C. E. (1999) *The arts as meaning makers: Integrating literature and the arts throughout the curriculum.* Upper Saddle River, NJ: Merrill Prentice Hall.

Goldberg, M. (2006). *Integrating the arts: An approaching to teaching and learning in multicultural and multilingual settings.* Boston, MA: Pearson.

Heacox, D. (2002) *Differentiating instruction in the regular classroom: How to reach and teach all learners, grades 3-12.* Minneapolis, MN. Free Spirit Publishing.

Hollingsworth, P. (2009). "Creative arts and words" in J. F. Smutny and S.E. von Fremd (Eds.), *Igniting creativity in gifted learners K-6: Strategies for every teacher* (p.246-252). Thousand Oaks: Corwin Press.

Landsberger, J. (2007.). *Guidance for teaching pupils gifted and talented in the arts.* Retrieved
    October 1, 2011, from www.creativegeneration.org.uk.
Protheroe, N. (2007). *Differentiating instruction in a standards-based environment.* Retrieved
    October 1, 2011 from www.naesp.org.
Tomlinson, C. A. (2000) *Differentiation of instruction in the elementary grades.* Arlington,
    VA. (ERIC Document Reproduction Services No. ED 443572).
Tomlinson, C. A., (1999). Mapping a route toward differentiated instruction. *Educational
    Leadership, 57* (1). 12-16.
Tomlinson, C.A. (1995). *Differentiating instruction for advanced learners in the mixed-ability
    middle school classroom.* Arlington, VA. (ERIC Document Reproduction Services No. ED
    359370).
Worley, B. B. (2006). Differentiation in the arts; What does this mean? *Understanding our
    Gifted, 18* (3), 3-5.

III

Differentiated Instruction and Other Considerations for Grades 5-12

Chapter Ten

Differentiating Instruction and Teaching for Higher-Level Thinking

The Thinking/Learning (T/L) System

Ervin F. Sparapani & Patricia S. Calahan

INTRODUCTION

It has already been established in previous chapters that the face of education in the United States in the twenty-first century has changed dramatically; and, although some people are advocating for a redesign of instruction and a redesign of schools (for example, Bellanca & Brandt, 2010), classrooms still look the same as they always have. Additionally, the emphasis, of instruction, as discussed particularly in Chapters 3 and 4, is on the standards and benchmarks of a discipline and how those standards and benchmarks are assessed to establish adequate yearly progress.

Further, school districts, for the most part, have restructured their curricula in order to focus specifically on common core standards and how those standards are assessed. Lost in this restructuring, however, is the uniqueness of the students. Teachers understand that students are different, but feel handcuffed by the standards, benchmarks, and high-stakes assessments, which is unfortunate. A way to picture this is the teacher being squeezed between the individual needs of the student and the one-size-fits-all idea that standardized testing implies. The Thinking/Learning (T/L) System discussed in this chapter gives teachers a way to plan lessons that allows for standardized testing scores to increase at the same time as allowing teachers to fulfill their moral and ethical obligation to help each child learn.

Here in the twenty-first century, teachers are faced with a twofold task. First, they must present information to their students in such a way that the students are successful on the high-stakes assessments. Second (as documented by Bellanca & Brandt, 2010), they must prepare students for success in the twenty-first century. The Partnership for Twenty-First Century Skills (Kay, 2010, p. xv) emphasizes higher-level thinking skills (specifically creativity and innovation, critical thinking, and problem solving) as twenty-first century skills that all people need for success.

The focus of this textbook is on differentiated instruction, and the key to a differentiated classroom is that all students are regularly offered choices. This chapter addresses differentiating instruction by presenting a system that differentiates while teaching for higher-level thinking. This system is the Thinking/Learning (T/L) System.

PLANNING FOR THE HIGHER-LEVEL THINKING CLASSROOM

As with anything in a classroom, in order to teach for higher-level thinking, planning is necessary. Often teachers (especially middle school and high school teachers) believe that they already teach for higher-level thinking, but such may not be the case (Nickerson, 1987; Costa, 1991). The first step to teaching for higher-level thinking in a classroom, however, is for teachers to believe that teaching for higher-level thinking is important (Onosko, 1992). Onosko (1992) interviewed teachers who are noted for teaching thinking skills in their classrooms. Such teachers believe that part of their job as a teacher is to teach "thinking." Teachers who do not teach thinking skills are a lot less likely to label part of their job as teaching students to think. Once a teacher makes the choice to teach thinking skills, the T/L System can give them a structure to use in their classrooms, and, in addition, the educational vocabulary to discuss and grow their ideas by sharing with others.

Thinking is hard work, and students often rebel when they have to "think." It is extremely difficult, for example, for a teacher to say "today" that "Tomorrow I am going to begin teaching for higher-level thinking" and have it happen. A mindset must be established in the teacher and in the students that says, "In this class everyone is expected to think, and perform, beyond the minimum," i.e., at higher levels. Before beginning to teach for higher-level thinking, then, teachers must prepare themselves and their students to allow higher-level thinking to be the center piece of instruction. There are three important components to this preparation. One component is to have an appropriate definition of thinking. The second component is establishing a classroom climate that is conducive to and encourages good thinking. The third component is the selection of a cognitive set that serves as a guide for instruction.

Definition of Thinking

In order for teachers to grow in their knowledge of a topic, such as thinking, however, they need to have a common vocabulary (as mentioned previously in the Introduction) by which to frame their ideas and discuss them with others. With this in mind, prior to beginning any lesson planning that teaches for higher-level thinking, a teacher should first have a definition of thinking that they understand, can articulate clearly, and informs their planning, both lesson planning and classroom planning. There are many definitions of thinking available, and some tend to believe that a definition of thinking is obvious; however, when one "thinks" about it, it is not so obvious. For instance, thinking is reflection; thinking is reasoning; thinking is critiquing; thinking is planning; thinking is problem solving; thinking is deciding; thinking is brainstorming; thinking is argument; thinking can (even) be daydreaming; and the beat goes on.

When determining a definition of thinking that "fits," consider what good thinkers do when they think. Glatthorn and Baron (1991) say that good thinkers welcome problematic situations and are tolerant of ambiguity. Good thinkers are self-critical and look for alternate possibilities. Good thinkers are reflective and deliberate. They search extensively for solutions. Good thinkers set goals, but they revise their goals when necessary, based on new information. Good thinkers are open to multiple possibilities, and constantly search for evidence that favors the favorite possibilities while also searching for evidence in opposition to the favored possibilities. In other words, good thinkers behave intelligently (Tishman, Jay, & Perkins, 1992).

That is the definition used with the T/L System, i.e., thinking is behaving intelligently. Behaving intelligently is (1) reasoning before acting, (2) asking questions and gathering information before forging ahead without purpose, (3) listening and hearing before doing. In other words, the person who behaves intelligently (the "good" thinker) can "figure out what to do, when they do not know what to do."

Classroom Environment for Thinking

While a teacher is framing their definition for thinking (which probably will take some "think" time), the teacher must also move forward with preparations for teaching for thinking. The teacher must prepare their students for a "thinking" classroom. To do this, a classroom culture (a classroom environment) must be established in which "thinking" can happen and is expected (Torff, 2011). Creating such a culture, however, which encourages good thinking (what Costa, 1991, refers to as "skillful" thinking) and allows for skillful thinking, takes time and preparation. Teachers need to create a classroom culture where students feel "free" to think (Hart, 2002; Sousa & Tomlinson, 2011).

On the part of the teacher, creating such an environment must be conscientiously deliberative, purposeful, and continuous. Depending on the classroom, this step just does not happen overnight. It can take a great deal of time; however, many teachers are stuck in the syndrome of "getting through the curriculum." For these teachers, taking the "time" to develop a climate for thinking interferes with "getting through the curriculum." If the teacher views the curriculum as a series of unrelated facts and concepts that can be taught with flashcards, then the students will view the curriculum that way too. If the teacher, though, sees the underlying links between the standards and the thinking behind the curriculum, then there is a chance their students will also see the links and learn more. The latter typically happens in a classroom that has a "culture of thinking."

To develop a "culture of thinking" classroom, here are three suggestions that work well, and can readily fit into the "getting through the curriculum" syndrome. The first suggestion is using the "habits of mind" (Costa & Kallick, 2000). Costa and Kallick (2000) have identified sixteen "habits" they believe are keys to skillful thinking. If the habits of mind are used, the teacher must begin by selecting one, and working on that one until it becomes a "habit" with the students. One of the "habits" is "persistence." If the teacher has selected "persistence" as the habit they want their students to use, they will know that "persistence" has become a "habit" when the teacher hears students using, with each other, the language of "persistence." The teacher will also know that "persistence" is becoming a "habit" when other teachers come to them and ask what they are teaching the students, because students are using "habit" language in the other teachers' classrooms, and usually habit language is not the typical student language.

When a "habit" becomes a "habit," the teacher then selects another "habit," while continuing to strengthen the first habit. Once the students have internalized at least three habits they probably have an attitude that allows for higher-level thinking. An atmosphere is now in place in the classroom where higher-level thinking is expected and probably happens on a regular basis.

A second suggestion is using the "thinking dispositions" that support higher-level thinking (Perkins & Tishman, 2010; Tishman & Andrade, n.d.; Tishman, Jay, & Perkins, 1993). Perkins and Tishman (2010, p. 1)) define a thinking disposition as a "tendency toward a particular pattern of intellectual behavior." Tishman, Jay, and Perkins (1993) identify seven dispositional behaviors. They are (1) being broad and adventurous, (2) sustaining intellectual curiosity, (3) clarifying and seeking understanding, (4) being planful and strategic, (5) being intellectually careful, (6) seeking and evaluating reason, and (7) being metacognitive. Perkins and Tishman (2010) claim that often good thinkers may have these dispositions, but may not be "disposed" to use them. Perkins and Tishman (2010) have suggestions for how teachers can develop a classroom environment in which students are disposed towards positive patterns of intellectual behavior. Once these intellectual behaviors become "habits," a classroom environment is in place that allows for and expects higher-level thinking.

The third suggestion (selecting a cognitive set) guides teachers' instructional practice within the classroom culture. The cognitive set must be one that the teacher understands and "fits" their instruction. Several cognitive "sets" (Bloom's taxonomy, Guilford's Structure of the Intellect, and Marzano, Brandt, Hughes, et al.'s core thinking skills) are briefly discussed in the next section.

HIGHER-LEVEL THINKING SKILLS

Before moving to the T/L System it is important to know something about thinking skills. In this section of the chapter, micro-thinking skills and macro-thinking skills are discussed. Micro-thinking skills are thinking skills which are used in the macro-thinking skills. Following the discussion of the micro-thinking skills, five macro-thinking skills will be reviewed that closely align with the partnership for twenty-first century skills (see Kay, 2010). These macro-thinking skills are information gathering, critical thinking, creative thinking, problem solving, and decision making.

Micro-Thinking Skills

The micro-thinking skills are skills such as those found in Bloom's cognitive taxonomy (Bloom, 1956) or Guildford's Structure of the Intellect (Presseisen, 1991). The micro-thinking skills are skills used in the macro-thinking skills (discussed below). Micro-thinking skills are skills considered basic (or essential) to good thinking.

Bloom's cognitive taxonomy has six levels (or cognitive categories), which include three lower-level thinking skills (knowledge, comprehension, application) and three higher-level thinking skills (analysis, synthesis, evaluation). Bloom's taxonomy is a main part of the T/L System, and is discussed in more detail later in the chapter.

Guilford's Structure of the Intellect (often referred to as Guilford's "cube") also has six levels (or cognitive categories), which include three lower-level thinking skills (units, classes relations) and three higher-level thinking skills (systems, transformations, implications). Guilford has taken the six categories and developed them into a cube that displays 120 possible ways of thinking. "Guilford is interested in both convergent and divergent operations, and his ultimate goal is a thorough exposition of the nature of intelligence" (Presseisen, p. 57).

A third set of micro-thinking skills is the "core thinking skills" introduced by Marzano, Brandt, Hughes, et al. (1988). Marzano, et al. provide eight core thinking skills, which are similar to those provided by Bloom and Guilford. The "core" thinking skills of Marzano, et al. include focusing skills, information gathering skills, remembering skills, organizing skills, analyzing skills, generating skills, integrating skills, and evaluating skills.

Macro-Thinking Skills

The macro-thinking skills are those thinking skills considered paramount to good thinking. For people to be successful in the 21st century, both in school and in the world, they must be proficient with the macro-thinking skills. Such skills include information gathering, critical and creative thinking, problem solving, and decision-making. Many who write about teaching thinking (e.g., Beyer, 1988; Baron & Sternberg, 1987; Halpern, 2003) believe that students should be explicitly taught the procedures for using each of the macro-thinking skills. The writers of this chapter agree with that. Some students seem to have the innate ability to gather the necessary information, to think critically or creatively, to problem solve adequately, or to make decisions appropriately. This, however, is not the case for all students. Most students need to be "taught" how to think, and this "teaching" needs to be done in the context of learning, not in isolation. What follows is a brief explanation of each of the macro-thinking skills.

Information Gathering

Information gathering addresses prior knowledge (remembering) and current (or new) knowledge. Information gathering, as a thinking skill, has the main function of determining what is already known about a subject and what needs to be known (current and future knowledge). Information gathering is used primarily to identify a body of information and understanding that information (the knowledge level in Bloom's taxonomy). Comprehension (working with knowledge to interpret and explain that knowledge), selecting (choosing the information needed), and classifying (ordering or categorizing the information) are also basic to information gathering. Information gathering is used to develop a knowledge base about a subject by remembering what has already been learned and then connecting that prior knowledge to new (or current) knowledge. The learner must have the necessary information (knowledge) to function adequately with the higher-level thinking skills, i.e., critical thinking, creative thinking, problem solving, decision making. For more on information gathering see Marzano, et al. (1988).

Critical Thinking

Critical thinking is one of the primary (perhaps the primary) higher-level thinking skills. Critical thinking involves deliberate analysis by using reasoning and judgment. It is judging the authenticity, worth, or accuracy of information. There are many important critical thinking skills. Critical thinking includes distinguishing between information that is verifiable fact and information that is value or opinion laden. Critical thinking is also necessary to distinguish information that is irrelevant. Critical thinking is necessary to determine the factual accuracy of a statement.

Critical thinking is an extremely important twenty-first century skill to develop, especially since people can use a search engine on the internet and get thousands of hits on a topic. While the internet has brought everyone to a large marketplace of ideas, it has also brought the need to develop the ability to reason and make a judgment about those ideas. In the past, editors (of books and magazines) serve as gatekeepers and only allow "worthy" information to be published for all to see. Now, however, all people need to develop the skills (the critical thinking skills) to be their own "editor."

Critical thinking is a close examination of information. Such an examination is used to determine the credibility of a source, to identify false or ambiguous claims or arguments, to detect bias or unstated assumptions, to recognize logical inconsistencies in reasoning, and to determine the strengths and weaknesses of an argument. Additionally, critical thinking is used to summarize quantitative information, grasp relationships between ideas, understand abstract critical elements in thinking, evaluate causal connections, and evaluate the relevance of data.

Creative Thinking

Creative thinking is the process of generating original or new thoughts, designs, or products. Creative thinking is inventive thinking, e.g., thinking "out of the box." Creative thinking is divergent thinking, i.e., working at the edge of one's competence. Interestingly, creative thinking is fairly close to the kinds of thinking used in problem solving. Perkins (1991) identifies three components for creative thinking. These are (1) ideational fluency (the ability to produce large numbers of appropriate ideas quickly and easily), (2) remote associates (the ability to retrieve information only remotely associated with the problem at hand, like "playing" detective), and (3) intuition (the ability to reach sound conclusions from minimal evidence).

There are four strategies important to strong creative (inventive) thinking. These are problem finding (paying attention to what problems should be addressed before attempting to solve a problem), using long searches (deferring closure and considering many alternatives), finding analogies, and brainstorming.

Creative thinking is required in a world where the high rate of change in society and technology requires that new ideas be developed because, in a constantly changing world, many ideas of the past no longer work. The development of creative thinking is closely related to the next section on problem solving.

Problem Solving

Problem solving is used where there is a "correct" answer and there is consensus about what that "correct" answer is. There are five main steps in problem solving. These are (1) recognizing that a problem exists (which is similar to problem finding), (2) representing the problem in an understandable way, (3) devising or selecting a plan to solve the problem, (4) executing and monitoring the plan as it unfolds, and making revisions as necessary, and (5) evaluating the results.

Decision Making

Decision making is evaluative, and used in situations which have a number of possible or workable answers to a particular situation. There are six main steps in decision making. These are (1) define the goal, or issue, to which an answer is needed, (2) identify alternatives for resolving the issue, (3) analyze/discuss the alternatives, (4) rank the alternatives, (5) evaluate/judge the highest ranked alternatives, and (6) choose and implement the one "best" alternative.

Everyone needs the micro-thinking skills to function adequately in the macro-thinking skills. The five macro-thinking skills explained above are all interrelated. The T/L System gives a way to combine these ideas into a workable differentiated instruction system for teachers to use in their classrooms.

DIFFERENTIATING INSTRUCTION AND THE T/L SYSTEM

Students and adults take in new information from their environments all the time. A teachers responsibility is to develop a classroom that gives the students good information to process and an environment that encourages them to explore the new information in a variety of ways.

Along with learning the basics of a subject, they need to learn how to construct their own knowledge while receiving information from the teacher (Friend & Bursuck, 2009). A rigorous yet appropriate curriculum will keep students engaged and motivated. A vital aspect to a successful, rigorous curriculum is the full implementation and encouragement of lessons based in higher-level thinking (Torff, 2011).

The T/L System differentiates instruction by designing lessons that focus on the five essential factors that must be considered when differentiating instruction and the three areas for differentiating instruction (see Chapter 2). With the T/L System, specific focus is placed on the uniqueness of the learner (a concern of teachers) and on higher-level thinking (a twenty-first century concern).

The T/L System has three interwoven components. Bloom's cognitive taxonomy is one component, which is selected because teachers are familiar with it and it "fits" the T/L System. A second component is the thinking skills, i.e., information gathering, critical thinking, creative thinking, and decision making. A third component addresses left-, right-, and whole-brain functioning.

The T/L System differentiates instruction by coupling specific levels of Bloom's cognitive taxonomy (knowledge/comprehension, application/synthesis, analysis, and evaluation) with four higher-level thinking skills (information gathering, critical thinking, creative thinking, and decision making) and left-, right-, and whole-brain modes of brain functioning.

The T/L System Conceptual Framework

The T/L System is conceptualized so that learners not only obtain a body of relevant knowledge (information gathering), they also process that knowledge in ways that engage them in higher-level thinking, i.e., critical thinking, decision making, and creative thinking. The T/L System conceptual framework (see Figure 10.1) shows how each of the thinking skills is linked to levels of Bloom's taxonomy. The conceptual framework also shows the tasks a learner is expected to perform for each of the thinking skills, and what the results are expected to be for each of the thinking skills. Fischer and Heikkinen (2010) capture this framework wonderfully. They say that learners conceive of information not as a ladder, building form one idea to the next, but as a web of independent strands or learning pathways.

It is important to remember that the T/L System conceptual framework displays the connections of thinking skill to taxonomy to task to result. The conceptual framework, however, does not show how the elements of the system function together. The conceptual framework, as shown in figure 10.1, appears linear and sequential; however, in practice it is neither linear nor sequential.

Understanding the Conceptual Framework

When designing the T/L System, Edwards and Sparapani (1994) have in mind how the brain processes information. The brain does not process information in a linear and sequential manner. A brain processes information in a

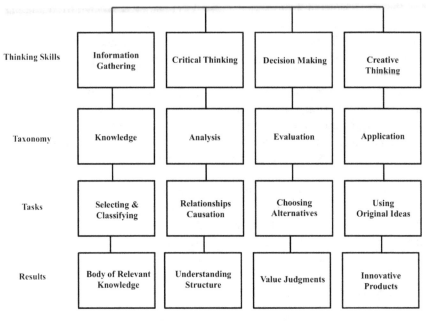

Figure 10.1. Conceptual Framework of the Thinking/Learning (T/L) System

manner that makes sense to that brain, and that brain only. That being said, a brain processes information in a manner that is random and non-linear. For example, right now, you are reading this page. You are gathering and processing the information, which is acquiring knowledge. At the same time, though, you are trying to make sense of the information (comprehension); you are judging the worth of the information (evaluation); and you are trying to decide (perhaps) how the information might be used (application). You are not thinking, "I am learning some knowledge. Now I need to understand it (comprehension). Now I need to apply it in some way (application), and, oh yes, now I have to think at higher-levels with it. I have to analyze it, synthesize it, and evaluate it." That's not the way the brain works with information. The brain automatically "jumps" randomly from knowledge and comprehension to evaluation to analysis to application and back to knowledge. This is experienced by teachers in classrooms when a student asks the teacher, "Why do we need to learn this?"

Edwards and Sparapani believe that Bloom's cognitive taxonomy is the most consistent with how the brain processes information, and how the T/L System functions. Bloom's cognitive taxonomy does not have to be thought of as either linear or sequential, which is the way it is usually understood by teachers, and the way it is typically used when teachers design lessons. To be consistent with how the brain processes information, Bloom's cognitive taxonomy can be imagined more like an atom. An example of how this can be "seen" is in figure 10.2.

At the center of an atom is a small, but heavy nucleus (knowledge/comprehension in the figure) with a cloud of tiny fast-moving electrons (application, analysis, synthesis, evaluation in the figure) orbiting around the nucleus. The nucleus also may have neutrons and protons (additional knowledge and comprehension).

The atom analogy is a good one because it shows how natural and fast-paced the thinking process is when new information comes into the brain. Making judgments and analyzing information and other important thinking skills are necessary for survival. Therefore, a teacher's job is to highlight the

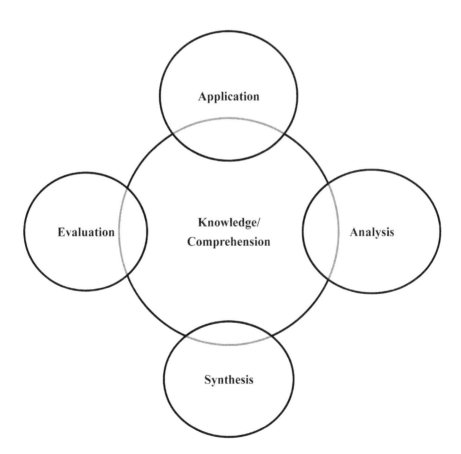

Figure 10.2. Bloom's Cognitive Taxonomy.

skills that students already have and further develop the skills necessary for success in the 21st century.

In an attempt to be "brain-based," and similar to the image of Bloom's cognitive taxonomy, Edwards and Sparapani have conceptualized the T/L System like a wheel. This "wheel" is explained in the next section.

How the T/L System Works

T/L System lessons differentiate instruction in such a way that the uniqueness of the learner is addressed while the learner gains a body of relevant knowledge and uses that knowledge to think at higher levels. Gaining the relevant knowledge (information gathering, the "K" in Figure 10.3) is at the center of the system. In order to use knowledge, the learner must first have the knowledge.

Once information is gathered, however, a teacher often goes to a new set of information, rather than engaging the student in higher-level thinking activities about the information already provided. With the T/L System, the students, after acquiring the information, are introduced to a path that leads to the perimeter of the wheel. Once students are on the perimeter, they never come back to the center, except to always use the information learned by thinking critically (analysis, "A^{1}" on Figure 10.3) and creatively (application/ synthesis, "A^{2}" on Figure 10.3), and making decisions (evaluation, "E" on Figure 10.3) about the worth of the knowledge. The teacher navigates the students around the perimeter of the wheel in any direction the teacher chooses. For instance, the teacher can go down the decision-making path to "E," stop there and have the students use the information by doing a decision-making activity.

To move the students from the center to the perimeter, and then around the perimeter of the wheel, the teacher poses appropriate questions. In order to get students to begin thinking in a decision making fashion, for instance, the teacher asks an evaluative question about the information. Once the learners have completed a decision-making activity, the teacher then must decide which direction to move the students next, either counter clockwise to critically think about the information or clockwise to creatively think about the information. The teacher asks a question about the information, then, that gets the students to begin thinking either critically or creatively.

Also, at each stop on the wheel, there is a "c," an "o" and a "p." The "c" is for content and context. The "o" is for outcome. The "p" is for process and product.

When teaching a T/L System lesson, the teacher must consider the "c" first, which is the content of the discipline and the context in which the instruction is to take place. Both content (the information to be taught) and the context (the "climate" of either the real world or the classroom) need to

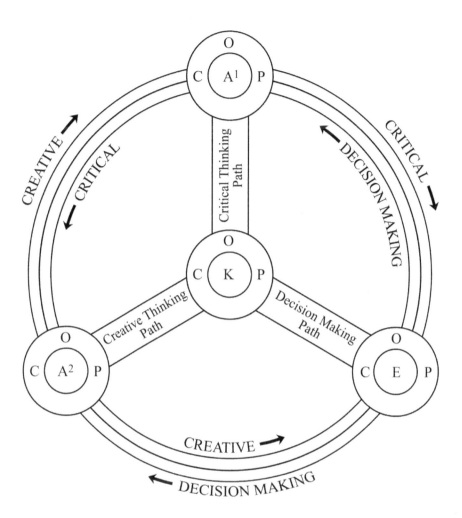

Figure 10.3. The Thinking/Learning (T/L) System Model.

be aligned appropriately. Outcomes (the "o") address lesson objectives and content area standards and benchmarks. All T/L activities must focus on the lesson objective(s) and lead to an in-depth understanding of the specific standards and benchmarks linked to the lesson. The processes and products (the "p") allow for differentiation among students. All processes in the T/L System need to address the essential questions of the lesson's unit and (1) be brain-based, (2) be at the appropriate level of Bloom's cognitive taxonomy, and (3) engage the students in skillful higher-level thinking. Further, each activity needs to result in a tangible product that demonstrates what students have learned.

The T/L System and Assessment

The culture of education today expects that teachers pay close attention to assessment. For instruction to be effective, however, it is imperative that assessment is done appropriately and consistently. Assessments need to not only address the objectives of a lesson and the essential questions of a unit, but the standards and benchmarks of the discipline as well. For the T/L System to effectively differentiate instruction, both formative and summative assessments are necessary. It is recommended that alternative assessments be used more often than traditional assessments.

Alternative assessments allow students to use their strengths to prove their understanding of the subject matter rather than being forced to comply with a very structured testing method that may only encourage one type of thinking and simple regurgitation of facts (Wolk, 1994). A powerful intellect is at the very heart of understanding both the content and context of information. A powerful intellect is the knowledge that allows a person to innovate, to think creatively, and to see issues from multiple perspectives, and find multiple solutions. In the 21st century, a powerful intellect may be the most important educational tool a teacher can teach a student.

Alternative assessments (like peer evaluations, exit cards, portfolio checks, journal entries, demonstrations) are excellent assessment tools. A reminder, though, is that when using alternative assessments, it is important expectations be made clear (as in a rubric), since many students are not used to alternative assessment. Rubrics are very helpful to students, and as teachers develop a rubric, the assignment often becomes clearer to the teacher.

Planning a T/L System Lesson

To plan a T/L System lesson, the teacher needs a lesson plan and "The Teaching/Learning (T/L) System Activities Selection Sheet." The "Activities Selection Sheet" can be seen in Table 10.1. A T/L System lesson is planned to be, ideally, one class period long. In practice, however, a T/L System lesson can last between one and three class periods.

The "Activities Selection Sheet" is used to engage students in thinking about the information that the teacher wants learners to understand. The "Activities Selection Sheet" is not the lesson plan. It is to be understood like a workbook, or, more accurately, a set of options the teacher can use to engage learners in higher-level thinking about the information found in the lesson.

The "Activities Selection Sheet" has six components. Component 1 includes the subject and the unit topic. Component 2 includes the standards and benchmarks that are addressed in the lesson. Component 3 includes the essential unit questions that focus the unit and the lesson, and, most specifical-

Subject:		Unit topic:	
Standards / benchmarks:			
Essential unit question(s):			
Lesson objective(s):			
Introduction:			
Activities			
	Information gathering activities	All learners participate in all information gathering activities.	
Of the following, learners participate in at least one in-class activity from each higher-level thinking area; additionally, one activity from one of the sections can be used as a homework assignment. Teachers select a different activity (left-, right-, or whole-brain dominant) in each section. The teacher can assign the homework or allow for learner selection.			
	Critical thinking activities	1. Left-brain dominant activity 2. Right-brain dominant activity 3. Whole-brain dominant activity	
	Decision making activities	1. Left-brain dominant activity 2. Right-brain dominant activity 3. Whole-brain dominant activity	
	Creative thinking activities	1. Left-brain dominant activity 2. Right-brain dominant activity 3. Whole-brain dominant activity	

**Table 10.1. The Teaching/Learning (T/L) System Activities Selection Sheet. ©
Edwards & Sparapani, 1993.**

ly, the assessments. Component 4 is the objective(s) for the lesson. Component 5 is the introduction to the set of activities. Primarily, the introduction is used to start the learners thinking about the lesson and the activities. Component 6 (the main component of the "Activities Selection Sheet") is the set of thinking activities that engage the learners.

The first set of thinking activities is the information gathering (knowledge/comprehension) activities, followed by the critical thinking (analysis) activities, the decision making (evaluation) activities, and the creative thinking (application/synthesis) activities. Additionally, in each set of activities, the teacher differentiates instruction by having a left-brain dominant activity (all the "a" activities), a right-brain dominant activity (all the "b" activities), and a whole-brain dominant activity (all the "c" activities).

When a teacher teaches a lesson following the T/L System "Activities Selection Sheet," because knowledge and comprehension are central and basic to learning and higher-level thinking, all learners complete the three information gathering activities. The teacher leads the learners through the information gathering activities in a traditional manner, but it is not necessary that the "a" activity lead to the "b" activity which leads to the "c" activity. The activities need to be independent (stand alone) so that they can be completed in any order. The main focus of the activities has to be on the lesson objective(s), which focus on the learning standards and the essential unit questions. Once the three information gathering activities are completed, the teacher moves the learners to the higher-level thinking activities. This is done by navigating to the outer perimeter of the circle (see Figure 10.3).

To complete the lesson, the teacher has learners do one of the critical thinking activities, one of the decision making activities, and one of the creative thinking activities. As with the information gathering activities, the "a," "b," and "c" activities under each higher-level thinking area do not build on each other. They are not ordered or sequential. The only requirements are that the activities are independent (stand alone) and refer back to the knowledge (the information gathering activities). Consequently, with a T/L System lesson, the teacher has, at minimum, three years worth of activities from which to choose.

LESSON EXAMPLES OF DIFFERENTIATING INSTRUCTION USING THE T/L SYSTEM

In this section, two examples of T/L System lessons are provided, a middle level (sixth-grade) science lesson about geological processes and a high school (eleventh-grade) English Language Arts lesson on Frankenstein. Names used in this section are fictitious. Any connection to an actual teacher is purely accidental.

Lesson One. Sixth-Grade Science

Mr. Jones is a sixth-grade science teacher who is expected to teach, as part of the sixth-grade earth science curriculum, the earth's geological processes. Typically, he introduces the sixth graders to the knowledge and then asks them to do a few exercises from a workbook, which is followed by a demonstration of a volcano erupting. Mr. Jones likes his students to work in teams. In fact, students in his classes always sit in groups. Because of that, this year Mr. Jones wants the students to do more than watch him do a demonstration and do exercises in a workbook. He still wants to teach to the standards, but he wants to use instructional practices that engage the students in activities that differentiate and provides them with opportunities to work independently (if they prefer) or with their group members. To do this, he decides to design and implement a T/L System lesson. This sixth-grade science lesson can be seen in Table 10.2.

Earth science: geological process	
Essential questions	How do geologic processes (weathering) affect the world? What effect does weathering of the world have on how people live in the world?
Michigan Grade-Level Content Expectations (based on National Science Standards)	1. E.SE.06.11 Explain how physical and chemical weathering lead to erosion and the formation of soils and sediments. 2. E.ST.06.41 Explain how Earth processes (erosion, mountain building, and glacier movement) are used for the measurement of geologic time through observing rock layers. 3. S.IA.06.12 Evaluate date, claims, and personal knowledge through collaborative science discourse.
Major objective	At the conclusion of the lesson, students will have in depth knowledge of the geologic weathering processes, while displaying deeper analysis and application skills.
Pre-assessment	What processes change the appearance or qualities of the world around us?
Introduction	View a 5-10 minute segment of an appropriate film on weathering and erosion.
Information Gathering (Knowledge/Comprehension)	1. Based on an Earth Science handout about physical and chemical weathering, list and summarize the given examples of physical and chemical weathering. 2. Utilizing the art supplies provided, visually express two of the geological weathering processes of your choice. Captions are allowed, but picture must support/tell the story! 3. Within your current small group complete the handout assignment by labeling the processes, and properly ordering the given supporting steps.
Critical Thinking (Reasoning/Analysis)	1. Based on our reading and discussion, write at least two complete paragraphs on how soil is a product of geological history. 2. As part of a homework assignment or class field trip, take a picture of any geological feature, investigate what conditions have led to its current state, and share with class. 3. Again in your small groups, complete a timeline diagram showing the general "rock cycle."

Table 10.2. Science, 6th Grade. © Edwards & Sparapani, 1993.

Decision Making (Evaluation)	1. Based on local geological landforms, describe the processes that you believe have led to this state. Submissions must be at least two pages in length. 2. Utilizing the magazines and newspapers in class or available in the library, find five articles or illustrations that show the impact of natural earth processes. 3. Working with your small group, complete the age estimation problems of the earth soil layers in the examples provided. Provide reasons/data for your decisions.
Creative Thinking (Application/Synthesis)	1. Based on the content and concepts covered, write a four paragraph (minimum) narrative on what you believe our area will look like in the near term future (ex: 500 years from now), and then in the far future (ex: 1 M years from now). Explain factors evaluated and basis for your conclusions. 2. With your small group, plan, produce, and perform a short play - approximately 5 minutes or less - demonstrating at least two of the weathering processes. At least three students must have roles to play, and only one may narrate! 3. Using the classroom art supplies and poster board provided, illustrate a soil/rock layer of our local area up to the current day, with your estimation of age and composition. For extra credit, add proposed future layers, reflecting global or regional changes you select.
Formative assessment	Completion of Information Gathering Activities
Summative assessment	Completion of final activity

Table 10.2 continued.

Comments on the Sixth-Grade Science Lesson

Notice in this sixth-grade earth science lesson that the activities all provide variety and challenge meant to engage the learner in not only learning about, but thinking about, what happens to the earth's surface as it erodes. The lesson begins with Mr. Jones asking the students (as a pre-assessment) what kinds of weather processes change the appearance of the world around us. This is followed with the students watching a brief segment (5-10 minutes) of an appropriate film that shows the effects of weathering and erosion on the earth's surface. Mr. Jones then begins the actual lesson.

It is important to notice that, in the lesson, all the activities address the essential questions for the lesson/unit as well as the content area standards. None of the activities seem to be "wasted" energy, or having the students "doing something for the sake of doing something" because it is "fun." All the activities are robust activities that are action-oriented, learner- and learning-oriented, and focused on the topic. Additionally, the information gathering activities provide the learners the knowledge needed, while the critical thinking, decision-making, and creative thinking activities engage the learner in skillful higher-level thinking, providing depth of knowledge.

This lesson is designed to last two to three class periods. The first class period addresses information gathering, while the next two class periods has the learners engaged in one each of the critical thinking, decision-making, and creative thinking activities.

Lesson Two. Eleventh-Grade English Language Arts

Mrs. Johnson is an eleventh-grade English Language Arts teacher. Each year, as part of the eleventh-grade English Language Arts curriculum, she teaches the novel *Frankenstein* (Shelley, 2000). This year, in addition to having the students read and discuss the elements of the novel, she decides to have the students grapple with the ethics of technology by getting the students to think about the role technology plays in their own lives. To do this she wants to differentiate instruction by using a higher-level thinking approach. She designs a T/L System lesson. This eleventh-grade English Language Arts lesson can be found in Table 10.3.

Comments about the Eleventh-Grade English Language Arts Lesson

As with the sixth-grade science lesson, notice that the activities in this English Language Arts lesson all provide variety and challenge meant to engage the learner in not only learning about, and thinking about, the novel, but the ethical uses of technology. The lesson begins with Mrs. Johnson asking the students (as a pre-assessment) four focusing questions about the role technology plays in people's lives, with special emphasis on how technology improves people's lives and the trade-offs people make for that improvement. Mrs. Johnson then begins the actual lesson by introducing the students to Mary Shelley (the author of *Frankenstein*) and the novel itself. Additionally, she has the students complete a survey she has made about the uses of technology, and then has the students watch a history channel documentary about the search for the "real" Frankenstein.

It is important to notice that, in the lesson, as with the sixth-grade earth science lesson, all the activities address the essential questions for the lesson/unit as well as the content area standards. None of the activities seem to be "wasted" energy, or having the students "doing something for the sake of doing something" because it is "fun." All the activities are robust activities

Frankenstein and technology	
Essential questions	What role does technology play in the lives of people? Are all uses of technology ethical?
Common Core Standards for ELA	1. Reading (9): Demonstrate knowledge of eighteenth, nineteenth, and early-twentieth-century foundational works of literature. 2. Writing (7): Conduct short as well as more sustained research projects. 3. Writing (10): Write routinely over an extended time frame (a single sitting or a day or two) for a range of tasks, purposes, and audiences. 4. Speaking and Listening (1): Initiate and participate effectively in a range of collaborative discussions (one-on-one, in groups, and teacher-led) with diverse partners in grades 11-12 topics, texts, and issues, building on others' ideas and expressing their own clearly and persuasively.
Major Objective	Students will start thinking critically about the role technology plays in their own lives.
Pre-assessment focus questions	1. What role does technology play in sustaining human life? 2. What issues are involved in creating, lengthening, & bettering life? 3. What is technology's role in society? 4. What are the trade-offs for technological advances?
Introduction	1. Read "Meet Mary Shelley" & "Introducing the Novel." 2. Students will complete a brief survey about the uses of technology. 3. Students will watch the first 10 minutes of the History Channel documentary titled, *In Search of the Real Frankenstein* to pique student interest regarding the themes of science and technology in Shelley's *Frankenstein*.
Information Gathering (Knowledge/Comprehension)	1. Create an outline that lists a minimum of 3 purposes/reasons for using technology today. Next, please list a minimum of 2 specific examples/pieces of technology that we utilize for each purpose. 2. With a partner, draw three "computer icons" - each icon displaying a different form of technology in today's society. 3. With a partner, create a timeline with illustrations that shows the progression/chronological order of technology inventions; list all examples that you can recall from early childhood to now.

Table 10.3. English 11. © Edwards & Sparapani, 1993.

Critical Thinking (Reasoning/Analysis)	1. Based on what we have learned, discuss in groups & be prepared to explain whether or not the advancement of technology outweigh the abuses. Record your answers on a "T" chart. 2. With a partner, create a collage of magazine picture/clippings that examines the various uses of technology today (i.e. preventing/curing diseases, cloning, communication) and examine what life would be like today if one of these items on your collage didn't exist. Your collage must include a minimum of 10 pictures; no white space should be showing. 3. Create a poster with 10 pictures from the Internet and/or magazines that show today's uses of technology. Paste each picture under the correct category (Using Technology for Beneficial Purposes vs. Abusing Technology) and discuss the items under each category in small groups.
Decision Making (Evaluation)	1. Write a one-paragraph journal entry addressing why we, as human beings, should be mindful of technology's role in society. 2. Create a storyboard, including 6 slides, that shows the potential consequences if one piece of today's technology was non-existent. 3. Decide which piece of technology is the most beneficial in today's society as a whole & create an illustrated concept map that shows a minimum of 6 uses for that piece of technology. Share your concept map with another student, and then choose one to share with the whole class.
Creative Thinking (Application/Synthesis)	1. Create an outlined plan that you will present to the high school principal that provides ways in which technology could be used to improve the school. 2. Create a PowerPoint presentation to be presented to the school board with ways that technology could be used to improve the facilities in the high school library. 3. With a partner, select 1 type of technology that is both beneficial to and abused by teenagers. Prepare a 5-10 minute debate that you will hold in small groups. You must create a visual to go along with your debate.
Formative Assessment	Completion of Information Gathering Activities
Summative Assessment	Completion of final activity

Table 10.3 continued.

that are action-oriented, learner- and learning-oriented, and focused on the topic. Additionally, the information gathering activities provide the learners the knowledge needed, while the critical thinking, decision-making, and creative thinking activities engage the learner in skillful higher-level thinking, providing depth of knowledge.

This lesson is designed to last about four to five class periods. The first two class periods address information gathering, while the next two or three class periods will have the learners engaged in one each of the critical thinking, decision-making, and creative thinking activities.

A third example of a T/L System lesson (another English Language Arts lesson) can be found in Chapter 5 (see Lesson 3 on *To Kill A Mockingbird*). Examples of T/L System lessons can also be found in Sparapani (2000).

WHAT TEACHERS SAY ABOUT THE T/L SYSTEM

After planning T/L System lessons, and using them in their classrooms, teachers have made comments like:

- It takes time to learn the T/L System, but once learned it is well worth it.
- It takes some time to plan the first two or three T/L System lessons, but after that the planning moves along quite smoothly.
- T/L System lessons take time to plan. Because of that a teacher may not want to design more than three or four T/L System lessons a semester.
- It is great to know that once a T/L System lesson is designed a teacher has twelve different activities from which to choose, enough for at least three-years worth of lessons.
- T/L System lessons seem to differentiate. When T/L System lessons are used, more students are actively engaged in the learning. Students who normally sit and watch or do nothing are involved and participating.
- The T/L System has high expectations for students and more than cover state-mandated standards and benchmarks.
- The T/L System gets both students and teachers to think at higher levels.

CONCLUDING THOUGHTS

Teachers typically agree that differentiated instruction addresses the needs of diverse learners. Teachers feel a legal and moral/ethical obligation to all the students in their classrooms. These same teachers, though, may have concerns about differentiated instruction. One concern is with how appropriately differentiated instruction addresses state-mandated standards and benchmarks for which teachers are held accountable based on the high-stakes tests of NCLB. Some teachers believe that differentiated instruction does not do an adequate job of addressing these state mandates.

A second concern is that differentiated instruction does not necessarily lead to higher-level thinking. Teachers who have this perception see differentiated instruction as "play" or "dumbing down" the curriculum. Other teachers believe that whether or not they use differentiated instruction practices, their students still are not able to think at higher levels and teachers, therefore, should spare these students the frustration (Zohar, 2003).

One way to address the concerns teachers have with differentiated instruction is to intentionally design lessons that teach for higher-level thinking. A process that differentiates and speaks to the concerns teachers may have with differentiated instruction, and provides rich, robust learning experiences, is the Thinking/Learning (T/L) System described in this chapter.

The T/L System differentiates instruction by deliberately concentrating on teaching for higher-level thinking. The T/L System differentiates instruction by combining specific levels of Bloom's cognitive taxonomy (i.e., knowledge/comprehension, analysis, evaluation, application/synthesis) with four higher-level thinking skills (information gathering, critical thinking, creative thinking, decision making) and left-, right-, and whole-brain modes of functioning. Each T/L System lesson includes the four levels of Bloom's taxonomy, the four higher-level thinking skills, and the modes of brain functioning. When a T/L System lesson is designed, the teacher has a total of twelve lesson activities from which to choose.

The purpose of the T/L System is to provide a mechanism for teachers to provide learners with a knowledge base of information and then, by using a variety of activities, moving learners to think at higher-levels about that information. Additionally, the T/L System is branching and cyclical (similar to the random manner by which the brain processes information), unlike most lesson designs (which tend to be linear and sequential).

The recommended procedure to teach a T/L System lesson is to do all the information gathering activities (so the learners "learn" the necessary knowledge base), followed by one of each of the activities from the other thinking skill sections. From the three remaining sections, the teacher selects a left-brain activity in one section, a right-brain activity in a second section, and a whole-brain activity in the third section. The result is that the learners experience six of the twelve possible activities. In effect, the teacher has a differentiated lesson with three-year's worth of activities.

Living in a generation of instant success, answers can be readily found at the click of a mouse. It may be the right answer, or it may be the wrong answer. The link between intellectual character and moral character (Tishman, 1995) is one on which teachers need to reflect. Having students think for themselves is a point that every teacher should make for the sake of the individual student and the future of the nation/world. Students oftentimes take what teachers say as the sole truth, and believe that the teacher is the sole provider of knowledge. Providing the students opportunities to seek their own insights, not only promotes an academic environment, but also promotes a higher level of thinking. Teachers need to move beyond the basics of Bloom's cognitive taxonomy. Higher levels of thinking are an essential life skill and a key element in a rigorous curriculum (Torff, 2011). Encouraging students to think rationally builds higher-order thinking skills, a real-world application of knowledge.

REFERENCES

Baron, J. B. & Sternberg, R. J. (1987). *Teaching thinking skills: Theory and practice.* New York, NY: W. H. Freeman and Company.

Bellanca, J. & Brandt, R. (Eds.). (2010). *21 st century skills: Rethinking how students learn.* Bloomington, IN: Solution Tree Press.

Beyer, B. K. (1988). *Developing a thinking skills program.* Nedham Heights, MA: Allyn and Bacon, Inc.

Bloom, B. S. (Ed.). (1956). *Taxonomy of educational objectives: Book 1 Cognitive domain.* New York, NY: Longman Inc.

Costa, A. L. (Ed.). (1991). *Developing minds: A resource book for teaching thinking* (Revised ed. Vol.1). Alexandria, VA: Association for Supervision and Curriculum Development.

Costa, A. L. & Kallick, B. (2000). *Discovering & exploring habits of mind.* Alexandria, VA: Association for Supervision and Curriculum Development.

Edwards, P. & Sparapani, E. F. (1994). *The thinking/learning system: A brain-compatible strategy for effective teaching of higher-order thinking and learning.* Arlington, VA. (ERIC Document Reproduction Service No. ED 374 396)

Fischer, K. W. & Heikkinen, K. (2010). The future of educational neuroscience. In D. A. Sousa (Ed.). *mind, brain, & education: Neuroscience implications for the classroom*, pp. 248-269. Bloomington, IN: Solution Tree Press.

Friend, M. & Bursuck, W. D. (2009). *Including students with special needs.* Upper Saddle River, NJ: Pearson Education Inc.

Glatthorn, A. A. & Baron, J. (1991). The good thinker. In A. L. Costa (Ed.). *Developing minds: A resource book for teaching thinking* (Revised ed. Vol. 1), pp. 63-67. Alexandria, VA: Association for Supervision and Curriculum Development.

Halpern, D. F. (2003). *Thought & knowledge: An introduction to critical thinking* (4th ed.). Mahwah, NJ: Lawrence Erlbaum Associates, Publishers.

Hart, L. A. (2002). *Human brain & human learning* (3rd ed.). Covington, WA: Books for Educators, Inc.

Kay, K. (2010). 21st century skills: Why they matter, what they are, and how we got there. In Bellanca, J. & Brandt, R. (Eds.). (2010). *21 st century skills: Rethinking how students learn*, (pp. xiii-xxxi). Bloomington, IN: Solution Tree Press.

Marzano, R. J., Brandt, R. S., Hughes, C. S., Jones, B. J., Pressiesen, B. Z., Rankin, S. C., & Suhor, C. (1988). *Dimensions of thinking: A framework for curriculum and instruction.* Alexandria, VA: Association for Supervision and Curriculum Development.

Nickerson, R. S. (1987). Why teach thinking? In *Teaching thinking skills: Theory and practice.* J. B. Baron & R. J. Sternberg (Eds.), pp. 27-37. New York, NY: W. H. Freeman and Company.

Onosko, J. J. (1192) Exploring the thinking of thoughtful teachers. *Educational Leadership, 49* (7), 40-43.

Perkins, D. N. (1991). What creative thinking is. In A. L. Costa (Ed.). *Developing minds: A resource book for teaching thinking* (Revised ed. Vol. 1), pp. 85-88. Alexandria, VA: Association for Supervision and Curriculum Development.

Perkins, D. N. & Tishman, S. (2010). *Patterns of thinking.* Available at www.pz.harvard.edu/Research/PatThk.htm.

Presseisen, B. Z. (1991). Thinking skills: Meanings and models revisited. In A. L. Costa (Ed.). *Developing minds: A resource book for teaching thinking* (Revised ed. Vol. 1), pp. 56-62. Alexandria, VA: Association for Supervision and Curriculum Development.

Shelley, M. (2000). *Frankenstein.* New York, NY: Signet Classics, New American Library.

Sousa, D. A. & Tomlinson, C. A. (2011). *Differentiation and the brain: How neuroscience supports the learner-friendly classroom.* Bloomington, IN: Solution Tree Press.

Sparapani, E. F. (2000). The effect of teaching for higher-level thinking: An analysis of teacher reactions. *Education, 121* (1), 80-89.

Tishman, S. (1995). *The concept of intellectual character and its connection to moral character.* Arlington, VA. (ERIC Document Reproduction Number ED 386 618)

Tishman, S. & Andrade, A. (n.d.). *Thinking dispositions: A review of current theories, practices, and issues.* Available at www.learnweb.harvard.edu/alps/thinking/docs/Dispositions.pdf.

Tishman, S., Jay, E., & Perkins, D. N. (1993). Teaching thinking dispositions: From transmission to enculturation. *Theory into Practice, 32* (3), 147-153.

Torff, B. (2011). Teacher beliefs shape learning for all students. *Phi Delta Kappan, 93* (3), 21-23.

Wolk, S. (1994). Project-based learning: Pursuits with a purpose. *Educational Leadership, 52* (3), 42-45.

Zohar, A. (2003). Higher order thinking skills and low-achieving students: Are they mutually exclusive? *The Journal of the Learning Sciences, 12* (2), 145-181.

Chapter Eleven

Using Technology to Differentiate Instruction

Amy M. Cooper & C. Rodney Williams

INTRODUCTION

Technologies surround us everywhere we look, at home, at work, while shopping, and in advertisements. It seems that almost every day there is a new technological device claiming to make our life easier, more productive, more entertaining, or more streamlined. Given the general public's fascination with these tools, it is no wonder that technology integration has become a 'buzz' word in educational conversations as well. Educational professionals, attempting to stay ahead of the curve, are working to understand the educational value and possible incorporation of many types of technologies into their classrooms. They are motivated by promises of increased student engagement, individualized pacing, and the ability to teach skills essential in today's world (Richtel, 2011).

The concept of differentiating instruction is also current in educational circles, and as with technology, it is likely here to stay (Smith & Throne, 2007). Previous chapters have shown the need for, and value of, differentiating instructional practices and activities in the classroom. Chapter 2 highlights three key principles to differentiated instruction. These key principles include (1) the reality that students differ in how they learn, (2) classrooms that foster active learning and problem solving are more effective, and (3) student construction of meaning is important. Offering choices in content, process, and product is a key piece to differentiating instruction, and technology offers tools that can enhance students' choices while also helping them learn 21st century skills. Goals for differentiating instruction may require the use of new tools and resources and may even require a shift in a teacher's personal philosophy or chosen style of presentation. In this chapter, we will explore how numerous technological tools can provide a new framework upon which instruction can be differentiated to meet the needs of diverse learners in the classroom.

A NEW FRAMEWORK

While some teachers justify technology integration for the sole reason that without it today's device-driven students would not be able to learn (Richtel, 2011), we believe a more holistic educational view is necessary. Most research on technology's effects on student learning and achievement are inconclusive, and critics assert that its costs outweigh its possible benefits (Richtel, 2011). Thus, educators are well-served to not consider technology integration in a vacuum, but rather determine how its use fits with the wider goals of education. Before a teacher adds a classroom set of the latest device to their classroom, we believe it is not only valuable, but necessary for them to identify the motivations for including the technology, and the learning goals that will be met through the use of the technology.

November (2010) promotes a clear framework through which teachers can determine the educational value of technology integration. He submits that there are two options; educators either automate, and simply use technology to produce the same educational products as always, or, allow new technologies to informate, or inform and redesign the way teachers 'do' education. The first option provides students the same choices, structure, and growth opportunities as they have had for years in educational systems; the second uses technology as the conduit through which students experience education in ways they likely have not before.

Sharaf and Musawi (2011) further suggest three roles that technology plays in learning. When viewed through the lens of November's (2010) differing frameworks these roles provide powerful perspectives about how technology is currently used in many schools and how it could be used in the future. The first role is management, likely classified as automating in nature, as computers provide for the automation of many systems, such as grades and attendance. The other two roles though, using technology as the medium for providing resources, and using technology as a method of delivering instruction, have the potential to fit within the informating model.

November (2010) best describes the difference between the two systems, "In an automating model, the technology is the vision. In an informating model technology is just the digital plumbing" (p. 4). When teachers automate, the use of technology produces the same student results because the lessons, goals, and learning outcomes do not change, students just use technology to carry out the old activities. As an example, "students [use] the computer as a $1,000 pencil with which to write a five-paragraph essay for a grade" (November, 2011, p. 4).

When teachers informate, however, they consider new ways of teaching and learning and their choice of technology is secondary, based solely on what technological tools best facilitate meeting the new learning goals. Teachers can ask themselves this question, "Do my students use technology because they should use computers in school and it makes some part of our routine easier or do my students use technology because it allows me to carry out new and different learning activities than I have been able to in the past?" November (2010) suggests that the best and only reason to incorporate technology is for the second reason.

Thus, as teachers make daily decisions about methods of instruction, sharing of resources, and assessment options with a goal of reaching the varied needs of all of their students, it only makes sense for them to consider what kind of digital plumbing helps them meet those goals. A variety of technological tools can provide either the method or the means to produce the differentiation teachers want and need to provide in their classrooms. Among the many arguments for incorporating technology into the classroom outlined in the following section, differentiating instruction is perhaps the most compelling.

REASONS TO INCORPORATE TECHNOLOGY

A common justification for including technology in instruction is that students are familiar with technologies; it is their world (Richtel, 2011). Research (e.g., Lenhart, Arafeh, Smith, & Macgill, 2008) finds that 85% of teenagers (aged 12-17) engage in electronic communication at least occasionally; and 94% are using the Internet, 63% on a daily basis. We are confident that a more recent study will show even higher percentages. But while it is true that students use technologies regularly, we do not believe that to be reason enough to incorporate it into the classroom. Another justification is the quickly growing mound of research (e.g., Jiang & McClintock, 2000; Liu & Su, 2011; Page, 2002; Schacter, 1999) legitimizing technology's value. As stated earlier, however, it is equally easy to find critics fearful that technology will not payoff, either monetarily or in increased test scores (Richtel, 2011).

The most convincing argument then is that technology integration can provide the means to meet the goals set forth in Chapter 2. Technological tools, used well, offer support to students' unique ways of learning, provide for a variety of choices in content, methods (process), and product, and create an environment where students can naturally and powerfully make meaning out of what they are learning. Students can create meaningful projects that have a wider audience than just their teacher and have value outside of the school building (Dorricott & Peck, 1994; MacBride & Luehmann, 2008). Technology integration also encourages the necessary 21st century skills of critical thinking, collaboration, and problem solving in students (Johnson & Johnson, 1996; Kafai & Ching, 2001).

CASE STUDIES

While it would be impossible to list all the possible ways that teachers can use technology to provide differentiation in today's classrooms, the following eight case studies will provide a variety of examples from which teachers can build their own technology integration models. (The following names, locations, and activities are fictitious, except in those cases where a citation is offered.)

Case Study 1. Middle School English/Language Arts

Mrs. Gregory believes that her eighth-grade English students need to start learning the process of writing a research paper. She has tried numerous approaches over the past few years but much to her disappointment not only have they resulted in poor papers, but students that are disengaged as well. Her students get bogged down and often lost in the process of outlining, note taking, summarizing, and organizing. Additionally, their synthesizing skills are poor. She is determined not to give up though, as she knows that the skills of researching, evaluating, summarizing, and synthesizing information are necessary 21st century skills, especially given the amount of information students now have access to through the simple click of a mouse (Luterbach & Brown, 2011). When she asks her department chair for ideas he suggests she look into an Internet-based research format called a WebQuest (http://www.webquest.org/index.php). She is intrigued by this idea, does some research of her own, and likes what she finds. She discovers that the goal of WebQuests is to provide direction and guidance to students as they use the Internet as a research tool in their efforts to solve a relevant or real-world problem (Polly & Ausband, 2009). She believes the outline that most Web-Quests follow of an introduction, task, information sources (resources), process, guidance, and conclusion will be helpful to her students since they will be guided step-by-step through the process (Dodge, 1997). Not only do Web-Quests offer a structure, they expand the learning activity by engaging students in multiple ways. WebQuests are more than simple Internet research; they can include interviews, role-playing, or competition, and the creation of newspapers, Power Points, or podcasts. Students practice explaining, describing, comparing, and contrasting in more creative ways. Mrs. Gregory is sold on the idea, but is now worried about how to create one, until she finds multiple WebQuest search engines full of WebQuests created by other teachers. Two such WebQuests can be found at http://www.nelliemuller.com/Junior_High_Webquests.htm and http://www.webquest.org/search/index.php. Now she can hardly wait to choose one and begin!

Identifying the Differentiated Instruction in English/Language Arts

In this case, Mrs. Gregory is struggling to make the research process relevant and interesting to middle school students. Her use of WebQuests provides a solution to this challenge. Students are presented with a relevant purpose and clear procedure for the learning activity which leads to increased student engagement. By using the Internet as the forum for much of the research, Mrs. Gregory is giving her students access to various additional multimedia formats that not only go beyond what a student would easily find at a library, but also provides additional interest to the student (Criswell, 2010). While the outline and process of a WebQuest are clear, other components are less structured, allowing for much student choice. In addition, students can work at their own pace, completing the activities and reviewing the material as much as they need. In some classes teachers may require that WebQuests be completed in groups or teams which provide students valuable practice in the skills of collaboration. Through solving the problem presented in the quest, students are actively learning, and when the quest provides varied activities and formats, it is more likely that something will interest each student.

Case Study 2. High School English/Language Arts

Mr. Ortiz, a tenth-grade English teacher, wants to revamp his unit on informational text. In the past it has been a small unit, including basic lessons in finding main ideas, outlining, and summarizing. But after meeting with his school's Advanced Placement (AP) English teacher he has a new perspective. She shows him how much of the AP curriculum covers informational text, reflecting the reality that much of the reading that students will do beyond high school will be this type.

Mr. Ortiz is now brainstorming new ideas for his unit and has started to look for Internet tools that might support his students in their learning. They tend to be disinterested in informational text, and their lack of engagement leads to poor work products. They struggle to find the main ideas and understand how those ideas fit together. Mr. Ortiz is excited to find two technological tools that he can use in his new unit. First is a tool that he will use as a pre-reading activity. Students will input text passages onto the Wordle website (http://www.wordle.net/) to create a word cloud. This is a visual array of all of the non-common words included in the text passage, displayed in various colors, sizes, and directions. In addition to the visual interest it brings to the text, the aspect that has the potential to be most valuable to Mr. Ortiz's students is that the size of each word in the word cloud is determined by its frequency in the passage. So words that appear more frequently in the text passage will be large, while those that appear less frequently will be small. This clear visual can help students easily identify key words and potentially main ideas as well. When students move into the "during-reading" phase, they will look for sentences that include these key words and start to make meaning out of the text. As a post-reading strategy, Mr. Ortiz plans to have his students use mind- or concept-mapping software (either Inspiration or the free, basic web-based https://bubbl.us/) to diagram how the main ideas of the passage are related. If using Inspiration, this mapping can be turned into a traditional outline with the click of a button. Mr. Ortiz looks forward to using these tools to enhance his unit and provide varied learning activities for his students.

Identifying the Differentiated Instruction in English/Language Arts

Mr. Ortiz uses various Internet and software tools to support students as they make meaning out of what they are reading. For students who struggle with reading comprehension, these tools can help them as they decipher the text and determine important points. In the past, teachers were limited in the formats they could use to share information with students. This is no longer the case. Digital forms of media provide teachers much flexibility, a flexibility that is invaluable in helping to meet students' varied instructional needs (Rose & Meyer, 2002). Not all students learn well from written text; therefore, the visual component that these tools bring to the learning activity will likely be appreciated by many students.

In addition to these benefits, Mr. Ortiz's students will be engaged in their learning because of the pre-, during-, and post-reading strategies he is incorporating into this unit. When students use the Wordle to identify key words before reading, they in essence create for themselves a purpose for their reading. When they move into the during-reading phase they already have an idea of what the passage is about and can focus on the next task of identifying how these words fit together into the main ideas of the text. The post-reading task draws all their learning together and challenges students to identify relationships between ideas. All three of these tasks are important when reading informational text.

Case Study 3. Middle School Mathematics

Mr. Phillips is a veteran seventh-grade mathematics teacher. It seems that every year his students are coming into his classroom with more varied math backgrounds than the year before. While he tries to include interesting activities and lessons in his class, he does not feel that he is meeting the needs of all of his students. Some continue to struggle no matter what he does, while others learn a concept the first time he teaches it and are ready to move on. In trying to teach to the middle, there are days when he believes instead that he is reaching no one.

Mr. Phillips attends a conference about technology and learns about Khan Academy (http://www.khanacademy.org/). This website is a complete resource of videos covering K-12 mathematics, high school science, and some history. It is also equipped with a mathematics knowledge map which organizes practice problems into color-coded topic nodes. When students are proficient in a topic they are directed to the next related topics. Students are only considered proficient when they have completed sufficient practice questions in a row correctly. Along the way students are supported in their learning through short videos and problem hints. There is also a 'Coach' feature that allows students to be monitored by a teacher, parent, or other mentor. When students associate themselves with a coach, their coach can then view detailed statistics about which topics the students are proficient in, what topics they completed the practice for without watching a video, which practice questions they received hints for during answering, how long they spent answering each question, and more. Students' interest in working the practice problems is maximized through a game-like structure where badges are awarded for different levels of success.

Mr. Phillips is eager to start using this resource with his students. He does not intend for it to replace his classroom teaching, but instead as a resource for struggling students and for those who are ready to move on to the next level. If the use of the site proves valuable, he might also choose to have his students watch a video and complete the related practice problems outside of class so that class time can instead be spent either addressing specific student needs one-on-one or with a full-class activity. (This concept is now known as the "flip" model and has been adopted by some school systems.) Since he can monitor their online progress, Mr. Phillips can choose an activity that he can be sure all students can complete successfully.

Identifying the Differentiated Instruction in Mathematics

The format of Khan Academy allows students to work at their own pace, moving ahead or reviewing material as much as they need. While a student is considered proficient after a sufficient number of correct answers, the student can continue to work additional problems in that topic area until the student is comfortable. A student can also return to that topic area later to review.

Mr. Phillips' use of this site mimics what Khan Academy founder Salman Khan (2011) calls the ability to humanize the classroom. Instead of giving the students a one-size-fits-all lecture, students can learn the material at their own pace outside of the classroom and receive individualized help on the areas that they are struggling when they come to the classroom. In this model student ability is measured by proficiency not by timing (whether they understand the material at the same time that everyone else does). Also, when students learn and practice the basics outside of the classroom, class time is freed up for extension and application activities that promote critical thinking and reasoning in students.

Case Study 4. High School Mathematics

Mrs. Wells is in her fifth year of teaching Algebra 2. The first few years were a challenge as she struggled to learn her course content and adopt classroom management strategies that worked for her. Now she finally feels as though she can begin to focus on adding depth to her course. She has always enjoyed math because it 'just makes sense' to her, but has quickly learned that that is not the case for some of her students. In addition, while a number of the students can learn a process and spout out a correct answer, they can rarely explain their mathematical thinking verbally, let alone offer clear mathematical connections to other topics or processes. Mrs. Wells wants to create an activity where students not only show their ability to carry out mathematical processes but must also explain their reasoning. She would also like her students to engage more with each other, asking questions of each other and reaching out to help struggling peers. After reading a convincing article about classroom blogging (MacBride & Luehmann, 2008), Mrs. Wells decides that a class blog might be a promising format through which both of these goals can be met.

She explains to her classes that each day it will be one student's responsibility to record a set of class notes, including key lesson points, examples, and the day's activities and post them on the blog (MacBride & Luehmann, 2008). The post must be detailed enough that an absent student can use the blog post as a catch-up lesson, so the blog has to include not only an outline but also detailed explanations of the processes and most importantly the 'why' behind them. To ensure that students are utilizing this new resource, the next day's blogger will be announced by the current day's blogger at the end of the post. That way, students will be required to read the post to find out if they are responsible for the next day's post.

In addition to the standard blog commenting feature, the blogging site that Mrs. Wells has chosen also has a chat feature in the side column. She encourages her students to use both of these tools to ask questions and clarify their thinking with classmates as they read the blogs. Mrs. Wells is nervous about this new venture because she has never used an Internet tool in the classroom before, but she is also very interested in the potential growth her students might make in their mathematical thinking and reasoning.

Identifying the Differentiated Instruction in Mathematics

In this case study, Mrs. Wells extends her classroom onto the Internet in order to challenge her students to grow in their mathematical reasoning and explaining skills. These Internet-based class activities offer her students a greater diversity of learning activities. The comment and chat features of the blogging site naturally creates the opportunity for conversation and collaboration among students. By providing both conversation tools she is meeting the varied pacing needs of her students. Those who appreciate immediate feedback and process new information more quickly will likely choose to use the chat feature, while the comments feature will serve those students who read new information and then need time to reflect on it, coming back later with a comment or question (Clough, 2008). Through the process of posting, questioning, and responding, students may naturally construct their own meaning of the mathematical ideas. Additionally, through the blog postings, not only is Mrs. Wells charging students with the responsibility of explaining class activities and new mathematical processes, she is also in essence creating an Internet-based student-produced textbook that her students can access anytime they need. The Internet provides anonymity that allows a student to read the same post as many times as he or she needs without fear of judgment from others (November, 2010). This is of great value to students as now they can review the content material that matches their level of understanding, thereby receiving the differentiated instruction they need to be successful.

Case Study 5. Middle School Science

Miss Schwinn's favorite life science unit is learning the parts of plant and animal cells. Every year she directs her students to choose one type of cell and make posters with pictures of each included part and an explanation of what each part does. This year one of her students asks if she can make a "yodio" (http://www.yodio.com/) instead of a poster. Miss Schwinn looks online to see what a "yodio" is and learns that it is a form of digital storytelling, where the user uploads pictures and then records voiceovers to describe or explain the pictures. She is intrigued by this idea and starts to research other digital formats that students can use for their projects.

Miss Schwinn discovers two other technological tools that will work well for the cell project, Prezi (http://prezi.com/), an online presentation tool, and video production software (www.techsmith.com/Camtasia; Windows Movie Maker). Miss Schwinn decides to allow her students to choose which format they want to use for the project. They may choose any of the technology-based ideas, or the original poster format, or ask her about any other idea they might have. Miss Schwinn is initially nervous about how she will grade the wide range of project formats, but she creates a rubric that highlights content requirements rather than format requirements. She includes a detailed list of cell parts and descriptions that must be included and realizes that her rubric will be easy to use regardless of what format students use for their presentations.

Miss Schwinn likes to post student work in her room so that students have an audience beyond just the teacher. Since this year's projects will likely be a mix of paper and digital, Miss Schwinn sets up a place on the class website where she can post the digital projects. As a closing activity to the unit, Miss Schwinn chooses to have her students write a multi-paragraph paper comparing and contrasting plant and animal cells. Since each student only does in-depth research into one of the types of cell structures, they will have to rely on the shared knowledge from classmates to complete the assignment. Miss Schwinn hopes that this added activity will provide her insight into her students' depth of knowledge of plant and animal cells.

Identifying the Differentiated Instruction in Science

In this case study Miss Schwinn utilizes a classic form of differentiation, student choice. Student choice is important not only because students can choose a format that they like and are good at, but they will likely choose a format that allows them to best demonstrate their knowledge. When students are working within their areas of strength, the conclusions that teachers make about student learning are the most valid (Tomlinson & McTighe, 2006). Therefore, Miss Schwinn may be able to make more accurate conclusions about students' learning this year than she has been able to in the past.

The supplemental activity Miss Schwinn asks her students to complete comparing and contrasting the two types of cells incorporates two 21st century learning skills, collaboration and critical thinking. While students may not be collaborating in a traditional sense, they are providing the resources and knowledge that their peers will need to complete the final piece of the assignment. Also, critical thinking is necessary to complete this activity as students not only consider their own knowledge but compare and contrast it with the knowledge they have learned from their peers.

Case Study 6. High School Science

Mr. Francisco teaches at a small rural school. Because Chemistry is a required class for all students and he is the only Chemistry teacher at his school, he sees a variety of students in his class each year. This year each section has at least three students with IEPs and one English Language Learner along with a handful of students whose parents think they need to be challenged more. Mr. Francisco struggles daily to determine how to meet the needs of all of his students during the same fifty-minute class period.

Mr. Francisco recently discovers the resources available through Apple's iTunes (http://www.apple.com/itunes/) and has found a variety of audio and video podcasts that he wants to share with the students in his class. Topics range from how the brain works, to biodiversity, to the discovery of Ibuprofen, as well as numerous others. Many are recorded by, or include interviews from, experts in their field of study. Mr. Francisco is considering recording some podcasts himself (http://audacity.sourceforge.net/) meant specifically for his struggling students, where he would read sections of the textbook to them, highlight important vocabulary, and show them how to use their textbook as a learning tool (Colombo & Colombo, 2007). In order to provide time for students to listen to and watch these resources, Mr. Francisco decides that one day every two weeks he will take his class into the computer lab and allow students to spend class time listening to or watching a podcast and completing a follow-up activity. Depending on the podcast, this follow-up activity could be content review questions, writing vocabulary words in a student's own words, or applying new scientific knowledge to a specific problem or scenario. Mr. Francisco will also post the podcasts on his class website for students and parents to review outside of the classroom.

Identifying the Differentiated Instruction in Science

In this case study, Mr. Francisco is very aware of his students individual learning needs and uses the technological medium of podcasts to help meet those needs. He provides a wide range of types of podcasts, as well as unique follow-up activities for each. All of the follow-up activities help students to actively engage with what they are learning and deepen their understanding of it. Students watching the application-based podcasts will need to think critically about what they have learned and determine how it applies to the problem or situation presented to them in the follow-up activity. Students re-learning fundamental skills or vocabulary will have an opportunity to reinforce their new knowledge. For all students, but especially English Language Learners or those who struggle to read informational text, audio and video files online can provide increased support for learning (Colombo & Colombo, 2007).

Case Study 7. Middle School Social Studies

Mr. Johnson is a sixth-grade social studies teacher. World geography, history, and culture are key pieces of the curriculum during this year and he wants to create a more authentic learning experience for his students. He finds three sister classrooms around the globe through the ePals Global Community (http://www.epals.com) and collaborates with these teachers to create blogs through which their classrooms can teach and learn from each other. To make the global connection real, Mr. Johnson and the other teachers set up initial meetings between their classrooms using Skype (http:// www.skype.com/intl/en-us/home). Once students have met (via Skype) they have many questions for each other. Mr. Johnson facilities a discussion between his students to decide what formats that they can use to answer other students' questions and teach them about American culture, geography, and history. They decide to use blog postings, podcasts, and student-produced videos. Then students choose which piece of the project they will work on, from researching information for blog postings, writing blog postings, reading and commenting on sister classroom blogs, creating podcasts or videos, to providing technical support for the different pieces of the project. Students come to class each day ready and eager to participate in this project and connect with their friends around the globe.

Identifying the Differentiated Instruction in Social Studies

Mr. Johnson actively engages his students in his content area by creating a worldwide network of learning. Instead of simply reading books or watching movies to learn about history and geography, his students meet real students in other parts of the world and learn directly from them. Students are engaged in the learning process because they are interested to learn from and about their peers. His students not only learn from their peers; they also act as teachers. Because of this students are motivated because there is then a clear purpose for their learning.

Mr. Johnson's students work collaboratively to determine how they will share their learning and knowledge with students around the globe. Then they choose what part of the project they would like to work on. By allowing this choice, Mr. Johnson ensures that his students are working in their personal areas of strength. Students who are tech-savvy can work on the website and production of media; students who prefer to write or research can contribute to the process in these ways. This case is supported by constructivist theory, i.e., the belief that students are most engaged in learning when they are actively constructing it, interested in it, and are involved in decision-making processes (Smith & Throne, 2007).

Case Study 8. High School Social Studies

Mr. Patil, a tenth-grade Social Studies teacher, is frustrated with his students' general lack of interest in history and geography. He loves learning about these topics but has struggled to foster the same engagement in his students. Recently, Mr. Patil has been reading about the use of Geographic Information Systems (GIS) in the Social Studies classroom. He learns that teachers are using GIS to integrate the study of history and geography in ways that proponents claim facilitate the development of students' complex under-standing of both subjects (Alibrandi & Sarnoff, 2006). He wonders if the use of this technological tool may also enhance students' interest in class activ-ities.

Two examples that Mr. Patil finds are of specific interest to him. In the first, students use census data from the Civil War era to construct maps illustrating the various economic aspects of the war. Students then use the maps to consider questions about the resources of the North and South and how they contribute to the final outcome of the war (Alibrandi & Sarnoff, 2006). Not only do students come away from this project with a greater understanding of the Civil War, but along the way they learn lessons in cartography and in evaluating data presented in various forms (tables, graphs, and maps).

The second example, focusing solely on geography, is entitled "Exploring Ocean Realms" (Lewandowski, 2000). The goal of the lesson is to "provide learners with the opportunity to (a) explore the concept of place, region, and system, (b) become aware of the locations of major world oceans, and their connections to rivers, estuaries, and watersheds, (c) investigate the physical processes that shape the oceans and all Earth systems to create, sustain, and modify ecosystems, and (d) raise questions and propose solutions for prob-lems related to human interaction with Earth's hydrologic system" (Lewan-dowski, 2000, p. 1). Students brainstorm the concept of "world oceans" and create concept maps (using Inspiration, or a similar tool) that detail their ideas as they explore and investigate topics related to Earth's oceanic sys-tems. After initial exploration of the topic, including some direct instruction on the part of the teacher, students formulate questions (individually or in teams) about the oceans that interest them. Key to the investigation is the requirement that students answer geographic questions related to world oceans. Using GIS software, students collect information and data that may help them answer the questions they pose. Finally, students are required to produce a poster that includes a GIS map with data relevant to their investi-gations along with appropriate captions and images. Students are also re-quired to individually produce a document detailing their learning from the activity. (This lesson, along with examples and rubrics can be found at http://www.mpcfaculty.net/tami_lunsford/SI_03_Institute/GIS/AlLewandowski_curriculum_products.htm.)

Mr. Patil plans to collaborate with the other social studies teachers in his department to discuss what he has learned about the potential of using GIS to expand students' learning in geography and history. He is confident that the use of GIS will prompt student interest as they see more real-world applica-tion of the topics they are studying.

Identifying the Differentiated Instruction in Social Studies

The activities detailed above and similar activities will provide Mr. Patil's students more authentic learning experiences through the use of GIS. Instead of 'learning' material, students act more as researchers and investigators. The second example is especially designed so that students have choices in inves tigating real-world questions of interest to them.

The lessons also require that students use 21st century learning skills of collaboration (if teams complete the project) and critical thinking to analyze data and extrapolate their analysis in order to pose possible solutions. Additionally, the data entry, map reading, and table reading skills that students use while completing these projects are useful skills in numerous real-world applications.

TECHNOLOGY IS NOT A MAGIC WAND

The above case studies show that a variety of technologies can be used to provide meaningful, authentic, and differentiated lessons and activities for students. Teachers should be aware, however, that the mere inclusion of technology does not imply that learning goals will be met (Andriessen, 2006, as cited in Lin, Hong, Wang, & Lee, 2011; Veerman, 2003, as cited in Lin, Hong, Wang, & Lee, 2011; Papanastasiou & Ferdig, 2006). Instead teachers need to be intentional about creating a classroom climate that supports using a variety of tools to accomplish learning. Remember, under the informating framework, technology is not the end goal, student learning is.

Additionally, if teachers such as Mrs. Wells (see Case Study 4) choose to start an 'online' branch of their classroom, they should be intentional about creating an online classroom climate. Students may not be immediately comfortable in this new realm (Smelser, 2002) even if they use the Internet often. If students primarily use the Internet for socializing, using it in an educational context will be new and will likely require some guidance. Also, teachers should be intentional about continuing to foster relationships with their students while in the online classroom. The relational part of face-to-face instruction should not be replaced by online experiences (Ward & Prosser, 2011).

TRAINING IN TECHNOLOGY

As with any new strategy or tool, appropriate training is necessary for its successful use. Technology is certainly not an exception. Training needs to be regular, and not only include training in the use of the tools but also the bigger picture of how these tools help teachers differentiate instruction

(Cobb, 2010). Teachers also need time to explore how they can use technology to adapt their current content into a product that will best meet student needs, and time to experiment with the new technologies themselves (Colombo & Colombo, 2007). As teachers investigate different technological tools it is important that they consider both the learning goal and the needs of the student so that appropriate choices are made (King-Sears, Swanson, & Mainzer, 2011). Depending on what technological tools are brought into the classroom, teachers may need to adapt their classroom management strategies (Cobb, 2010). Also, certain tools provide for different teacher-student interactions (National School Boards Foundation, 2002), and thus teachers benefit from time spent discussing how to best facilitate teaching and learning in these new environments. Given appropriate training and time, teachers will be prepared to use new technologies in ways that engage and challenge students in and beyond their subject areas.

CONCLUDING THOUGHTS

Today's students come from a variety of backgrounds and cultures and bring to the classroom a wide range of experiences, strengths, and weaknesses. Teachers have an important responsibility to meet students where they are, support them in their learning throughout the year, provide engaging and meaningful learning activities, and train students in skills they will need for their futures. While technology is abundant in today's world, research (e.g., Software & Information Industry Association, 2011) shows that the greatest strides made in school integration are in using technology to provide Internet access for communication, administrative and instructional needs, to keep student data secure, and to ensure student privacy. The area of least change is in using technological tools to differentiate instruction in order to meet the personalized instructional needs of all students. As November (2010) points out, schools are using technology to automate, not informate. It is time for this to change.

Powerful technological tools exist today; tools that allow students to learn in ways they have not before. These technological tools connect students with other students around the globe so that they can engage in meaningful sharing of knowledge. They allow students greater choice in product, so that they are working within their strengths. They provide students easy access to needed reinforcement wherever they are in their understanding, and encourage students to collaborate with one another to solve problems. Today's technologies provide teachers with methods and means to change the way education is done, to meet the varied needs of students, and to send students from their classroom better prepared to meet the challenges they will find beyond the classroom. Yet, despite all of the notable technological tools available to students today, still newer and different tools will be available to them tomorrow. Therefore, it is not about the specific technological tools, but rather teachers using whatever means are available to affect powerful and lasting learning in students.

REFERENCES

Alibrandi, M. & Sarnoff, H. M. (2006). Using GIS to answer the 'whys' of 'where' in social studies. *Social Education, 70* (3), 138-143.

Clough, G.W. (2008). Wanted: Well-rounded students who can think. *Educational Digest, 74* (2), 58-62.

Cobb, A. (2010). To differentiate or not to differentiate? Using internet-based technology in the classroom. *The Quarterly Review of Distance Education, 11* (1), 37-45.

Colombo, M. W. & Colombo, P. D. (2007). Blogging to improve instruction in differentiated science classrooms: The need for highly qualified science teachers who can differentiate instruction for diverse learners is acute. *Phi Delta Kappan, 89* (1), 60-63.

Criswell, C. (2010). Music technology: Making a music lesson out of online research. *Teaching Music, 18* (3), 26-27.

Dodge, B. (1997, May 5). *Some thoughts about webquests.* Available at http://webquest.sdsu.edu/about_webquests.html.

Dorricott, D. & Peck, K. L. (1994). Why use technology? *Educational Leadership, 51* (7), 11-14.

Jiang, Z. & McClintock, E. (2000). Multiple approaches to problem solving and the use of technology. *The Journal of Computers in Mathematics and Science Teaching, 19* (1), 7-20.

Johnson D. W. & Johnson R. T. (1996). Cooperation and the use of technology. In D. H. Jonassen (Ed.). *Handbook of research for educational communications and technology* (pp. 1017-1044). New York, NY: Macmillan.

Kafai, Y. B. & Ching, C. C. (2001). Affordances of collaborative software design planning for elementary students' science talk. *The Journal of the Learning Sciences, 10* (3), 323-363.

Khan, S. (2011). *Let's use video to reinvent education.* Available at http://www.ted.com/talks/salman_khan_let_s_use_video_to_reinvent_education.html.

King-Sears, M. E., Swanson, C., & Mainzer, L. (2011). Technology and literacy for adolescents with disabilities. *Journal of Adolescent and Adult Literacy, 54* (8), 569-578.

Lenhart, A., Arafeh, S., Smith, A., & Macgill, A. R. (2008). *Writing, technology and teens.* Washington, D.C.: Pew Internet and American Life Project.

Lewandowski, A. (2000). *Exploring ocean realms.* Available at http://www.mpcfaculty.net/tami_lunsford/SI_03_Institute/GIS/Al_Lewandowski/Ocean_World_Lesson1_ALewandowski.pdf.

Lin, H-S., Hong, Z-R., Wang, H-H., & Lee, S-T. (2011). Using reflective peer assessment to promote students' conceptual understanding through asynchronous discussions. *Educational Technology & Society, 14* (3), 178-189.

Liu, H-C. & Su, I-H. (2011). Learning residential electrical wiring through computer simulation: The impact of computer-based learning environments on student achievement and cognitive load. *British Journal of Educational Technology, 42* (4), 598-607.

Luterbach, K. J. & Brown, C. (2011). Education for the 21st century. *International Journal of Applied Educational Studies, 11* (1), 14-32.

MacBride, R. & Luehmann, A. L. (2008). Capitalizing on emerging technologies: A case study of classroom blogging. *School Science and Mathematics, 108* (5), 173-183.

National School Boards Foundation. (2002). *Are we there yet? Research and guidelines on schools' use of the Internet.* Available at http://grunwald.com/pdfs/ARE-WE-THERE-YET-GRUNWALD.pdf.

November, A. (2010). *Empowering students with technology* (2nd ed.). Thousand Oaks, CA: Corwin Press.

Page, M. S. (2002). Technology-enriched classrooms: Effects on students of low socio-economic status. *Journal of Research on Technology in Education, 34* (4), 389-409.

Papanastasiou, E. C. & Ferdig, R. E. (2006). Computer use and mathematical literacy: An analysis of existing and potential relationships. *Journal of Computers in Mathematical and Science Teaching, 25* (4), 361-371.

Polly, D. & Ausband, L. (2009). Developing higher-order thinking skills through webquests. *Journal of Computing in Teacher Education, 26* (1), 29-34.

Richtel, M. (2011, September 4). In classroom of future, stagnant scores. *The New York Times*, p. A1.

Rose, D. H. & Meyer, A. (2002). *Teaching every student in the digital age: Universal design for learning.* Alexandria, VA: Association for Supervision and Curriculum Development.

Schacter, J. (1999). The impact of education technology on student achievement. *Milken Exchange on Educational Technology.* Available at http://www.mff.org/pubs/ME161.pdf.

Sharaf, A. & Musawi, A. (2011). Redefining technology's role in education. *Creative Education, 2* (2), 130-135.

Smelser, L. M. (2002). *Making connections in our classroom: Online and off.* Arlington, VA. (ERIC Document Reproduction Service No. ED 464 323)

Smith, G. & Throne, S. (2007). *Differentiating instruction with technology in K-5 classrooms.* Eugene, OR: International Society for Technology in Education.

Software & Information Industry Association. (2011, August 10). *2011 SIIA Vision K-20 survey results.* Available at http://www.siia.net/visionk20/pages/progress.html.

Tomlinson, C. A. & McTighe, J. (2006). *Integrating differentiated instruction: Understanding by design.* Alexandria, VA: Association for Supervision and Curriculum Development.

Ward, A. & Prosser, B. T. (2011). Reflections on cyberspace as the new 'wired world of education. *Educational Technology & Society, 14* (1), 169-178.

Chapter Twelve

Response to Intervention (RTI)

A System to Meet the Needs of All Students in Grades 5-12

Deborah L. Smith

INTRODUCTION

American schools have been working with a wide variety of students since the turn of the century, when child-labor laws grow stricter. At this same time, when an influx of immigrant students pour into our schools, there is an emphasis on Social Darwinism which provides "a scientific basis for seeing some groups of people as being of lesser social and moral development than others" (Oakes, 1985, p. 21). Education is seen as a way to "Americanize" newcomers and teach them the values that are believed to guide good citizens (Oakes, 1985). So, all school-age children are encouraged and eventually required to attend public schooling, but all are not treated equally.

After World War II it became politically incorrect to assume that certain groups of people were inferior, so schools developed IQ tests and standardized tests and used these for placement purposes. In this way, the myth of meritocracy was born because ethnic minorities and low-income students generally tested poorly on IQ tests and standardized tests, and this 'proved' that they were correctly placed in the lowest tracks at schools across our nation (Oakes, 1985; Zemelman, Daniels, & Hyde, 1998). Students whose first language was not English were given IQ tests in English and then labeled 'retarded' when they failed the test. In this way, the tracks created at many schools produced situations where ethnic minorities and students of poverty consistently sat in classes where expectations were lowered. Historically, special education classrooms and lower-track classrooms housed a disproportionate number of poor and minority students, and did not serve the purpose of remediation.

Tracking continues on in many schools throughout the twentieth century and is still prevalent today, even though research has shown that tracking results in substantial differences in the day-to-day learning opportunities provided to children (Oakes, 1985, Blau, 2004; Burris & Garrity, 2008). Those students who are in higher tracks are consistently exposed to great literature, expected to learn more advanced vocabulary, and taught critical-thinking skills and problem-solving skills, while those in lower tracks are more likely to focus on workbooks, memorization exercises, and cover topics in less depth.

Studies (for example, Oakes, 1985; Blau, 2004; Burris & Garrity, 2008) repeatedly show that students who are tracked are provided with unequal learning opportunities. In higher tracks the teachers tend to be more enthusiastic and establish a positive classroom environment. Teachers tend to spend less time on discipline and establishing routines and require students to complete more homework. In contrast, teachers in lower-track classrooms tend to be more critical, and put more emphasis on getting students to be on time, follow directions, and stay quiet (Oakes, 1985). And, rather than provide the remedial services necessary, the achievement gap between those in low tracks and high tracks increases each year. Thus, low track classes have not served their purposes; "To the contrary, these practices did not even enable minority students to sustain their position, relative to white students, in the district's achievement hierarchy" (Oakes, 1999, p. 232).

In 1954 when the Supreme Court made their monumental Brown vs. The Board of Education decision, the national policy for educating students with special needs began. Since then public schools in America progressed with continually evolving ideas on how best to meet the needs of all students in an environment that was fair and just. In 2004, when the Individuals with Disabilities Education Act (IDEA) was reauthorized, the government included the phrase "least restrictive environment" and the impetus for inclusion was reinvigorated. The original IDEA in 1975 set the stage for mainstreaming and subsequent reauthorizations moved the language and ideas forward toward an inclusive education system that treated students fairly. Progress in the laws that govern education was more rapid than progress in the educational practices in some ways, but they led us in the right direction.

Differentiation has always been a necessary aspect of teaching, but the increasing inclusion of special education students into regular education classrooms has made it a top priority in American schools, and the adoption of Response to Intervention (RTI) systems have been a common outcome. RTI is a system that prepares teachers for the convergence of general education classes and special education students (Reeves, Bishop, & Filce, 2010).

RESPONSE TO INTERVENTION

Response to Intervention (RTI) is a tiered system for intervention based on classroom progress monitoring that allows for early identification of students who have difficulties meeting academic or behavioral standards. This system is approved by IDEA in 2004 as a legitimate method for identifying and supporting students who need assistance, but it is not intended to be used solely as a system for identifying or assisting students with special education needs. RTI is based on the premise that all children can be successful if provided with the proper support. RTI is focused on differentiation of instruction for all students with a system in place for identifying students who need help meeting specific learning objectives. Figure 12.1 (available at http://www.rcoe.k12.ca.us/edServices/rti2.html) shows how RTI is often represented. The figure illustrates the three tiers of RTI, and shows what they have in common and how each tier differs.

Tier One

The tiers of RTI are often presented as a pyramid, where the first tier represents the general education classroom with students receiving differentiated instruction, using curriculum that is based on scientifically-proven strategies of instruction. It is estimated that 80-85 percent of all students will reach proficiency with this level of instruction (Fisher & Frey, 2010). This tier is seen as providing high quality universal instruction to all students. Elements of Universal Design for Instruction (UDI) are considered at this tier so that different ways of learning are considered when learning activities are designed and the framework of lessons helps to maximize learning for all. The principles behind UDI guide teachers to ensure that learning is inclusive and accessible to all learners (Thomas, 2009).

Lessons in Tier One are designed to maximize learning for all. This is imperative if an RTI system is to be effective. To ensure quality core instruction, that is, "instruction that encompasses all areas of language and literacy as part of a coherent curriculum that is developmentally appropriate for preK-12 students and does not underestimate their potential for language and literacy learning" (IRA, 2010, p. 3), teachers must spend time establishing a clear and coherent purpose for each lesson. These purposes should be stated in terms of goals and should come directly from the expected standards for their subject area and grade-level (Fisher & Frey, 2010). Once the purpose of each lesson is clear, it must be implemented in a way that engages all learners in the classroom. Teachers at all grade levels and in all content areas "believe it is desirable to attend to learner variance as they teach" (Tomlinson & McTighe, 2006, p. 39). Yet, very few teachers are able to put this desire for differentiated instruction into practice. In order for this to occur, teachers can

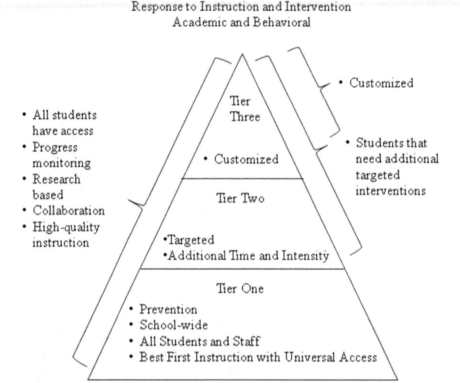

Figure 12.1. RTI Pyramid.

present a model of instruction that includes the following four principles of effective instruction (Sadker & Sadker, 2005):

1. The first principle is maximizing academic learning time. Students spend the majority of their classroom time 'on task'. A teacher is given a limited amount of time with students and they need to make the most of every minute. Considering the value of each planned activity and eliminating any that are not clearly productive is one way that teachers can ensure quality instruction.

2. The second principle is having a classroom structure that is clear and positive. Students learn best in an environment that allows them to focus on learning. In order to make sure the classroom is structured the teacher must make sure classroom rules and routines are posted and followed; disruptions are minimal and the classroom layout is carefully arranged to promote learning.

3. The third principle is providing an academic structure for lessons, including activation of background knowledge, modeling, guided practice, independent practice, and extension of learning. "Into," "through," and "beyond" component are needed for each lesson and unit presented in the classroom. Teachers can ask, "How will I get my students 'into' the materials or prepare my students to learn? How can I guide my students 'through' the materials or help them to process what they are learning? How can I get students to go 'beyond' the lesson and apply what they have learned in new situations and reflect upon their own learning?" Asking these questions can guide teachers to plan lessons with academic structure, and thus engage all learners in their classrooms.

4. The fourth principle is providing variety in content and process. There are many ways that students learn, and teachers need to incorporate all of these into their classrooms. Teachers can include (a) cooperative learning structures, (b) strategies that students can transfer across subject areas, (c) workshop approaches, (d) active learning, (e) authentic experiences, (f) integrated units, (g) graphic organizers, (h) summarization practice, or (i) explicit vocabulary instruction. The more variety provided in content and processes the more chances that students will succeed as teachers attempt to address the various learning styles represented in their classrooms.

Another component of Tier One is "universal screening." As each curriculum (or content area) standard is taught in the classroom, students are monitored for their progress and those who do not meet standards after receiving quality instruction are given additional assistance at the Tier Two level. This process of assessing students, analyzing the data to determine who is not reaching proficiency, intervening to guide students back toward proficiency, and then re-assessing to monitor progress is an ongoing cycle in the RTI system.

Tier Two

Students who do not make adequate progress with the general education curriculum are identified by their teachers and are provided with strategic research-based interventions designed to help students reach proficiency. Examples of possible interventions (e.g., "check-and-connect," "self-collection of data," and "word study") will be described later in this chapter. These interventions are normally delivered to a small group of students within the regular education classroom, and are short in duration. The intervention can be delivered by the regular classroom teacher, or by a trained team-member. Approximately 15 percent of all students in a school implementing RTI are expected to need these "tier two" interventions. This targeted intervention is meant to be supplemental to the regular classroom curriculum rather than serve as a replacement. Students receiving "tier two" interventions still participate in the regular classroom learning activities.

Tier Three

Those students who do not respond to the interventions provided at the "tier two" level progress on to the final tier. This group should be a small percentage (5%) of students who still lag behind peers in achievement levels. Students at this level receive very intensive research-based interventions either in a one-on-one format or in very small groups. Examples of possible interventions (e.g., "anecdotal records," "SG4R," and "writing-to-learn") will be described later in this chapter. This group is likely to receive their interventions from a specialist or a special education teacher. Interventions at the Tier Three level are also a supplement to regular classroom learning activities rather than a replacement, and are provided until students reach proficiency. Those students who do not respond to Tier Three interventions are referred for special education testing to determine if more formal and intensive interventions may be necessary.

At each tier on the RTI pyramid, there is an emphasis on universally monitoring student progress. In order to do this teachers must have valid and reliable means of assessing student achievement, and the results must be available quickly so that interventions can occur. RTI interventions often involve prepackaged programs such as *Language!* (Greene, 2009), *Read 180* (Scholastic, 2011), or *REWARDS* (Archer, Gleason, & Vachon, 2006). While these programs often boast of impressive rates of improvement on standardized testing, they do not help individual teachers whose schools have not purchased the programs or teachers who are less focused on teaching students to read than on teaching students to learn through reading. "An important switch occurs in fourth grade in that instruction moves from learning to read to reading to learn, which results in a focus on reading comprehension that lasts throughout the remaining grades" (Burns & Gibbons, 2008, p. 68). Thus, teachers whose students can read but who still need to work on comprehension skills and increase proficiency rates need interventions that are not just focused on basic literacy. A basic level of proficiency is expected for students in reading and computational skills, so the interventions presented here are for students who have some basic skills in place. Students in grades 5-12 who struggle with basic decoding skills or computational skills at these grade levels need to be referred to a specialist for a formal assessment process.

INTERVENTIONS

Most RTI systems have interventions that are both social/behavioral and academic since the reasons that students fail to reach academic proficiency can be related to either of these factors. While there are numerous interventions in the literature for elementary students, there are very few mentioned for students at the middle school or high school levels. The focus and implementation of RTI systems is much more prevalent at the elementary level, and additional research is needed to determine the best interventions possible at the middle and secondary levels. The following interventions are suggested as ways to guide students in grades 5-12 who are at any of the tier levels. Students will need interventions at all levels, and the ones presented here can be adapted for whole-class, small group, or individual implementation. Each of these interventions provides a way to learn more about students academically or behaviorally, and can be used to differentiate lessons to meet students' various needs. Whether under a formal RTI system, or as an individual teacher, it is always important to identify students who struggle with learning and differentiate instruction to help those students grow.

SOCIAL/BEHAVIORAL INTERVENTIONS

Check-and-Connect

Check-and-Connect is a social intervention that involves a monitor/advocate working to build a level of trust with the students (Sinclair, Christensen, & Thurlow, 2005). This advocate monitors students' engagement and progress, and keeps education salient for the students. The core elements of a "check-and-connect" intervention include (1) relationship building, (2) routine monitoring, (3) problem solving, and (4) commitment. Relationship building includes (1) building a relationship with the students' family to make sure a support system is in place that extends beyond the school personnel and (2) building a relationship with the student so that the student knows that s/he has an advocate at the school who cares about them and who is looking out for their interests.

This advocate monitors students' routines, such as attendance and grade performance, while guiding students to monitor their own academic and behavioral progress. In addition, this advocate talks with the student about progress, problem-solves potential pitfalls, and teaches conflict-resolution skills (Sinclair, et al., 2005). The advocate must be committed to connecting with the student and continuing to check on progress in order for this intervention to be successful.

Anecdotal Record

Students whose behavior interferes with achievement are in need of interventions that directly relate to the disruptive behavior. An "anecdotal record" is a written record kept in a positive tone. It can track a student's academic or behavioral progress, but in this case a teacher will focus on the behavioral possibilities. The teacher observes and records (keeps an anecdotal record of) the student's actions, interactions, and work throughout the class period as activities are occurring.

Possible uses for anecdotal records include:

1. Planning a conference to talk with a student or the parents about progress;
2. Determining a plan of action to correct a behavioral issue in the classroom;
3. Diagnosing why or at what point a student is experiencing difficulty.

Some tips for keeping appropriate anecdotal records are:

1. Focus in on a specific behavior and keep the note brief;
2. Keep observations objective and specific;
3. Record anecdotal information frequently (daily if possible);
4. Record anecdotal information at various times to get a complete profile;
5. Create a form that works for the purpose of keeping such records;
6. Keep paperwork organized and dated for each day.

Possible Format:

Table 12.1 shows one format that can be used for keeping anecdotal records. It is meant to be adapted for teachers' classroom use.

Self Collection of Data

While teaching middle school years ago the writer of this chapter started the year with a skills-assessment that provided her with instant feedback on the English Language Arts (ELA) skills that the students had mastered. She made a chart with all the skills along one side and student numbers across the top, and put stars in each cell where mastery had been achieved. She made this chart for herself, and yet before class students were often clustered around the poster tracing the line down from their student number to see which skills they had mastered and which they had not. Students were focused on getting stars all the way down the list and would ask her to test them again regularly after a lesson in which a particular skill had been covered. These students were motivated by seeing their progress each week, and

Name: _____

Date: _____

Time of Class:_____

Observed Event or Behaviors:

Student Quotes:

Teacher Interventions:

Student Response:

Table 12.1. Anecdotal Record Example.

learned to keep track of their own achievement, set goals for themselves, and reflect on their progress.

One way to organize students' self-collection of data is for individual students to have a chart of the standards they are expected to achieve for a unit of study so they can monitor their progress, and self-report and reflect as the chart is updated. For example, a student can receive this chart (see Table 12.2) at the beginning of a new unit that is designed to cover the standards listed. Students can complete the chart as they progress through the unit, and keep track of their own progress.

While the three behavioral interventions listed here would need to be adapted to the specific behavioral needs of students, they provide an overview of what a teacher can and should do when students' behavioral issues interfere with learning. Making students responsible for their own goal-setting and record keeping can empower students and provide a catalyst for improvement. Making personal connections with students can help teachers understand the students' perspectives and relate lessons more directly to students' lives; and, record keeping can provide teachers with tangible evidence that can allow for increased objectivity when dealing with disruptive behaviors. All three of these interventions can assist in developing a positive

7th Grade Common Core Standards (Content Areas)	Activities in this unit that focus on this standard…	How did you progress on standards?	What can you do to become fully proficient?
Determine the central ideas or information of a primary or secondary source; provide an accurate summary of the source distinct from prior knowledge or opinions.			
Determine the meaning of words and phrases as they are used in a text, including vocabulary specific to domains related to history/social studies.			
Analyze the relationship between a primary and secondary source on the same topic.			
Write informative/ explanatory texts, including the narration of historical events, scientific procedures/ experiments, or technical processes. Use precise language and domain-specific vocabulary to inform about or explain the topic.			

Table 12.2. Students' Self-Collection Chart.

classroom environment where all students are expected to achieve; and, when implemented in a classroom where a positive atmosphere has already been achieved, they can guide students toward self-monitoring their behaviors so that these are less likely to interfere with academic achievement.

ACADEMIC INTERVENTIONS

The key to academic intervention is to use research-based strategies that make sure students who are not achieving get the time and focused attention needed to succeed, and that this progress is continually monitored. In some cases, additional time and small-group or one-on-one tutoring may be all that is needed to assist a student who does not meet an academic standard the first time it is covered. Sometimes, the materials just need to be presented in a slightly different format to meet the students' learning styles. Sometimes, prior knowledge is lacking and building that can be enough for a student to master a concept. The following interventions are research-based strategies that can be adapted for many situations and learners.

Word Study

New vocabulary can often interfere with comprehension in content-area texts, and lack of comprehension clearly interferes with proficiency. A "word study" is one way for students to analyze new words, and it teaches students their options when they encounter any difficult vocabulary. Teachers should model this process and then monitor students' progress on their word studies. Table 12.3 shows a Word Study format that a teacher can use in any subject-area class.

SG4R

Another possible intervention for students who need focus when reading their textbook is SG4R, which has been successfully implemented by schools in Brockton, Massachusetts, as a part of their school-wide literacy initiative (Fitzgerald, Hochholzer, Love, & Szachowicz, 2010). This tool can be used as a way to encourage students to apply research-based strategies to their content-area textbooks. Table 12.4 provides an example intervention for using the SG4R strategy.

The SG4R intervention (Fitzgerald, et al., 2010), can guide students to process new material by setting a purpose for the reading, connecting the text with the students' prior knowledge, and directing students to apply the new knowledge, which can increase the topic's relevance.

Writing-to-Learn

"Writing-to-learn" can also be an effective intervention strategy. Writing goes beyond procedural knowledge, and beyond demonstrating content knowledge; it can be used to explore the very processes by which we learn. Change-Wells and Wells (1995) define metacognition as "knowledge about one's own mental processes and the control of those processes to achieve one's intended goal" (p. 58). Metacognition is more than just "thinking about thinking" as it has been commonly defined. It involves analyzing, drawing conclusions, and putting into practice one's learning. Writing can be a powerful tool for exploring thinking on any topic, and when used as a way to

Word Study

New Word: Write a word from the reading that you do not know here.

> [   ]

Word parts (prefix, root, suffix): Separate the words into 'parts' if any are used, such as 's' for plural or 'tri' for three.

> [   ]

Meaning of word parts: Define the word parts you found in the box above. If you do not know the meanings, ask three classmates before asking the teacher.

> [   ]

Predicted Meaning: Take a guess at what the word means, based on the definitions of the word parts and the context of the reading.

> [   ]

Prediction Check: Use the dictionary, thesaurus, or the text glossary to find out the meaning of your word and compare this definition with your prediction.

> [   ]

Table 12.3. Word Study Format.

engage students in understanding their own mental processes, can be a cata-lyst for growth. Journaling or logs about learning experiences with guided questions to lead students to metacognition is one way to incorporate "writ-ing-to-learn" into any classroom. Prompts to guide students' metacognition can include:

1. What were the steps you took in solving the problem/answering the question?

Survey: What type of text/document are you reading? What are the main sections?	
Goal: What is your reason for reading this text? What do you plan to learn? What objective is linked with this reading?	
Recall: What do you already know about the topic? What do the sections and headings remind you of?	
Record: As you read, what new concepts or vocabulary words seem important?	
Revise: Has the information changed what you know about the topic? Did you have any misconceptions? Explain.	
Reflect: How is this information useful in school or life? How can I use this new knowledge?	

Table 12.4. SG4R Graphic Organizer.

2. There is not only one answer to today's question. Consider how someone could reasonably come up with an answer that is different than yours and explain.
3. What parts of this activity were easy and what parts were difficult for you?
4. If you were to teach another student what you learned today, how would you go about that? How would this process change if you were teaching a young child? How would this process change if you were teaching an adult?
5. How would you evaluate your thinking for this lesson? Why?
6. How could you use what you learned today over the weekend? How could you use what you learned in another class?

Metacognition is a strong predictor of academic success and problem solving ability (Theide, Anderson, & Therriault, 2003). Writing about their thinking processes is one way to intervene so that students are more likely to become proficient.

Academic interventions can take on many forms. For most students reading self-selected, high-interest pieces that are directly related to the learning goals can aid understanding. Questioning can be another powerful tool as can graphic organizers, partner-learning, think-alouds modeled by the teacher, and cooperative learning. The key to selecting the right intervention is to know the students and to continually monitor progress. This is not a process that should be undertaken alone. Support systems should be in place at schools so that teachers have input from specialists and administration as they decide who would benefit from interventions and how and when they should intervene.

CONCLUDING THOUGHTS

RTI is clearly linked with differentiation. It is a system that has been developed as a way to identify students who need more focused time and attention. It has been developed in response to language that states students should be given the opportunity to learn in the "least restrictive environment" and yet it has developed into a system designed to impart high expectations for all. "Proponents of RTI say the process has changed education because of its focus on catching problems early, and on improving education for all students" (Samuels, 2011, p. 3). This new system is seen by many as a replacement of remedial education programs that have had minimal impact on the improvement of student achievement. Just imagine education and schools as being a transformative agent for students of all backgrounds and you can imagine the potential impact of RTI.

It is not necessary to have a formal RTI system in place in order to benefit from the concepts of RTI. If all teachers took steps to monitor students' progress and put into action research-based interventions whenever students do not meet proficiency levels, then there would be more learning happening in all classrooms. Ideally, teachers will have the opportunity to do this in a supportive environment where specialists help to plan and implement interventions and students' progress is monitored with input from administrators and teachers working together. As educators though, we cannot wait for this to happen. RTI is based upon providing scientific-based instruction for all students, teaching responsively and differentiating, and continually monitoring students' learning. These are not new concepts in education, but they are key concepts, and when taken together they can be the basis for improved learning for all.

REFERENCES

Archer, A. L, Gleason, M. M., & Vachon, V. (2006). *REWARDS: Multisyllabic word reading strategies, intermediate level.* Frederick, CO: Sopris West.

Blau, J. R. (2004). *Race in the schools: Perpetuating white dominance?* Boulder, CO: Lynne Rienner Publishers.

Burns, M. K. & Gibbons, K. A. (2008). *Implementing response-to-intervention in elementaryand secondary schools: Procedures to assure scientific-based practices.* New York, NY: Routledge.

Burris, C. C. & Garrity, D. T. (2008). *Detracking for excellence and equity.* Alexandria, VA: Association for Supervision and Curriculum Development.

Chang-Wells, G. & Wells, G. (1995). Dynamics of discourse: Literacy and the construction of Knowledge. In E. A. Forman, N. Minick, & C. Addison Stone (Eds.), *Contexts for learning:*

Sociocultural dynamics in children's development (pp. 58-90). Oxford, UK: Oxford University Press.

Fisher, D. & Frey, N. (2010). *Enhancing RTI: How to ensure success with effective classroom instruction and intervention.* Alexandria, VA: Association for Supervision and Curriculum Development.

Fitzgerald, T. J., Hochholzer, N., Love, C. J., & Szachowicz, S. (2010). *Designing literacy initiatives for whole school improvement in grades 7-12.* Rexford, NY: International Center for Leadership in Education.

Greene, J. F. (2009). *Language! The comprehensive literacy curriculum.* Frederick, CO: Sopris West.

International Reading Association (IRA). (2010). *Response to intervention: Guiding principles for educators from the International Reading Association.* Newark, DE: International Reading Association.

Oakes, J. (1985). *Keeping track: How schools structure inequality.* New Haven, CT: Yale University Press.

Oakes, J. S. (1999). Limiting students school success and life chances. In A. C. Ornstein & L. S. Behar-Horenstein (Eds.), *Contemporary issues in curriculum* (pp. 227-234). Needham Heights, MA: Allyn & Bacon.

Reeves, S., Bishop, J., & Filce, H. G. (2010). Response to Intervention (RtI) and tier systems: Questions remain as educators make challenging decisions. *Delta Kappa Gamma Bulletin, 76* (4), 30-36.

Samuels, C. A. (2011). RTI: An approach on the march. *Education Week, 30* (22), 2-6.

Sadker, P. & Sadker, D. (2005). *Teacher, schools, and society* (7th ed.). New York, NY: McGraw Hill.

Scholastic Publications. (2011). *A compendium of Read 180 research.* New York, NY: Scholastic Inc.

Sinclair, M. F., Christenson, S. L., & Thurlow, M. L. (2005). Promoting school completion of urban secondary youth with emotional and behavioral disabilities. *Exceptional Children, 71* (4), 465-482.

Thiede K. W., Anderson M. C., & Therriault, D. (2003). Accuracy of metacognitive monitoring affects learning of texts. *Journal of Educational Psychology, 95* (1), 66-73.

Thomas, C. A. (2009). *Universal design for transition: A roadmap for planning and instruction.* Baltimore, MD: Paul H. Brookes Publishing Co.

Tomlinson, C. A. & McTighe, J. (2006). *Integrating differentiated instruction and understanding by design: Connecting content and kids.* Alexandria, VA: Association for Supervision and Curriculum Development.

Zemelman, S., Daniels, H., & Hyde, A. (1998). *Best practices: New standards for teaching and learning in America's schools.* Portsmouth, NH: Heinemann

Chapter Thirteen

Dropouts and Differentiation

Toward Understanding and Prevention

Brian J. Smith

INTRODUCTION

In the second decade of the twenty-first century, it is clear that educational success is more important than ever for a youth's individual life trajectory and for the larger community (Hallam & Rogers, 2008). Being an uneducated adult in today's knowledge- and technology- based world is an incredibly disadvantaged status. Such adults are unlikely to be gainfully employed, and will earn far less over the course of their lifetime compared to educated adults (Payne & Slocumb, 2011; Plank, DeLuca, & Estacion, 2008). Furthermore, although a recent executive order signed by President Obama will enable states to 'opt out' of the No Child Left Behind (NCLB) 2014 deadline regarding student proficiency (Dillon, 2011), NCLB has had a widespread impact on community expectations and school culture and policies. Schools and teachers are being held accountable for the achievement of all students (Franklin, Harris, & Allen-Meares, 2008; Hondo, Gardiner, & Sapien, 2008). Thus, for students, for schools, and for communities, preventing dropout is critically important; in short, student dropout causes a myriad of individual and social harms.

This chapter discusses how differentiation can play a role in addressing the dropout phenomenon. First, an overview of the data on dropouts in the United States will be provided; this overview includes a presentation of how social class and race/ethnicity correlate with dropping out, as well as a discussion of how disadvantageous it is to be a dropout. Next, a theoretical framing of dropping out will be presented, including the importance of individual factors, and social level factors. The final part of the chapter explores

how differentiated instruction can play a role in addressing the dropout problem. This final section suggests that dropouts and the dropout phenomenon
present unique challenges which are well suited to be addressed by a differentiated approach to instruction.

DROPOUT DATA IN THE UNITED STATES

It is difficult to accurately estimate the dropout phenomenon in the United
States. There are some variations and discrepancies across states regarding
the reporting and compilation of high school graduation statistics, and, in
addition, students sometimes return to school after leaving (Easton, 2008;
Hondo, et al., 2008; Payne & Slocumb, 2011; Warren & Halpern-Manners,
2009). Importantly, there are different ways to measure dropping out; the
category of 'event dropout' refers to how many students dropout in a given
school year; the category of 'status' dropout refers to how many youth and
young adults of a certain age (typically 16 – 24) have not completed high
school and are not currently enrolled in high school or a GED program
(Chapman, Laird, & KewalRamani, 2010). Regardless of how dropping out
of school is measured, it is clear, as the following data demonstrate, that
dropping out of school is an extremely important social problem in the U.S.
that needs to be addressed (Barton, 2005; Horvat & Davis, 2011; Swanson,
2008).

Well over half a million youth drop out of school each year in the United
States. The U.S. ranks seventeenth in the developed world in high school
graduation rates; a full 30% of youth in the United States do not graduate 'on
time' (Easton, 2008; Payne & Slocumb, 2011). Every single day, approximately 7000 teens drop out of school (Jackson & Cooper, 2007).

Government data on the 'event dropout' rate for private and public
schools illustrated that 3.5% of students dropped out of public or private
schools during the 2007-2008 school year (Chapman, et al., 2010). Government data regarding the 'status dropout' category showed that in 2009 8% of
16-24 year olds (about 3 million individuals) in the U.S. were not enrolled in
school and did not already have a GED or high school diploma (Chapman, et
al., 2010). Government data on the 'event' dropout rate for public schools
indicated that there were 607,789 dropouts during the 2008-2009 school
year, representing 4.1% of students in grades 9-12 (Sillwell, Sable, & Plotts,
2011). About one-third of dropout events occurred in grade 12, with the
remaining numbers spread relatively evenly across grades 9-11 (Sillwell, et
al., 2011). Interestingly, more than 50% of dropouts in the year 2000 came
from only 14% of high schools, commonly referred to as 'dropout factories'
(Payne & Slocumb, 2011).

It is not difficult to envision the social significance of the dropout problem when one considers that there are three million older teens/young adults in the U.S. who lack a high school degree or GED. Such individuals are not, as a general rule, on track for a comfortable, high quality life.

Race/Ethnicity and Social Class

Given the structural inequalities, which constitute the U.S. society, it is not surprising that certain race/ethnic groups and social classes are overrepresented in dropout statistics. Those living at the bottom of the social class ladder are more likely to be surrounded by a myriad of social forces (e.g., community violence, dysfunctional social institutions, deviant peer groups, lack of adult role models, visible alternative/criminal activities, substandard schools), which decrease the likelihood of being successful at school and hinder school success. Quite simply kids living in poverty are more likely to drop out of school (Hallam & Rogers, 2008; Janosz, Archambault, Morizot, & Pagani, 2008). Data on the 'event' dropout rate from 2008 show that youth from low income families are more than four times (4x) more likely than those from high income families to drop out of school; the income correlated 'event' dropout rates are low income family, 8.7%; middle income family, 3.0%, and high income family, 2.0% (Chapman et al., 2010).

Youth from certain race/ethnic groups are overrepresented in dropout statistics, and only about one out of every two African-American or Hispanic youths graduate from high school on time (Payne & Slocumb, 2011). White and Asian/Pacific Islander youth are actually underrepresented in dropout statistics; social class correlations and a cultural emphasis on education can explain this underrepresentation. For public high schools, the race/ethnicity event dropout rates, for the 2008-2009 school year, are, Asian/Pacific Islander, 2.4%; White, 2.7%; Hispanic, 6.0%; American Indian/Alaska Native 6.3%; and, Black, 6.6% (Stillwell, et al., 2011). Minority youth, specifically Blacks and Hispanics, also constitute a higher percentage of status dropouts in the United States. In 2008, the 'status' dropout rate by race/ethnicity is, Asian/Pacific Islander, 4,4%; White, 4.8%; Black, 9.9%; American Indian/ Alaska Native 14.6; Hispanic, 18.3% (Chapman, et al., 2010).

A comparison of the U.S. total population percentages with the total status dropout population percentages also illustrates the overrepresentation of minority youth. Overall, Hispanics are most likely to be 'status dropouts' (Behnke, Gonzalez, & Cox, 2010; Hill & Torres, 2010). In 2008, the U.S. population percentages by race/ethnicity for 16-24 year-olds are, American Indian/Alaska Native, 0.8%; Asian/Pacific Islander 4.0%; Black, 14.3%; Hispanic, 17.9%; and White, 61.1% (Chapman, et al., 2010). Compare this with the race/ethnicity percentages of the total 'status' dropout population, American Indian/Alaska Native, 1.4% ; Asian/Pacific Islander, 2.2%; Black,

17.9%; Hispanic, 40.9% ; and White, 36.7% (Chapman, et al., 2010). Correlations with race/ethnicity and social class position can explain why
American Indian/Alaska Native, Black, and Hispanic youth are overrepresented in dropout statistics.

Given the knowledge and technology-based nature of today's economic
world, it comes as no surprise that those who drop out are likely to suffer
from multiple social and economic disadvantages throughout their lives
(Horvart & Davis, 2011; Ream & Rumberger, 2008). Dropouts are more
likely to be poor, be unemployed, have low self-esteem, have poor health, be
involved in criminal activity, end up under the control of the criminal justice
system, and be non-productive members of society (Behnke, et al., 2010;
Easton, 2008; Payne & Slocumb, 2011; Plank, et al., 2008; Sum, Khatiwada,
McLaughlin, & Palma, 2011). Ultimately, those who drop out are more likely to live on the social and economic boundaries of society as adults, with all
the difficulties that come along with such a marginal existence. The cost of
dropping out, for both the dropouts and society, is quite high. As a general
rule, youth do not grow up saying "I want to be a dropout when I grow up."
In order to adequately understand dropping out of school, we need to understand the factors which correlate with dropping out.

UNDERSTANDING DROPOUTS

Empirical research has demonstrated that there is truly a multitude of factors
which play a role in putting kids at risk for dropping out of school; these
factors include individual level issues such as home problems and pregnancy;
school issues such as poor quality, poor performance, and negative social
interactions at school; neighborhood level factors such as low SES, high
levels of negative peer associations, violence, drugs, and crime; and, family
factors such as low SES, and abuse and/or substance abuse (Behnke, et al.,
2010; Hondo, et al., 2008; Janosz, et al., 2008; Payne & Slocumb, 2011;
Plank, et al., 2008; Ruffolo, 2008; Smink & Schargel, 2004; Staff & Kreager,
2008).

Dropouts are likely to be students of color, poor, living in poverty, male,
have failed a grade, read significantly below grade-level, score at the bottom
on standardized tests; and, before they drop out, they are more likely to
already be enrolled in remedial courses, sitting there disengaged and getting
into trouble. These "students not only never realize their promise but believe
a myth that suggests they have no promise" (Jackson & Cooper, 2007, p.
244). The myriad of problems faced by many at-risk students is daunting and
can seem overwhelming. In order to facilitate an understanding of dropouts
within the context of influencing factors, theorists and researchers have
framed the issue as a process of disengagement from school.

Process and Engagement

Theorists and researchers stress that dropping out of school should be understood as a process which leads to disengagement from school. An at-risk student does not simply decide one day, spontaneously, to drop out of school. Rather, the decision to drop out represents the final outcome of a process of "diminishing school engagement" that has taken place over time (Archembault, Janosz, Fallu, & Pagani, 2009; Ensminger, Lamkin, & Jacobsen, 1996; Finn, 1989; Payne & Slocumb, 2011; Plank, et al., 2008; Ream & Rumberger, 2008; Wehlage, Rutter, Smith, Lesko, & Fernandez, 1989). The concept of engagement, or lack thereof, is the central organizing principle for theoretical perspectives on dropping out of school (Janosz, et al., 2008; Ream & Rumberger, 2008). Scholars use different concepts such as "bonding" or "connectedness" when theorizing or researching about student engagement with school (Archembault, et al., 2009). Research findings have consistently demonstrated that not being engaged with school (both academically and socially) increases the likelihood of dropping out of school (Janosz, et al., 2008; Ream & Rumberger, 2008).

Students need to feel invested in their school and have a sense that there is a "place" for them there. While the numerous risk factors faced by many dropout youth are relevant for understanding dropping out, there are specific school issues that fuel a process of disengagement from school. Research documents that both academic performance and social standing at school are important for understanding the extent of a student's engagement with school. Finn's (1989) perspective is widely cited as seminal for understanding how a student becomes disengaged from school. Rather straightforwardly, and rather significantly for this chapter, Finn (1989) and other theorists and researchers (e.g., Archembault, et al., 2009; Janosz, et al., 2008; Perreira, Harris, & Lee, 2006; Plank, et al., 2008; Wehlage, et al., 1989) posit that one reason why students disengage from school is due to poor academic performance and a lack of interest in the curriculum; in short, curriculum "matters" (Hallam & Rogers, 2008). Behnke, et al.'s (2010) research with Hispanic students finds that "students saw academic challenges as an important factor for school dropout" (p.410). Behnke, et al. write that their "findings are consistent with those of other large-scale studies of dropout, which generally place academic challenges as a leading factor" (p. 400). Plank et al.'s (2008) research documents that academic factors are especially important early in high school (9th grade), but social factors (peer influence) become more important in the later high school years. Smink and Schargel (2004) state "poor academic performance linked to retention in one grade is the single strongest school-related predictor of dropping out. One report indicated that out of every ten dropouts, nine had been retained at least one year" (p. 33). Easton (2008) notes that being retained more than once "almost guarantees the student will eventually drop out" (p. xvi). Research on dropouts highlights the importance of having "culturally responsive" curriculum with minority, at-risk students (Behnke, et al., 2010; Hill & Torres, 2010; Hondo, et al. 2008).

In addition, and related to academic performance, students who do not feel they are socially "integrated" into school are more likely to drop out; involvement in extracurricular activities and even being, to some extent, "popular" can matter (Behnke, et al, 2010; Hondo, et al., 2008; Janosz, et al., 2008; Staff & Kreager, 2008). Those who do not feel like they "belong" at school often view school as a "negative experience" (Lee & Breen, 2007, p. 341). Thus, while academic success is important for school engagement, how a student feels about their standing in the social world of the school is also important.

DROPOUTS AND DIFFERENTIATION

This final section presents the relevancy of differentiation for working with students at risk for dropping out (as well as those who have dropped out and are returning to a traditional or alternative school). First, a very brief overview of differentiation is provided (see Chapter 2 for detailed specifics on differentiated instruction); next, how differentiation is particularly well- suited for dropouts and those at risk for dropping out is discussed.

Differentiated Instruction

Differentiation in instruction is based upon the premise that students are unique individuals and should be at the "front" of the learning process (Hall, 2011; Tomlinson, 1999; Tomlinson & McTighe, 2006). The differentiated instruction framework involves just what its title implies, having different types of instructional process and curriculum for different students. While there must be an awareness of and attention given to general standards, the process of instruction and the particular curriculum utilized to reach those standards varies according to unique, individual learners (Tomlinson & McTighe, 2006). The curriculum and process is flexible according to student needs, rather than expecting different students to conform to a preset process and or rigid curriculum formats (Hall, 2011). Hall (2011) states, "to differentiate instruction is to recognize students varying background knowledge, readiness, language, preferences in learning, interests, and to react responsively" (p. 3). Tomlinson (1999) discusses the concept of differentiation:

> In differentiated classrooms, the teacher is well aware that human beings share the same basic needs for nourishment, shelter, safety, belonging, achievement, contribution, and fulfillment. She also knows that human beings find those

things in different fields of endeavor, according to different paths. She understands that by attending to human differences she can best help individuals
address their common needs..... In a differentiated classroom, the teacher
unconditionally accepts students as they are, and she expects them to become
all they can be (p.10).

Dropouts and Differentiated Instruction

When educators examine who tends to drop out of school and the contributing factors which lead to the decision to dropout, the relevancy and preventa-
tive potential of differentiated instruction can be seen. As discussed earlier,
dropouts are likely to face a plethora of social problems; these problems
often include individual, family, community, and economic issues. Thus,
teachers should not think that differentiation can be a panacea for addressing
dropping out of school. Yet, at the same time, teachers know that engagement with school is perhaps the key factor for understanding the process of
becoming a dropout; furthermore, research has documented that school engagement can be directly linked with school performance. Students who have
dropped out have often performed poorly at school. Thus, it seems more than
reasonable to posit that differentiation has a role to play in preventing dropping out of school.

A differentiated instruction approach can be a catalyst for helping students perform well academically and reach their full potential. It offers a
curriculum and process that is individualized and student-centered; thus, increasing the likelihood that the student will become engaged with school.
While schools can also function to maintain social inequalities, they can also
be places where lower-class kids can achieve and get on a path to a better and
higher SES adult life (Horvart & Davis, 2011). Given the general school
challenges that poor youth face, and the extent to which they are likely to
drop out of school, a differentiated instruction approach appears to be an
excellent way to attempt to educationally engage them.

Scholars suggest that differentiated instruction is useful for addressing the
dropout phenomenon. Janosz, et al. (2008) write that "interventions" for
potential dropouts "need to be differentiated" (p. 35). In his discussion of the
dropout problem and successful alternative school programs, Dupper (2008)
writes that addressing "the academic needs of these youth requires a hands-
on, experiential curriculum that is tailored to the unique learning style of
each student" (p. 27). Hallam and Rogers (2008) write that "schools need to
be proactive in tailoring the taught curriculum to meet student needs" (p.
285). Hallam and Rogers (2008) also note that "one of the main factors
associated with school failure and pupils who drop out of education is the
mismatch between the academic curriculum offered by the school and the
interests and skills of the students" (p. 162).

Differentiated instruction is also well suited to the special nature of the dropout population in the United States. Consider the case of Hispanic youth; as noted earlier, these youth represent more than 40% of the total 'status' dropout population in the United States. Hispanics often attend the worst schools in the poorest districts (Hill & Torres, 2010). Hispanics often have very high educational aspirations, and hope to "make it" but have the highest dropout rate (Hill & Torres, 2010).

Hondo, et al.'s (2008) research on Hispanic dropouts discusses the importance of a "culturally responsive," differentiated instruction approach for working with (potential) dropouts. In Hondo, et al.'s study, dropouts view school as an "unrewarding experience" and "did not feel valued by the schools they attended" (pp. 10-11); the school presents a 'color blind curriculum and pedagogy" (p. 107). Hondo, et al. (2008) write that "if the diverse students in our public schools do not see themselves as well represented in the curriculum, instruction, and staff they can erroneously conclude that schooling is not for them" (p. 116); they also note that "differentiated instruction can be a way to allow teachers to attend to the individualized learning needs of students within the regular heterogeneously grouped classroom" (p. 133).

CONCLUDING THOUGHTS

It is important to highlight a few obvious, yet important, issues regarding differentiated instruction. Such instruction cannot take place in a vacuum; there must be an awareness of attending to the wider staff and school context. Researchers have consistently demonstrated the importance of high expectations, caring teachers, and a supportive, flexible school community when addressing the dropout phenomenon (Dupper, 2008; Hallam & Rogers, 2008; Hondo, et al., 2008; Lee & Breen, 2007).

Regarding minority youth, researchers have documented the need for bilingual, support staff (Behnke, et al., 2010; Hill & Torres, 2010). Finally, as noted earlier, some research has documented that the older a student gets (later high school years), the more important peer influences are for understanding the decision to drop out. Academic disengagement seems especially important for understanding dropping out early in high school. Consequently, when teachers are thinking about implementing differentiated instruction, it is fair to say that the old adage "the earlier the better" rings true.

Differentiated instruction, with its individualized framework, has the potential to enable at risk students to perform well. Performing well at school means a student is more engaged. A more engaged student is less likely to drop out.

REFERENCES

Archambault, I., Janosz, M., Fallu, J., & Pagani, L. (2009) Student engagement and its relationship with early high school dropout. Journal of Adolescence, 32 (2009), 651-670.

Barton P. E. (2005). One third of a nation: Rising dropout rates and declining opportunities. Princeton, NJ: Policy Information Center, Educational Testing Service.

Behnke, A., Gonzalez, L. & Cox, R. (2010). Latino students in new arrival states: Factors and services to prevent youth from dropping out. Hispanic Journal of Behavioral Sciences, 32, 385–409.

Chapman, C., Laird, J., & KewalRamani, A. (2010). Trends in high school dropout and completion rates in the United States: 1972–2008 (NCES 2011-012). Washington, D.C.: National Center for Education Statistics, Institute of Education Sciences, U.S. Department of Education. Retrieved September 28, 2011 from http://nces.ed.gov/pubsearch.

Dillon, S. (2011, September 22). Obama to waive parts of No Child Left Behind. New York Times. Retrieved September 28, 2011 from http://www.nytimes.com/2011/09/23/education/23educ.html.

Dupper, D. (2008). Guides for designing and establishing alternative school programs for dropout prevention. In C. Franklin, M. Harris, & P. Allen-Meares. (Eds), The school practitioner's concise companion, (pp. 23-34). New York, NY: Oxford University Press.

Easton, L. (2008). Engaging the disengaged: How schools can help struggling students succeed. Thousand Oaks, CA: Corwin Press.

Ensminger, M. E., Lamkin, R. P., & Jacobson, N. (1996). School leaving: A longitudinal perspective including neighbourhood effects. Child Development, 67, 2400-2416.

Finn, J. D. (1989). Withdrawing from school. Review of Educational Research, 59 (2), 117-142.

Franklin, C., Harris, M., & Allen-Meares, P. (Eds.). (2008). The school practitioner's concise companion to preventing dropout and attendance problems. New York, NY: Oxford University Press.

Hall, T. (2011). Differentiated instruction and implications for UDL instruction. Wakefield, MA: National Center on Accessible Instructional Materials. Retrieved September 28, 2011 from http://aim.cast.org/learn/historyarchive/backgroundpapers/differentiated_instruction.

Hallam, S. & Rogers, L. (2008). Improving behavior and attendance at school. Berkshire, England, UK: Open University Press.

Hill, N. & Torres, K. (2010) Negotiating the American dream: The paradox of aspirations and achievement among Latino students and engagement between their families and schools. Journal of Social Issues, 66 (1), 95-112.

Hondo, C., Gardiner, M., & Sapien, Y. (2008). Latino dropouts in rural America: Realities and possibilities Albany, NY: SUNY Press.

Horvat, E. & Davis, J. (2011). Schools as sites for transformation: Exploring the contribution of habitus. Youth and Society, 43, 142-170.

Jackson, Y. & Cooper, E. (2007). Building academic success with underachieving adolescents. In K. Beers, R. Probst, & L. Rief (Eds.), Adolescent literacy: Turning promise into practice, (pp.242-256). Portsmouth, NH: Heinemann.

Janosz, M., Archambault, I., Morizot, J., & Pagani, L. (2008). School engagement trajectories and their differential predictive relations to dropout. Journal of Social Issues, 64 (1), 21-40.

Lee, T. & Breen, L. (2007). Young people's perceptions and experiences of leaving high school early: An exploration. Journal of Applied and Community Social Psychology, 17, 329-346.

Payne, R. & Slocumb, P. (2011). Boys in poverty: A framework for understanding dropouts. Bloomington, IN: Solution Tree Press.

Perreira, K. M., Harris, K. M., & Lee, D. (2006). Making it in America: High school completion by immigrant and native youth. Demography, 43, 511-536.

Plank, S., DeLuca, S., & Estacion, A. (2008). High school dropouts and the role of career and technical education: A survival analysis of surviving high school. Sociology of Education, 81 (4), 345-370.

Ream, R. & Rumberger, R. (2008). School engagement, peer social capital, and school dropouts among Mexican American and Non-Latino White students. Sociology of Education, 81,
   109-139.

Ruffolo, M. (2008). Enhancing skills of students vulnerable to underachievement and academic
   failure. In C. Franklin, M. Harris, & P. Allen-Meares. (Eds), The school practitioner's
   concise companion, (pp. 13-21). New York, NY: Oxford University Press.

Smink, J. & Schargel, F. P. (2004). Helping students graduate: A strategic approach to dropout
   prevention. Larchmont, NY: Eye on Education.

Staff, J. & Kreager, D. (2008). Too cool for school? Violence, peer status and high school
   dropout. Social Forces, 87, 445-471.

Stillwell, R., Sable, J., & Plotts, C. (2011). Public school graduates and dropouts from the
   common core of data: School year 2008–09 (NCES 2011-312). Washington, D.C.: U.S.
   Department of Education, National Center for Education Statistics. Retrieved September 28,
   2011 from http://nces.ed.gov/pubsearch.

Sum, A., Khatiwada, I., McLaughlin, J., & Palma, S. (2011). No country for young men:
   Deteriorating market prospects for low-skilled men in the United States. Annals of the
   American Academy of Political and Social Science, 634, 24-55.

Swanson, C. B. (2008). Cities in crisis: A special analytic report on high school graduation.
   Bethesda, MD: Editorial Projects in Education Research Center.

Tomlinson, C. (1999). The differentiated classroom: Responding to the needs of all learners.
   Alexandria, VA: Association for Supervision and Curriculum Development.

Tomlinson, C. & McTighe, J. (2006). Integrating differentiated instruction and understanding
   by design. Alexandria, VA: Association for Supervision and Curriculum Development.

Warren, J. & Halpern-Manners, A. (2009). Measuring high school graduation rates at the state
   level: What difference does methodology make? Sociological Methods and Research, 38, 3-
   37.

Wehlage, G., Rutter, R., Smith, G., Lesko, N., & Fernandez, F. (1989). Reducing the risk:
   Schools as communities of support. New York, NY: Falmer Press.

Chapter Fourteen

Differentiated Instruction

*Strategies for Students
with Moderate and Severe Disabilities*

Dorothy Squatrito Millar

INTRODUCTION

Educating students with moderate and severe disabilities is a challenge. "Challenges" is a term that summarizes what educators continually encounter from an array of fronts. Current reform agendas posed by legislation (including No Child Left Behind and Individuals with Disabilities Education Improvement Act, especially with regard to the use of evidence/research- based practices and increasing student achievement) have produced unprecedented efforts to ensure that educators are able to meet the needs of, and effectively instruct, a diverse student population. This diversity is evidenced by the variety of student cultures, languages, economic levels, and disabilities, with each student possessing varying needs and abilities (Friend & Bursuck, 2011; Kennedy & Horn, 2004; Vaughn, Bos, & Schumm, 2010). With great challenges, comes great opportunity. Something to keep in mind is that since their inception, classrooms have never categorically been homogeneous. Quite some time ago, it is estimated that a teacher should expect to have a ten-year range in reading ability across same-age students in a traditional class (Singer & Donlan, 1989).

Given that educators have a long standing history of educating diverse students, they are well-positioned to adjust their instruction that aims to enable each student to have access to a high quality education where they can continually acquire knowledge and develop skills. These students include those who have moderate and severe intellectual or developmental disabilities. In order for all students to truly learn, it is essential that educators (1) uphold high expectations for each student; (2) provide effective instruction to make it such that each student can take advantage of having a rich and high quality curriculum; (3) collaborate with others to establish goals that will enable each student to grow as much as he or she can, and to acknowledge the growth when it occurs; and (4) create and sustain a classroom environment where all students are valued, respected, engaged, and develop skills that prepare them for a future of continued learning (Friend & Bursuck, 2011; Vaughn et al., 2010; Lawrence-Brown, 2004; Wolfe & Hall, 2003).

Numerous evidence-based educational approaches exist that educators can employ to meet the unique needs of students and to capitalize on their learning. As presented in previous chapters, using varying instructional strategies is a key element for differentiating instruction, which can benefit students with a range of needs and ability levels (Neber, Finsterwald, & Urban, 2001), learning styles, cultural/linguistic backgrounds (Vaughn, et al., 2010), and disabilities, including moderate and severe intellectual or developmental disabilities (Lawrence-Brown, 2004; Wolfe & Hall, 2003). This chapter provides strategies and examples regarding how to align individualized education program (IEP) content with common core and state adopted standards in addition to differentiating instruction and planning multilevel lessons that are manageable in a standards-based instructional context. Supports emphasized within this chapter are directed to students with moderate and severe intellectual or developmental disabilities; however, the information is relevant and applicable to meeting the needs of all students in a diverse general education classroom.

STUDENTS WITH MODERATE AND SEVERE DISABILITIES

The No Child Left Behind (NCLB) federal legislation specifies that states may count up to 1% of students participating in its assessment system as proficient using alternate assessments founded on alternative achievement standards (Courtade & Browder, 2011). Federal policy denotes this 1% of students as having "significant cognitive disabilities" and affords the opportunity to each state to decide the eligibility criteria for determining which students are to be counted within the 1%. The state criteria cannot simply be based on a disability label, i.e., a student who has a label of "severe cognitive impairment" does not automatically qualify as a student who should take an alternative assessment. In actuality, students from every federal disability category may have severe levels of disabilities, hence be considered as part of the 1% (NCLB, 2002). This chapter focuses on students who have moderate to severe intellectual or developmental disabilities that may be accompanied by other disabilities including sensory or physical impairments, e.g., autism, traumatic brain injury. Further, this chapter uses the phrase 'intellectual disability' rather than 'cognitive disability' as federal law will change its reference of 'mental retardation' to 'intellectual disability' within the near future (Courtade & Browder, 2011).

Inclusion and Students with Disabilities

The inclusion of students with moderate and severe intellectual or developmental disabilities as the construct pertains to general education classrooms has become increasingly prevalent (Friend & Bursuck, 2011; Gartin, Murdick, Imbeau, & Perner, 2002; Kennedy & Horn, 2004; Vaughn, et al., 2010). Although the term inclusion is used regularly in the world of education, the interpretation of the construct varies. Frequently, inclusion has been synonymously used with mainstreaming. The two constructs, however, should not be equated.

Mainstreaming typically refers to students receiving a large portion or the majority of their education in a special education self-contained or resource (pull-out) room, and participate in the general education setting only when deemed appropriate (Vaughn, et al., 2010). When in the general education setting, the students who have a disability may or may not receive supports or accommodations; hence, mainstreaming is often viewed as leaving students to either 'sink or swim' in the situation (Vaughn, et al., 2010).

Inclusion, in comparison, is actually a philosophy that supports the belief that all students, regardless of ability or disability, have an important role in the general education system. Friend and Bursuck (2011) suggest the following inclusion foundations, (1) all students are to receive education in the school and classroom that they would attend if they had no disability; (2) the law of natural proportion (that is, representative of the school district at large) is to be observed regarding the number of students with disabilities enrolled in each school and classroom; and (3) honor a zero-reject philosophy such that no student is excluded on the basis of type or extent of disability. Additional aspects pertaining to the inclusive philosophy are that school and general education placements are age- and grade-appropriate such that no self-contained special education classes exist; special education supports exist within the general education class and in all educational environments; and that all students should have access to the general education curriculum and state adopted standards (Friend & Bursuck, 2011).

It should be noted that the Individuals with Disabilities Education Improvement Act of 2004 (IDEA, 2004), the main special education law, does not mandate or use the term inclusion but rather strongly encourages consideration of appropriate placement of students with disabilities in general education settings. The purpose of IDEA is to ensure that all students with disabilities, in the least restrictive environment (LRE), have available to them a free and appropriate public education that emphasizes special education and related services designed to meet their unique needs and prepare them for further education, employment and independent living (IDEA, 2004, [602(d)(1)(A)]). Essentially, inclusion is an interpretation of LRE. The legislation is updated approximately every five years to determine what works as well as what needs clarification.

DEVELOPING STANDARDS-BASED INDIVIDUALIZED EDUCATION PROGRAMS (IEPS)

As a result of the IDEA amendments and NCLB, educators begin to focus on promoting and ensuring access for all students, including students with moderate and severe intellectual or developmental disabilities, to the general education curriculum, as well as state and local assessments. Alternative assessments are to be considered as a possible option for 1% of students, where participation in the state large-scale assessments, even with accommodations, is deemed inappropriate (NCLB, 2002). Schools are accountable for assessing all students they serve to determine the extent to which students are achieving and meeting grade-level standards. In 2010, most states adopt the Common Core Standards for mathematics and language arts. The standards are sorted by grade level per content area and define the knowledge and skills all students should acquire during their K-12 schooling. In addition to the Common Core Standards, most states have established additional standards in content areas such as science and social studies (Courtade & Browder, 2011).

STANDARDS AND STUDENTS WITH DISABILITIES

Students, regardless of the severity of their disability, are predicted to learn the same standards that have been developed for their grade level placement (Courtade & Browder, 2011). As an example, a student with a moderate intellectual disability in sixth grade is expected to focus on sixth-grade standards. If, however, a student is unable to participate in the general assessment, the student may take an alternative assessment that addresses some areas of the core standards.

When alternatives are needed, it is essential that a collaborative team of individuals work together, including general education and special education teachers, parents, and students themselves. Each team member is responsible for learning about the assigned grade-level standards for the student. Assigned grade level is based on the student's chronological age, in contrast to an instructional grade that is based on the student's present level of performance. Some states provide special curricular planning resources (often referred to as curricular frameworks, extended standards, or alternative achievement standards) directed to those students who are planning to take the state alternative assessment.

The extended standards are aligned with the general education standards a state has adopted and if available, are posted on the state's education website. Focusing on assigned grade-level and extended standards can be quite a daunting challenge; therefore, it is essential that the Individualized Education Program (IEP) team collaborate to align a student's IEP goals with targeted standards, while also identifying instructional supports, accommodations, and assistive technology that may assist the student (Courtade & Browder, 2011).

IEP Requirements

An individualized education program (IEP), as a requirement of IDEA, specifies the special education services a student with a disability must receive. The IEP is to include (1) a statement of the student's present levels of academic achievement and functional performance; (2) a statement of measurable annual goals, including academic and functional goals, designed to meet the student's needs that result from the student's disability to enable the student to be involved in and make progress in the general education curriculum; and (3) for students with disabilities who take alternate assessments aligned to alternate achievement standards, a description of benchmarks or short-term objectives (IDEA, 2004, [34 CFR 300.320(a)] [20 U.S.C. 1414(d)(1)(A)(i)]). In addition, the IEP is to include a description of how the student's progress toward meeting the annual goals described in IDEA (2004) 34 CFR 300.320 will be measured and when periodic reports on the progress the student is making toward meeting the annual goals will be distributed to IEP team members. IDEA (2004) also states that IEPs provide:

> A statement of any individual appropriate accommodations that are necessary to measure the academic achievement and functional performance of the child on State and district-wide assessments consistent with section 612(a)(16) of the Act; and if the IEP Team determines that the child must take an alternate assessment instead of a particular regular State or district-wide assessment of student achievement, a statement of why the child cannot participate in the regular assessment and why the particular alternate assessment selected is appropriate for the child (IDEA, [34 CFR 300.320(a)] [20 U.S.C. 1414(d)(1)(A)(i)]).

Beginning with the first special education federal legislation that was passed in 1975, educators along with members of a team have been creating IEPs. The difference between then and now is the emphasis, i.e., teams are to create IEPs that have goals that promote student learning of the state-adopted general education standards. It should be emphasized that an IEP should not include a goal for every standard in every content area, but rather the aim is to provide opportunities for students to learn the general education curriculum content to the fullest extent possible.

Students with disabilities are not necessarily given this opportunity in the recent past as the majority of educators solely teach a life-skills curriculum as replacement for the general education curriculum (Courtade & Browder, 2011; Friend & Bursuck, 2011; Gartin, et al., 2002; Lawrence-Brown, 2004; Vaughn, et al., 2010; Wolfe & Hall, 2003). Although life skills are essential for students to become autonomous, the opportunity to learn general education content standards may show that students can learn more than previously expected, as these students have little or no opportunity to learn age-appropriate academics (Courtade & Browder, 2011; Friend & Bursuck, 2011).

PRIORITIZING STANDARDS AND IEP GOALS

An IEP is not intended to define all instruction, and it should not be considered a curriculum (Courtade & Browder, 2011). An IEP, rather, should be viewed as a mechanism to help determine priorities regarding what students should learn and be able to do. Without question, determining what academic skills to teach students with moderate and severe intellectual or developmental disabilities can be daunting.

In an effort to assist with this challenge, Courtade and Browder (2011) have suggested that IEP teams consider the following six guidelines when identifying IEP goals and aligning them with state-adopted standards:

1. Be knowledgeable about the standards the state has adopted (e.g., Common Core standards for mathematics and language arts; or state created standards) and know the 'assigned level' standards (chronological grade) in relation to the instructional level.
2. Be knowledgeable with the state-adopted alternative assessments and whether alternate achievement standards (sometimes referred to as extended standards) are an option for students when developing IEP goals. Alternate standards should be aligned with the content standards, and not differ from the main content areas.
3. Ensure that planning is focused on the student. When considering how to support a student, it is essential to always keep at the forefront the student's preferences and needs, as well as their skills in academics, communication, and other functional daily living.
4. Consider both specific academic and broader access goals. In order to do this, it may be helpful for the IEP team to know the highlights of the curriculum to help them prioritize goals. Specific questions to

consider in relation to instruction are discussed below (See section on Continuum of Considerations).

5. Once academic content is determined, each team member should ask the question: "is it really academic?" It is not uncommon for the essence of academics to become obscured, and goals for the student to shift and therefore not be aligned with core standards. As an example, an English language arts reading standard cannot necessarily be considered aligned with a communication IEP goal. The team will need to spend time to make the alignment between student goals and content standards. This non-alignment can be addressed by following guideline six.

6. Be aware that not all IEP goals need to be aligned with academic standards. It may be that students with moderate and severe intellectual or developmental disabilities have need of therapy and need specific life-skill instruction. As an example, a student may need to learn to independently use a wheelchair. It may not be worth the time to try to align a mobility IEP goal with that of a mathematics or language arts standard (see Courtade & Browder, 2011, for detailed descriptions of guidelines).

To exemplify how a standards-based IEP can be developed, consider Nathan's educational situation. For several years, Nathan, who is twelve years-of-age and in sixth grade, has been successfully included in general education classrooms. Although not necessarily expected to learn at the same pace as his classmates, Nathan continues to progress as he aims to achieve the individualized educational goals that have been identified for him by a collaborative team consisting of educators (both general and special education teachers), a speech therapist, his parents, and Nathan himself. Nathan's achievement is demonstrated through the state's alternative assessment because it does not seem appropriate that he participate in large-scale assessments, even if given accommodations. His report card documents the progress he has made toward IEP goals that have been aligned with the Common Core State Standards which his state has adopted. These standards aim to define the knowledge and skills all students should acquire during their K-12 education careers in language arts and mathematics. His IEP goals are also aligned with the science and social studies standards his state designed. In addition to the academic areas, Nathan's IEP goals address his life-skill needs including hygiene, social interactions, vocational preparation, recreational involvement, and everyday living tasks, e.g., preparing simple meals, using money to purchase items. The collaborative team assembles on a fixed schedule, and as needed, to identify ways for Nathan to actively and meaningfully take part in lessons that might be too challenging at first glance. The team also determines how to align the general education lessons with Nathan's IEP goals. Nathan is a student with Down Syndrome and moderate intellectual disabilities.

Nathan enjoys most lessons that involve the use of computers. He hopes to work with them when he completes his public schooling. Although he is unable to consistently count objects or identify numbers without assistance, he can use manipulatives, calculators, and computer applications to some degree as he computes simple addition and subtraction problems. Nathan likes to have coins and dollar bills in his wallet as he enjoys purchasing things. He does need assistance with counting the appropriate amount of bills and finding the correct change while shopping or using a vending machine. He is able to write the majority of consonant letters and reads forty-five basic sight words. The words are mainly daily living terms, e.g., Enter, Push, Stop. With pictures and controlled sight words, Nathan can read short passages. Interestingly, he is able to read words specific to astronomy, biology, and dinosaurs. He can also read, again with picture cues, some basic recipes. He does well with using the microwave, but has no experience with stoves or ovens. Nathan is social, outgoing, and well-received by the majority of people he interacts with at school. Although social, his speech is often difficult to understand; he uses his 'tablet' to aid with making requests, answering questions, as well as sharing various 'apps' he has downloaded on the device. The 'tablet' is a recent educational find for Nathan. Not always understood by others, at times, Nathan becomes frustrated. He has shown his frustration by hitting and pushing. The 'tablet' has opened new doors for Nathan and there are many skills yet to be discovered. The technology may also provide Nathan with ways to further develop skills that are already in his repertoire.

Nathan had his mathematics IEP goals aligned with a targeted set of general education standards. To create the IEP, the first step of Nathan's team was to become knowledgeable with the assigned grade level general education standards, which for Nathan was grade six. The team also reviewed assessment results to determine his present level of education performance pertaining to mathematics. Given the information, the team targeted a selection of mathematics related IEP goals for Nathan. The IEP goals were adapted from Courtade and Browder (2011):

1. Nathan will divide a group of at least 20 items into 1-5 sets, as well as identify the number that represents each set for at least 8/10 trials a day, for 5 consecutive days. As a result, Nathan will also split these sets to display division of fractions and ratios for at least 8/10 trials a day, for 5 consecutive days. (Mathematics: Ratios & Proportional Relationships, Standard 6.1; Number System, Standard 6.1).

2. Nathan will solve 3-digit math problems for at least 8/10 trials a day, for 5 consecutive days. He will use a calculator to: enter each number,

the operation, the equals sign, and determine the answer. (Number System, Standard 6.3).

While determining the content standards, the team also identified ways that Nathan could participate in selected common core standards in Mathematics, grade 6. The examples are adapted from Courtade and Browder (2011).

1. Regarding the Common Core Standard 6 in the section Ratios and Proportional Relationships, item 1 "Understand the concept of a ratio and use ratio language to describe a ratio relationship between two quantities," the team thought Nathan might participate in relevant unit and lesson plans by applying the concept of ratio to planning a pizza party. If for every one pizza, 6 people can be fed, could he determine, by using a graphic organizer, how many pizzas would be needed to feed 12 to 20 peers? Refer to Nathan's IEP Goal 1.

2. Regarding mathematics Common Core Standard 6 in the section Number system, item 1 "Interpret and compute quotients of fractions, and solve word problems involving division of fractions by fractions, e.g., by using visual fraction models and equations to represent the problem," the team thought Nathan could focus on fractions that were used during cooking. As an example, given 8 tablespoons of butter (1 stick), how many tablespoons (and sticks) are needed when a recipe calls for 1 cup of butter? See Nathan's IEP Goal 1.

3. Regarding mathematics Common Core Standard 6 in the section Number System, item 3 "Fluently add, subtract, multiply, and divide multi-digit decimals using the standard algorithm for each operation" the team suggested that Nathan could monitor a simple budget by using a calculator to add, subtract, multiply and divide by entering digits and then using the correct symbol (+, -, x) and =. In applying these skills, Nathan will become more fluent in number recognition. Refer to Nathan's IEP Goal 2.

DIFFERENTIATING INSTRUCTION

Once a standards-based IEP is developed, differentiated instructional planning moves to the forefront as IEP team members further identify the supports students with moderate and severe intellectual and developmental disabilities can receive while being integral members within the general education classroom. Tomlinson and Kalbfleisch (1998) have indicated that differentiated classrooms are responsive to each student's ability level, varying interests, and diverse learning styles. Unlike mainstreaming, inclusive education that utilizes differentiated instruction will not isolate or exclude students with moderate and severe disabilities because they are unable to stay at the pace of their grade-level peers. To better ensure that students with disabilities are learning to their absolute potential, it is essential that they have continuous access to the general education curriculum and environments (Vaughn, et al., 2010).

Continuum of Considerations

Differentiated planning and instruction begins with high-quality general education lessons that (1) encourages dynamic learning, including hands-on experiences, cooperative learning, and real life applications of concepts/skills; (2) connects content with students' interests, communities, and experiences; (3) are aligned with the state-adopted standards; and (4) address the various learning styles of students (Lawrence-Brown, 2004; Wolfe & Hall, 2003).

Once furnished with a high-quality lesson, it is then that differentiation within that lesson becomes more of an emphasis. It should not be expected that major changes to a lesson are necessary simply because a student has a moderate or severe disability. The following points provide a continuum of considerations, based on the work of Wolfe and Hall (2003), to deliberate when considering changes in a lesson for students with moderate and severe disabilities who are included in general education settings.

Five considerations, adapted from Wolfe & Hall (2003):

1. Can the student participate in and perform the same tasks while using the same materials already incorporated into the general education lesson? That is, can the student participate without specialized changes being made to participate in the general curriculum lesson? Does the lesson clearly align with at least one goal written into the student's standards-based IEP? (Same activities, same standards, same objectives, same setting).

2. Can the student participate in and perform the same tasks, however, might benefit if provided some easier steps or minor modifications to aspects of the general education lesson? Again, consider whether the lesson is aligned with at least one goal found on the student's standard-based IEP. (Same activities, same standards, different (related) goals, same setting).

3. Can the student participate in and perform the same tasks incorporated into the general education lesson, but have the student use different materials? That is, are there aspects of the lesson that can be met by the student, even if they are not fully germane to the main lesson objectives, and also align to some extent with an IEP goal? That is, are there skills that can be learned by the student that embedded within the

general education lesson, and address IEP goals? (Similar activity, different (related) goals, same setting).

4. Does the student need to participate in and perform a different task, but may have the same theme as peers? This consideration emphasizes a functional curriculum that can be addressed in the general education classroom. Even though class lesson and activities can be unrelated to a goal on the student's IEP, the student stays in the general education setting. (Different activities, different (related) objectives, same setting).

5. Does the student require a different theme and a different task than designed in the general education lesson? This is the least desirable scenario; however, there may be times when a functional curriculum and IEP goals would be better addressed outside the general education classroom. (Different activities, different (unrelated) goals, different setting).

The first consideration is that simply no changes are needed, and that the lesson as designed, addresses the most effective ways to deliver instruction to the diverse group of students in the classroom. At the other end of the continuum of consideration for the student with moderate and severe intellectual and developmental disabilities, and others who may benefit from the change from the original lesson, is to temporarily have the students learn needed skills outside of the classroom. The continuum of considerations provides a series of questions designed to help educators and IEP team members make decisions regarding the most effective way to differentiate instruction during content standards-based units and lessons.

Collaborative Planning

Differentiating instruction is not new, as good teaching has always involved adapting lessons so that the needs of diverse learners are met. A key part of effectively differentiating instruction, especially when educating students who have moderate and severe intellectual or developmental disabilities, is through collaborative problem solving. Again, the team must be familiar with the general education state-adopted standards, as well as the curriculum and the student's standards-based IEP goals (Friend & Bursuck, 2011; Vaughn, et al., 2010; Wolfe & Hall, 2003).

Wolfe and Hall (2003) offer two stages of planning for special and general educators when considering how to ensure that education is meaningful to a student. The two stages provided by Wolfe and Hall (2003), however, have separate and unique roles for each type of educator. Here, the preplanning and planning stages, have been adapted and are presented in Table 14.1.

Briefly, during the preplanning stage, each IEP team member considers the content area of the unit, lessons, and activities to determine their key components. Once the components of the unit have been identified, the team then considers the student's IEP goals and how the goals can be addressed in

Stage 1. Preplanning Questions for each IEP Team Member to Consider	1. What are the goals of the unit and lesson? 2. What is the knowledge and skills students should obtain? 3. What are the component activities that will be used in each lesson of the unit? 4. Is it clear how the activities pertain to achieving the unit goal? 5. Will activities involve: cooperative learning groups and individual learning? 6. What materials are needed for the activities (e.g., computer, internet, poster boards)? 7. How will each student demonstrate their knowledge and skills (e.g., written report, oral presentation, quizzes)? 8. How often will assessment occur (both formative and summative)? 9. What are the IEP goals of students who have a disability? 10. What aspects of the unit, lessons, and activities can address IEP goals? 11. What are the abilities and limitations of the student with regard to cognitive level, behavior, motor skills, communication and social interaction abilities? 12. What level on of the continuum of consideration hierarchy is most appropriate? 13. What, if any, changes may be needed to ensure the students is actively and meaningfully participating in instruction?
Stage 2. Planning and Discussion as a Team	1. Based on the sharing of responses of each team member that address the questions listed above, what consensus has been reached on the IEP goals that can be addressed during the unit and subsequent lessons? 2. What adaptations, accommodations, or supports, if any, will be used (e.g., co-teaching, personal assistant, technical devices)? 3. How will student progress be assessed? 4. How will the student's progress towards achieving IEP and other goals be communicated to all IEP team members (e.g., informal meetings, weekly/monthly fixed team meetings, report cards)?

Table 14.1. Preplanning and Planning Considerations. List adapted from Wolfe & Hall (2003).

the general education content-area unit. In the preplanning stage, the IEP team members think about ideas before holding a group meeting. In the second planning stage, the team meets to determine the IEP goals that will be targeted per lesson, what instructional methods are planned, if additional differentiated methods are needed, what adaptations or accommodations, if any, will be necessary, what additional supports may be needed, and how student progress will be examined.

To continue with Nathan's situation, Table 14.2 presents how the continuum of considerations and planning stages can be implemented.

Nathan's IEP is comprised of a number of goals across both academic content and life skills areas, e.g., communication, self-determination, hygiene, leisure/recreation, and social interactions. Using segments of Nathan's IEP, the educators along with IEP team members design an instructional plan to ensure that one lesson can address more than one of his IEP goals. The examples in Table 14.3 focus on the mathematics content area. As demonstrated in this example, the IEP goals that are addressed differ across activities relative to the content taught on any particular day. In addition, considerations of additional support needed or required to implement instruction (i.e., adaptive equipment, additional personnel, and technical support) are shared. By collaborating and thinking through the continuum considerations and planning sessions, a majority of Nathan's IEP goals can be addressed during mathematics sessions.

An additional strategy that team members can use is that of a matrices, where each student who has IEP goals can be displayed. Matrices can provide a visual chart regarding how IEP goals align with general curriculum content standards and helps to ensure that each of the students who have IEP goals are systematically scheduled and addressed. These matrices can also assist with dialogue among IEP team members as they consider ways to differentiate instruction needs and thinking of possible adaptations.

IDENTIFYING STRATEGIES AND MONITORING STUDENT PROGRESS

It is essential that effective instruction is provided to all students, especially when considering standards and IEP goals pertaining to students with moderate and severe intellectual and developmental disabilities. Effective instruction options are numerous. The following section provides strategies to differentiate instruction that may enable students to learn while monitoring their progress, and begins by emphasizing the importance of educators collaborating with the student and their family.

Common Core 6th Grade Mathematics Standard	Section Number System, item 3: "Fluently add, subtract, multiply, and divide multi-digit decimals using the standard algorithm for each operation."
Day 1: One hour	1. Activity for entire class: work on budgeting for a holiday gifts. 2. Amount to work with $250. 3. Students assigned to small collaborative learning groups. 4. 5 people on gift list (to be identified by team). 5. Determine strategy about how to portion monies per person on list. 6. Identify items per person. 7. Materials: paper & pencil, ads (newspaper, online), internet, textbooks. 8. Activity for Nathan: monitor a simple budget by using a calculator to add, subtract, multiply and divide by entering digits and then using the correct symbol (+, -, x) for 1 person with a $20 budget.
Additional IEP goals to be addressed during activity	1. Functional academics/reading: read and identify ads and amount of specific gift items. 2. Communication: Initiate conversation with group members while using tablet. 3. Social skills: Take turns interacting with peers during group work.
Day 2: One hour	1. Team completes budget. 2. Team prepares oral presentation (presentation will be 10 minutes). 3. Activity for Nathan: continue to monitor a simple budget by using a calculator to add, subtract, multiply and divide by entering digits and then using the correct symbol (+, -, x) for 1 person with a $20 budget.
Additional IEP goals to be addressed during activity	1. Social skills: Take turns interacting with peers during group work, prepares PowerPoint slides.
Day 3: One hour	1. Small groups make presentations
Additional IEP goals to be addressed during activity	1. Functional academics/math: keeps time for group and notifies when time is complete. 2. Communication: presents to class his responses via his tablet and PowerPoint slides. 3. Social skills: take turns interacting with peers during small and large group interactions.

Table 14.2. Implementing the Continuum of Considerations. Adapted from Courtade & Browder (2011) and Wolfe & Hall (2003).

Student and Family Involvement

Although the importance of collaborating has been emphasized throughout this chapter, ensuring active participation by students who have moderate and severe developmental or intellectual disabilities and their family members in educational planning cannot be stressed enough. Students and family members can be key team participants when it comes to deciding a student's IEP content, assessments, and instructional strategies, and may also be a source of information that pertains to the student's culture, religion, language, and experience (Downing 2008; Turnbull, Turnbull, Erwin, & Soodak, 2006). Students and family members can also provide information regarding the student's interests, concerns, and future goals that can guide educational programs.

The collaboration between student, family, and school is essential to increase the likelihood that a student will have a productive learning experience. To assist with facilitating student-family-school collaboration efforts, a number of processes have been designed, including pioneering processes such as person-centered planning (Pearpoint, Forest, & O'Brien, 1996) and choosing outcomes and accommodations for children (Giangreco, Cloninger, & Iverson, 1998). A major aim of these processes is to ensure that teams are student centered when having discussions and making plans. It should be noted that the role of family will change as the student ages, particularly when the student reaches the age of majority and the educational rights previously afforded to the parents are transferred to the student (Millar, 2009). During planning discussions, it is essential that students, family members, and all IEP team participants are reminded that the student should be the driving force during discussions as they become older, especially when transition from the age of being a child to that of an adult occurs (Millar, 2003, 2007).

Assistive Technology

IDEA (2004) defines assistive technology as any item, piece of equipment, or product system that is used to increase, maintain, or improve functional capabilities of individuals with disabilities and can be used in educational settings to provide a variety of accommodations or adaptations. Assistive technologies encompass a range of devices from "low tech" that typically do not require batteries or electricity (e.g., pencil grip, photo album that has pictures with the aim of helping a student communicate) to "high tech" that can vary in cost, e.g., calculators, tape recorders, computer software applications. A variety of assistive technology can be used to modify delivery of instruction, act as materials during lessons, as well as, provide students with a means to demonstrate what they know. Common devices include audio books (teachers can record lessons, students can talk out their answers to questions), screen reading programs, voice recognition software to support written expression, and simulation software to illustrate content concepts (Obremski, Palmer, Wehmeyer, et al., in press).

Depending on the ability of the student, it may be helpful for a student to have ways to demonstrate their knowledge in a manner that differs from their peers. For example, some students with moderate and severe disabilities may not be able to verbally express their knowledge, hence need to use a communication device such that they can point to a response with their fingers or push a button. It may also be the case that some students lack motor control necessary to use their hands and, rather, rely on their eye-gaze to indicate a response (Ketterer, Schuster, Morse, & Collins, 2007; Browder, Flowers, & Wakeman, 2008). For any assistive device to be used effectively by a student, systematic instruction will be needed (See section below on Evidenced-Based Instruction). Instruction will be needed not only by the student, but so too will the adults and peers in the classroom. To learn more about possible assistive devices, state department of education websites often provide links to organizations that offer services.

Applications

In recent years, a number of technology devices have become available (e.g., smart phones, tablets) that are not previously accessible to the mainstream and there is a new emphasis on finding educationally-related applications that can be used by IEP team members and students alike. Educators can use applications to support instructional delivery, modify activities, and help students convey what they have learned. These devices are increasingly becoming more common place and when used, do not single out the student who has a disability (Wehmeyer & Tasse, in press). In fact, such devices may help the students to further develop their skills and assist them in interacting with others. Nathan, as an example, could use his tablet to share applications he downloads during lessons to show what he knows to his teachers, parents, and peers. He could also share various applications while conversing with peers.

Because this area is relatively new, research is needed to systematically determine the extent to which applications assist students. Until then, applications in the classroom can be systematically investigated to determine specific student impact. Also, applications continue to be designed to meet the needs of students as traditional assistive devices have, and continue to be, expensive, and do not always meet a student's needs (Stock, Davies, Wehmeyer, & Lachapelle, 2011). For example, a father recently designed an application for his son who has autism, such that he could create simple sentences by selecting from a row of virtual flashcards that represent nouns and verbs. The application allows parents and educators to customize the flashcards, uploading their own photos, typing in their own text and recording their own voices (Palmer, Wehmeyer, Davies, & Stock, in press). Applications such as this are continually being designed, and technology devices are increasingly being used by families, educators, and service providers that aim to ensure the person who has a disability is as self-sufficient as possible and enjoy a quality of life (Palmer, et al., in press).

Blended Teaching and Learning – Flipped Instruction

Although no vast research base exists, there has been an increase in the use of blended teaching and learning, also referred to as "flipped" instruction (Means, Toyama, Murphy, Bakia, & Jones, 2010). Blended teaching typically refers to combining online and traditional face-to face methods where teachers assign short online video lectures for homework, students can work at their own pace, and then have students participate in discussions and hands-on activities while in class. Video lectures can be presented in a number of ways. For example, there is software that allows teachers to speak over their lecture slides, and even write on the slide while online, then archive the lecture. Even though not all students may have access to computers, this teaching strategy is one to consider as initial results indicate that students do as well or modestly better than simply using face-to-face instruction (Means, et al., 2010).

Evidence-Based Instruction

A number of evidence-based practices, such as systematic instruction, have been developed that are highly recommended when teaching students who have moderate and severe intellectual or developmental disabilities, (Downing, 2008; Snell & Brown, 2006; Westling & Fox, 2009). Systematic instruction involves identifying target skills, teaching by prompting and reinforcing the desired skills within typical age-appropriate environments, while constantly evaluating student progress. Systematic instruction can be used to teach academics (e.g., reading, mathematics processes, science lab procedures) (Browder, Spooner, Ahlgrim-Delzell, Harris, & Wakeman, 2008; Browder, Trela, & Jimenez, 2006; Browder, Wakeman, Spooner, Ahlgrim-Delzell, & Algozzine, 2006; Courtade, Spooner, & Browder, 2007).).

Systematic instruction can also be used to teach essential life skills (e.g., communication, self-care, self-determination), and can occur in general education classrooms as well as in the community (Downing, 2008; Falkenstine, Collins, Schuster, & Kleinert, 2009; Jimenez, Browder, & Courtade, 2008; Snell & Brown, 2006; Westling & Fox, 2009). Frequently used types of systematic instruction are time delay and hierarchy prompts, i.e.., "least to most" intrusive prompts, "most to least" intrusive prompts.

Time Delay

Time delay is a systematic, essentially errorless learning, instructional procedure (Snell & Brown, 2006; Westling & Fox, 2009). With time delay, student errors are minimized as the instructor teaches accurate responses by pointing, then modeling the correct response, and allowing the student to imitate the model.

As an example, consider an instructor wanting to teach vocabulary words that will be used in an upcoming science unit. At first, the instructor points to the word and immediately states the word. The student is then to state the word following the instructor model. The instructor gradually increases the time delay between pointing to a word and giving the correct answer. The instructor reinforces the student's response by restating the desired term. The aim of this method is to have the student anticipate the correct response between the point cue and when the instructor gives the response. Time delay has been effectively used to teach academic skills (e.g., reading, mathematics, science) as well as life-skills (Browder, Ahlgrim-Delzell, Spooner, Mims, & Bates ,2009; Snell & Brown, 2006; Westling &d Fox, 2009).

Hierarchy Prompts

With the "least to most intrusive prompts" instructional strategy, the instructor identifies a hierarchy of up to four prompts that are considered to be "least to most" intrusive, e.g., indirect verbal prompt "what is next?;" model with direct verbal prompt "pour the water into the bowl" while demonstrating the task; "pour the water into the bowl" while providing gentle hand over hand physical guidance (Snell & Brown, 2006; Westling & Fox, 2009). The aim is to provide ample opportunities for the student to respond and eventually not need any instructor prompts.

In comparison, using a "most to least" intrusive instructional approach may seem appropriate, particularly when there is concern that a student will make an error or not have the motor skills in their repertoire. Using the same example of pouring water into a bowl, with "most to least," the instructor first provides a direct verbal cue while providing "hand over hand" support such that the student can perform the task. When the student demonstrates that they have the motor skills, the "hand over hand" physical support is systematically eliminated. Then, the next type of prompts may include the instructor pointing or modeling the task when giving direct verbal cues (Snell & Brown, 2006; Westling & Fox, 2009).

Cooperative Learning

Cooperative learning is an effective differentiated instructional strategy which involves placing students into small teams. Each team should consist of students that have varying ability levels, and use a number of well thought out activities that aim to augment student understanding of the content. Each member of a team is responsible for learning the content as well as helping their teammates. Ideally, students work through assignments until all group members successfully understand and complete them. Considering Nathan again, as he works on mathematics standards and goals, he could be assigned to a heterogeneous, small-group game, and work on his goals while his classmates work on more advanced objectives. When students are accountable for each team member's achievement with regard to accomplishing unit and lesson goals, both academic skills and interpersonal relationships are more likely to improve (Johnson & Johnson, 1999).

Personal Assistance

Personal assistants can refer to paraprofessionals, volunteers, as well as peers. When properly supervised, support from others can serve the purpose of providing access to grade-level curriculum. Caution should be taken, however, to avoid development of unnecessary dependencies on personal assistance (Downing, 2008).

Service Dogs

Personal assistants that may not regularly be used in inclusive classrooms are service dogs. This support is commonly associated with students who have vision impairments, but has more recently been shown to help students who have autism or other special needs. As an example, a student who is prone to violent tantrums when upset might be calmed by a dog since the animal can be taught to hold its ground while preventing the student from bolting the scene. The time required to train service dogs can be lengthy, as can be helping other individuals in the educational setting acclimate to the dog; however, the benefits provided to students, educators, and others may be warranted in the long run (Viau, Arsenault-Lapierre, Fecteau, et al., 2010).

COMMUNITY-BASED SERVICE PROJECTS AND AUTHENTIC INSTRUCTION

As previously noted, it may be that in addition to addressing content standards in an IEP, students with moderate and severe disabilities may need to work on functional life-skills (e.g., independent living skills, vocational/job skills) (Lawrence-Brown, 2004) that are directly related to a student becoming as self-reliant and self-sufficient as possible. The IEP team is charged with prioritizing and balancing these goals with the student's assigned grade level academic goals.

It is essential that content standards not be overly emphasized at the expense of a student further developing life skills. By addressing prioritized goals, the educators and IEP team members will most likely feel assured that the student will receive an appropriate education. Functional life-skill goals for students with moderate and severe intellectual and developmental disabilities can be addressed with no or minimal changes in emphasis in lessons and activities planned for an entire class lesson or unit when a teacher focuses on real-life applications of general curriculum content. Functional academics can include identifying the correct number on a bus, reading bathroom signs to find the correct room prior to entering, communicating to a doctor symptoms of concern, or using a wheelchair on a sidewalk. Authentic instruction or applied curriculum can actually be of benefit to all students in a heterogeneous, diverse classroom (Hamill & Everington, 2002; Miller, Shambaugh, Robinson, & Wimberly, 1995).

As an example of authentic instruction, Miller, et al. (1995) described a project that was conducted in a middle school science course where students enhanced the knowledge of science content when working in collaboration with a local botanical garden. In addition to learning content, students had the opportunity to make connections across disciplines such as science, math, geography, and language arts by actually creating self-sustaining ecosystems, growing plants for landscaping, and creating brochures and trail maps for the botanical garden. The number of benefits that resulted from this learning experience impacted a wide range of diverse students.

Community-based, service projects, and authentic instruction should not be viewed as add-ons to an already full lesson plan, but rather as an effective way of teaching the general education curriculum content and skills that would be taught in traditional, passive lessons. For students with moderate and severe intellectual and developmental disabilities, this instruction provides opportunities for them to also learn life-skills goals that are of priority as found on their IEP's. Opportunities in the real world are essential and need to be frequent, since students with moderate and severe disabilities do not necessarily generalize or transfer skills learned in isolation or within the actual context of which a skill is needed. Although it may be a challenge to include Nathan in a middle school science unit that traditionally has relied on lecture, textbook, and worksheets, a project, such as the botanical garden project, will help all students, and Nathan can have several opportunities to work on his IEP goals. It may also be that Nathan can surprise his teacher and potentially further his social and technology skills, beyond those identified in an IEP. For example, using his tablet, Nathan can take pictures of plants and his peers, and ultimately make a closed-captioned slideshow that can be used at an open house and for garden publications.

ADDITIONAL DIFFERENTIATED INSTRUCTIONAL STRATEGIES

Because each student is unique, there is no "one-size-fits-all" approach to differentiating instruction specific to students who have moderate and severe intellectual or developmental disabilities. It is recommended, therefore, that the strategies provided in previous chapters in this text be viewed as possible ways to help students who may also have a disability. Adapting materials, extending timelines/due dates, providing options to students to show what they know (e.g., allowing students to make oral as opposed to written presentations), adding picture cues, highlighting important information, changing font sizes, using theatre, music, and movement, arranging the physical environment, are all ways to differentiate instruction if the instruction will help students learn, regardless if the student has a disability. Whenever teaching, it is essential that educators reflect on what they are doing, as well as determine the extent to which students are learning.

Progress Monitoring

Continuous monitoring of instruction by collecting and using quality data to monitor student progress is essential to sound teaching. For the majority of students in a diverse general education classroom, the assessments typically incorporated into lessons (e.g., quizzes, reports) may serve this purpose. Students with moderate and severe intellectual or developmental disabilities will have IEP goals, and hence may need additional assessments to determine learning. It is best when assessments are practical such that they can consistently be used in the general education classroom. The systematic instruction approaches discussed above have monitoring strategies embedded (Halverson & Neary, 2001). Chapters in this text also provide ways that instructors can efficiently collect and analyze data.

CONCLUDING THOUGHTS

As first presented in this chapter, educators are continuously faced with challenges, and with these challenges come new opportunities. Challenges also, however, may bring unintended consequences. With regard to differentiated instruction, caution should be taken to ensure that any unintended consequences are minimized by understanding that needs, whether they have a disability or not, will vary from student to student (Courtade & Browder, 2011; Friend & Bursuck, 2011; Gartin, et al., 2002; Lawrence-Brown, 2004; Vaughn, et al., 2010; Wolfe & Hall, 2003).

Educators and members of an IEP team must ensure that each student, including those that have a moderate or severe intellectual or developmental disability, meaningfully and actively participate in the general education settings. Needs will vary from unit to unit, lesson to lesson, age to age, and grade level to grade level. All responsible for educating students should reflect on the extent to which they have hope and high expectations for each person with whom they have the privilege of working.

It is also imperative that education is a collaborative process and that ongoing and effective collaboration among general and special educators, family members, and students themselves is critical to successful inclusion and for planning instruction that is differentiated. Educating students with significant needs can be daunting and time-consuming. It is important, therefore, that all who facilitate learning maintain a proper perspective and be mindful of these "keeping perspective" tips.

Five suggestions to keep responsibilities manageable:

1. It takes a village. Educating youth, particularly students with moderate and severe intellectual and developmental disabilities, is not a one person task or one person's responsibility. When a student with a disability is to receive general education and special services, the goals for the student are determined by an IEP team which typically consists of the student, parents, general and special educators, and other service providers (e.g., therapists, social worker). Collectively, the team should determine how to best meet the needs of a student are determined.

2. Not all students require specialized, individualized, and involved planning. A disability should not be equated with the need for major curriculum or lesson revisions. By collaborating, the IEP team will become more efficient at deciding which supports are needed for individual students of concern. As an example, Nathan needed adaptations made to reading materials (e.g., picture cues, audio recordings of text), but he had the same supports (e.g., calculator) as his peers during math lessons.

3. Prioritize. While keeping the big picture in mind, do things in manageable chunks. When thinking that everything needs to be done immediately, a situation may become overwhelming, and odds are that few things will be actually accomplished. By collaborating, situations may not seem so ominous. With team members, prioritize, and begin with the highest priority.

4. "It's not fair!" Interestingly, when some students with disabilities are provided additional support, it is not uncommon for students and adults to question if such support is 'fair' given that not all students are receiving the same support. Simply remind the questioners—if someone fell and broke a leg, hence needed a cast and crutches, does that mean everyone should be given a cast and crutches? Supports are

actually provided to make things 'fair' and to somewhat level the playing field.

5. Create a Differentiated Instructional Portfolio. Given that the diversity of student classrooms will continue, it may help to develop a portfolio and keep a list of ideas and strategies that might be used at some point. This portfolio could be in a traditional file format, but now with technology, the portfolio could actually be a website. Potential resources include websites, colleagues (including those in grade levels above and below the one being taught), families, and students.

Inclusion of students with moderate and severe intellectual or developmental disabilities requires the access to, and meaningful delivery of, the general education curriculum. This chapter addresses a number of aspects for instruction, one of which is the continuum of considerations, now that students with disabilities are included in the general education system. When educators and IEP team members collaborate and review the continuum of considerations, they can include students with moderate and severe intellectual or developmental disabilities in general education settings in meaningful ways.

REFERENCES

Browder, D. M., Ahlgrim-Delzell, L., Spooner, F., Mims, P. .J., & Bates, J. N. (2009). Using time delay to teach literacy to students with severe developmental disabilities. *Exceptional Children, 73*, 343-364.

Browder, D. M., Flowers, C., & Wakeman, S. Y. (2008). Facilitating participation in assessments and the general curriculum: Level of symbolic communication classification for students with significant cognitive disabilities. *Assessment in Education: Principles, Policy, & Practice, 15*, 137-151.

Browder, D. M., Spooner, F., Ahlgrim-Delzell, L., Harris, A., & Wakeman, S. (2008). A meta-analysis on teaching mathematics to students with significant cognitive disabilities. *Exceptional Children, 74*, 407-432.

Browder, D. M., Trela, K. C., & Jimenez, B. (2006). Increasing participation of middle school students with severe disabilities in reading of grade appropriate literature. *Focus on Autism and Other Developmental Disabilities, 22*, 206-219.

Browder, D. M., Wakeman, S. Y., Spooner, F., Ahlgrim-Delzell, L., & Algozzine, B. (2006). Research on reading for individuals with significant cognitive disabilities. *Exceptional Children, 72*, 392-408.

Courtade, G., & Browder, D.M. (2011). *Aligning IEPs to the common core state standards for student with moderate and severe disabilities.* Verona, WI: Attainment Company, Inc.

Courtade, G., Spooner, F., & Browder, D. M. (2007). A review of studies with students with significant cognitive disabilities that link to science standards. *Research and Practice in Severe Disabilities, 32*, 43-49.

Downing, J. E. (2008). *Including students with severe and multiple disabilities in typical classrooms: Practical strategies for teachers* (3rd ed.). Baltimore, MD: Brookes Publishing Co.

Falkenstine, K. J., Collins, B. C., Schuster, J. W., & Kleinert, H. (2009). Presenting chained and discrete tasks as non-targeted information when teaching discrete academic skills through small group instruction. *Education and Training in Developmental Disabilities, 44*, 127-142.

Friend, M. & Bursuck, W.D. (2011). *Including students with special needs: A practical guide for classroom teachers* (6th ed.). Upper Saddle River, NJ: Merrill/Prentice Hall.

Gartin, B. C., Murdick, N. L., Imbeau, M., & Perner, D.E. (2002). *How to use differentiated instruction with students with developmental disabilities in the general education classroom. DDD Prism Series.* Arlington, VA: Council for Exceptional Children, Division on Mental Retardation and Developmental Disabilities.

Giangreco, M. F., Cloninger, C. J., & Iverson, V. S. (1998). *Choosing outcomes and accommodations for children.* (2nd ed). Baltimore, MD: Paul H. Brookes.

Halverson, A., & Neary, T. (2001). *Building inclusive schools: Tools and* strategies for success. Needham Heights, MA: Allyn & Bacon.

Hamill, L. & Everington, C. (2002). *Teaching students with moderate to severe disabilities: An applied approach for inclusive environments.* Upper Saddle River, NJ: Merrill Prentice Hall.

Individuals with Disabilities Education Improvement Act (IDEA). (2004). *P.L. 108-446, 20 U.S.C. §§ 1400 et seq., C.F.R.*

Jimenez, B. A., Browder, D. M., & Courtade, G. R. (2008). Teaching an algebraic equation to high school students with moderate developmental disabilities. *Education and Training in Developmental Disabilities, 43,* 266-274.

Johnson, D. & Johnson, R. (1999). Making cooperative learning work. *Theory into Practice, 38* (2), 67-73.

Kennedy, C. H., & Horn, E. M. (2004). *Including students with severe disabilities.* Boston, MA: Pearson Education.

Ketterer, A., Schuster, J. W., Morse, T. E., & Collins, B. C. (2007). The effects of response cards on active participation and social behavior of students with moderate and severe disabilities. *Journal of Developmental and Physical Disabilities, 19,* 187-199.

Lawrence-Brown, D. (2004). Differentiated instruction: Inclusive strategies for standards-based learning that benefit the whole class. *American Secondary Education, 32,* 34-62.

Means, B., Toyama, Y., Murphy, R., Bakia, M., & Jones, K. (2010). *Evaluation of evidence-based practices in online learning: A meta-analysis and review of online learning studies,* Washington, D.C.: Department of Education, Office of Planning, Evaluation, and Policy Development.

Millar, D. S. (2009). Comparison of transition-related IEP content for young adults with disabilities who do or do not have a legal guardian. *Education and Training in Developmental Disabilities, 44,* 151-167.

Millar, D. S. (2007). "I never put it together:" The disconnect between self-determination and guardianship-implications for practice. *Education and Training in Developmental Disabilities, 42,* 119-129.

Millar, D. S. (2003). Age of majority, transfer of rights and guardianship: Considerations for families and educators. *Education and Training in Developmental Disabilities, 38,* 378-397.

Miller, P., Shambaugh, K., Robinson, C., & Wimberly, J. (1995). Applied learning for middle schoolers. *Educational Leadership, 1,* 22-25.

Neber, H., Finsterwald, M., & Urban, N. (2001). Cooperative learning with gifted and high-achieving students: A review and meta-analysis of 12 studies. *High Ability Studies, 12*(1), 199-214.

No Child Left Behind Act (NCLB) of 2001. (2002). *Reauthorization of the Elementary and Secondary Education Act, P. L. 107-110, §2102(4), 115 Stat. 1425.*

Obremski, E.S., Palmer, S., Wehmeyer, M. L., Davies, D., Stock, S., Lobb, K., & Bishop, B. (in press). Technology and people with intellectual disability: Utilization and barriers. *Intellectual and Developmental Disabilities.*

Palmer, S. B., Wehmeyer, M. L., Davies, D., & Stock, S. (in press). Family members' reports of the technology use of family members with intellectual and developmental disabilities. *Journal of Intellectual Disability Research.*

Pearpoint, J., Forest, M., & O'Brien, J. O. (1996). MAPs, Circles of Friends, and PATH: Powerful tools to help build caring communities. In S. Stainback and W. Stainback (Eds.), *Inclusion: A guide for educators* (pp. 67 -86). Baltimore, MD: Paul H Brookes.

Singer, H. & Donlan, D. (1989). *Reading and learning from text.* Hillsdale, NJ: Erlbaum.

Snell, M. E. & Brown, F. (2006). *Instruction of students with severe disabilities.* (6th ed.). Upper Saddle River, NJ: Pearson Education.

Stock, S. E., Davies, D. K., Wehmeyer, M. L., & Lachapelle, Y. (2011). Emerging new practices in technology to support independent community access for people with intellectual and cognitive disabilities. *Neurorehabilitation, 28,* 1-9.

Tomlinson, C. & Kalbfleisch, M. L. (1998). Teach me, teach my brain: A call for differentiated classrooms. *Educational Leadership, 2,* 52-55.

Turnbull, A. P., Turnbull, H. R., Erwin, E., & Soodak, L. (2006). *Families, professionals, and exceptionality: Positive outcomes through partnerships and trust* (5th ed.). Upper Saddle River, NJ: Merrill/Prentice Hall.

Vaughn, S. R., Bos, C.S., & Schumm, J. S. (2010). *Teaching students who are exceptional, diverse, and at risk in the general education classroom* (5th ed.). Upper Saddle River, NJ: Merrill Prentice Hall.

Viau, R., Arsenault-Lapierre , G., Fecteau , S., Champagne, N., Walker, C., & Lupien, S. (2010). Effect of service dogs on salivary cortisol secretion in autistic children. *Psychoneuroendocrinology, 35,* 1187-1193.

Wehmeyer, M. L., & Tasse, M. (in press). Support needs of adults with intellectual disability across domains: The role of technology. *Journal of Special Education Technology.*

Westling, D. L., & Fox, L. (2009). *Teaching students with severe disabilities* (4th ed.). Upper Saddle River, NJ: Merrill/Pearson.

Wolfe, P. S., & Hall, T. E. (2003). Making inclusion a reality for students with severe disabilities. *Teaching Exceptional Children, 35,* 56-60.

Index

CPSIA information can be obtained
at www.ICGtesting.com
Printed in the USA
LVHW081747020722
722641LV00015B/1184

9 780761 865544